Helping and
Human Relations

Helping and Human Relations

A PRIMER FOR LAY AND PROFESSIONAL HELPERS

VOLUME I
Selection and Training

ROBERT R. CARKHUFF
CENTER FOR HUMAN RELATIONS
AND COMMUNITY AFFAIRS
AMERICAN INTERNATIONAL COLLEGE

Holt, Rinehart and Winston, Inc.
New York · Chicago · San Francisco · Atlanta · Dallas
Montreal · Toronto · London · Sydney

To my parents

FOREWORD

Most books in this area are woven around one point, often not the author's, and often not substantive. These volumes on helping and human relations offer as their basic fabric an overwhelming number of substantive points. This difference alone marks them as the foremost contribution to theory, research, practice, training, and selection in helping, but they are also general and specific extensions to human relations. For these and many other reasons these books have to be both an embarrassment and a source of new hope and potency to the professional committed to increasing sources of human benefit. The implications for the concerned lay public are perhaps even more profound in that Professor Carkhuff has developed a perspective so broad in scope and so rooted in deep, clear sensitivity that his work is directly applicable to human relations problems in education, community affairs, racial relations, industry, government, and other professional and lay helping efforts.

There is full recognition that in time of crisis for the individual and society there can be no substitute for delivery. There can be no delegation of responsibility by preoccupation with process alone. The systematic, step-by-step development of propositions and corollaries based on a large body of research evidence exposes our efforts to hide behind our theories. These volumes render impotent the argument that the human relations area is too complex, mystical, and lacking in substantive knowledge. They meet fully the criteria of meaning and rigor. They are complete to the point of dealing with the limits and extensions of what is known and not known.

Helping is no longer a brilliant verbal game played by people who emphasize the pathology of others to avoid exposing their own impotence, nor is it a means of enlarging one's tolerance for abuse. Professor Carkhuff breaks free of these traditional choices by being open to an intense pace of learning, relearning, immense energy, and work. Further he puts together the necessity to nurture and to risk in a complete person. The masculine and feminine aspects are not mutually exclusive in his treatment, but rather integrated aspects of an integrated life style. Helping is not acceptance alone; it often involves active destruction of those forces denying helper and helpee personal emergence.

For the first time we have a comprehensive model for helping, a psychology of personal emergence that goes beyond our preoccupation with pathology. (Works on the psychology of adjustment only present a *relatively* palatable neurotic.) In the first volume we have a distinct set of guidelines for discriminating what is facilitative and what is deteriorative; guidelines for implementing effective research, practice, selection, and training; operationalized directions for action and philosophy; comprehensive and detailed treatment of the potential contributions of the helper, helpee, and contextual and environmental conditions; comprehensive and detailed treatment of the potential contributions of the trainer, trainee, and contextual and environmental conditions for training and selection of useful discrimination devices, validated scales, preferred modes of treatment; and I could go on and on listing the "firsts." However, it will suffice to say that all of the above and the many topics I have not listed are considered in terms of their relevance to the task, population, level of talent, and the press of crises.

In the second volume, the unique contributions focus on complete operational expositions of effective helping. Professor Carkhuff spells out the relationships among the critical helping variables—exploration, understanding, and action. He then develops these aspects of the process and outcome to incorporate operational treatments of crises in life and the developmental process as applied to basic aspects of the person. The entire volume is further concretized with detailed reports dealing with applications developed from preferred modes of treatment and a uniquely creative integration of training and practice. Here the author develops the evidence and rationale for employing effective interpersonal communications and training as a preferred mode of treatment for a wide variety of helpee populations. The section dealing with implementation and inquiry is valuable not only to the professional, but also to others less fully trained, whom it helps to make systematic and meaningful studies of their work. In an area that has often asked its workers to choose between theory and practice, meaning and rigor, practice and research, this section makes the only potent contributions to a resolution of these "classic" conflicts. In addition these chapters may be profitably read for their contributions to a meaningful philosophy of science. For the social scientist and those engaged in social action there are fully new approaches to theory and practice with groups and communities based upon the deepest levels of description and understanding.

All the superlatives apply; more so in that the completed package blends into a comprehensive treatment of the areas. Each volume can stand alone as a classic; together they constitute a monumental landmark in the history and future of all helping and human relations efforts, be they one-to-one relationships, groups, or large-scale social action programs in communities, government, or industry.

It will be difficult for the reader to believe that all this comes from one man—a complete man—but that is what he will have to live with and that will be part of his growth.

No review will do this work justice. It must be lived with, for each new reading brings with it fresh new challenges, directions, and understandings of old mysteries.

Volumes like these cannot be produced without having great impact on our view of man in all his mysteries, strengths, and weaknesses. Further, constructive and creative personal and interpersonal growth are no longer beyond our comprehension and realization. Many things are now possible. We can fill the gap between the demands of crises and the lack of competent people to meet them. We can look to efficacy and delivery rather than credentials only. We can effectively select and train. We can see through the games and smoke screens of those who avoid facing the issue of delivery by attacking those who do. We can hope to begin to taste the rewards of full living and deeper interpersonal relationships with our children, spouses, friends, students, and any out there who will reach when we do.

We can no longer continue finding ourselves, as the author puts it, "searching for help yet rejecting it in its most efficacious forms, calling for light yet preferring darkness to exposure, crying for life yet choosing death." In summary, "Those who can use their resources seek to populate their worlds with helpers; those who cannot, populate their worlds with helpees"!

With the publication of this work there is no place to hide. The choice is made clear: to act to reconstruct the human condition or to die like fools.

Bernard G. Berenson, Ph.D.
Professor of Psychology
State University of New York at Buffalo

PREFACE

The would-be helper faces issues he has never before faced. Unfortunately, all too frequently he is led to believe that his mentors have faced and resolved these issues—usually they have not. The critical issues comprise the three R's of helping: (1) the *right* of the helper to intervene in the life of another; (2) the *responsibilities* of the helper once he has intervened; and (3) the *role* the helper must assume in helping another individual and, concomitantly, the various role conflicts he encounters in attempting to implement the responsibilities implied by intervention. Many practitioners in the field assume rather than question right; the issue of responsibility is usually raised only superficially, for example, in questions concerning whether or not a counselor may see a client outside of the formal counseling session; and questions having to do with roles and role conflicts are too frequently summarily dismissed as examples of the conflicts between institution and individual, and the effects of age and role reversals in helping.

RIGHT

A person with emotional problems seeks help. In some way or in some area of his life he is living ineffectively. He has not been able to resolve his difficulty in living on his own or in conjunction with the persons available to him in his environment. He comes for help with the expectation that the helper can help him to live more effectively. His implicit assumption is that, given the same problems, the helper would be able to find a more appropriate and healthier resolution. The prospective helper, in turn, says that he can help the person with problems to live more effectively. His implicit but almost universally unexplored assumption is that he himself is living effectively or, at a minimum, more effectively than the helpee. That is, given the helpee's difficulties, the helper would be able to find more appropriate and healthier resolutions than the helpee has been able to work out for himself. To be sure, the helper cannot have experienced all of the problems of all of the people who come to him for help. However, the essential proposition upon which the helping process is based—and without which it cannot take place—is that the helper must be functioning at higher levels than the helpee in the relevant areas of concern. The majority of helpers never face directly the problem of the right of intervention. If helpees could know the levels of functioning of their helpers, many of them would never appear for help in the first place, or if they did they would terminate the process immediately.

If the helper is functioning himself at minimally facilitative and self-sustaining levels—and here we have evidence that the modal level of functioning of counselors and therapists is far below this point—there is no real question of right. That is, if the helper is himself a productive and creative person who is moving toward higher levels of functioning and actualization, then he knows that there are no real alternatives to helping persons who are similarly struggling to grow. Such a helper does not even raise the question of right in the same manner as his ineffective counterpart. *Only the person who is alive and growing can enable the struggling person to choose life at the life and death crisis points. He knows that when he makes it possible for another person to choose life he increases his own probabilities of continuing to choose life.*

Unlike the healthy practitioner who strives for wholeness and desires to relate to persons who are similarly committed, the less effective helper functions out of his own need to find some sense of temporary "completion" in his relationship with the helpee: he seeks in the therapeutic relationship experiences that have been unfulfilled in his daily living; he finds an intimacy that he cannot find elsewhere; he feels "good" finding people with problems similar to or worse than his; and he finds rewards in helping which he cannot find in his own life. A helper of this kind *needs* the helpee, perhaps more than the helpee needs him—remove the helpee and the helper must once again experience the agonizing pains of incompletion that led him to assume the role of helper in the first place.

RESPONSIBILITY

The issue of responsibility of intervention follows from the question of right of intervention. The individual who intervenes out of need proceeds in the helping process out of need. He acts in a distorted manner that reflects his incompletion, and he follows procedures that are calculated, whether consciously or unconsciously, to satisfy his own neurotic needs. He employs the orientations and techniques that offer him the most satisfactory temporary sense of completion. In the manner in which he discharges his responsibility *the incomplete person assures himself that no one can have more than he can.* At best the helpee's level of functioning finds an upper limit in the level of functioning of such a helper; at worst the helpee deteriorates in a relationship with an authority figure who is continually subtracting from the responses of the helpee and, in fact, compounding the helpee's own distortions of himself and his world.

The healthy person, on the other hand, having intervened in the lives of persons who have meaning to him, is committed to giving real help. In terms of the goals that he and the helpee have determined are meaningful for the helpee, he is committed to doing whatever is necessary to accomplish these goals. Such a helper is not bound by any single system or orientation; he is guided by the helpee's constructive change or gain. The attitude of the healthy person toward others is a function of his attitude toward himself: the effective helper will do anything for his helpee that, given the same circumstances, he would do for himself. In the manner in which he discharges his responsibility—indeed, in the manner in which he lives his life—*the healthy person teaches his helpee to be no less than he can be at a given moment in time.*

ROLE

Many different roles are thrust upon the practitioner in the helping process. The question of roles involves responding differently to different persons—that is, the helper may be one person with A, quite a different one with B, and still a different one with C. Those who perform the helping function out of unfulfilled needs are dominated by these roles and are constantly looking for rules to guide them with particular individuals and in particular situations. In addition, such persons are always asking whether their role calls for institutional allegiance or individual allegiance. A sophisticated person would not seek help from such a helper because, in his urgency to resolve his problems, he is not concerned with the welfare of the helper or with the establishment; indeed, such a helpee is frequently in some way the victim of the establishment.

On the other hand, persons for whom counseling is a way of life, that is, those whose lives are committed to their own growth as well as to that of others, reject the imposition of roles beyond those dictated during the initial moments of contact with the helpee. When the helpee enters the helping process the helper, having accepted him, is committed to do all that he can that translates to helpee benefits. *Helping is for the helpee, and only concomitantly does it incorporate benefits for the helper.* Effective helpers do not deny the power implicit in their role in the therapeutic relationship because of its realistic base; that is, they are functioning at more effective levels than their helpees, and they accept the helpees' recognition of them as agents of change because they can involve the helpees in a therapeutic process leading to constructive change. Their movement in all of their human relations, however, is from role to person; it is perhaps best exemplified in the movement from initial unconditional calculation to avoid the potentially deleterious effects of premature communication of counselor values and attitudes to the often *very conditional quality of healthy human relationships, in which neither person allows himself or the other to be less than he can be.*

The two volumes of this text attempt to make operational the critical phases of effective human relations, keeping fully in focus the questions of right, responsibility, and role in intervening in the life of another person. Volume I builds upon the empirical and experiential bases of evidence for effective helping and makes translations to both selection and training. Given the present development of our knowledge of effective helping, I have attempted, in primer form, creatively and pragmatically, to make effective selection and training operational. In order not to detract from my main purpose, I have summarized the literature as simply and as succinctly as possible, often in propositional form. The previous work upon which these volumes build may be employed meaningfully as supplementary reading, although these volumes go considerably beyond earlier sources in their creative development of the constructs of effective helping, training, and selection.

Part One examines the present state of affairs in the helping profession, emphasizing particularly the potential sources of effectiveness of both lay and professional programs.

Part Two presents a model for the development of psychological health and psychopathology. In addition, it examines the factors that influence the success of the treatment program—the helper, the helpee, and contextual and environmental variables.

The focus of Part Three is the development of procedures for selecting effective helpers. Special attention is given to methods of assessing the communication and discrimination of conditions related to constructive helpee change or gain.

Part Four attends to the development of effective training procedures, including in particular the implementation of discrimination and communication training and the development of effective courses of action and preferred modes of treatment.

Part Five presents a summary and overview and develops a model for a formula for effective selection and training.

These volumes are dedicated to the development of effective lay as well as professional practitioners. Indeed, much of the evidence concerning training and treatment favors lay personnel and thus takes counseling and psychotherapy out of the realm of mystical arts where the helping profession for too long has been relegated. These texts, then, are meant not only for the traditional helpers—social workers, counselors, clinicians, psychiatrists, and other professionals in the area of human relations, such as nurses, educators, lawyers, and ministers—but also for lay persons concerned with effective helping. They should also serve those whose lives are most influenced by the helping process, the helpees themselves. Finally, while a private reading may contribute substantially to the development of effective helpers, *this text is meant to be used under the guidance of an experienced professional, one who is equipped to handle all modes of practice and inquiry.*

In the preparation of this book I am in debt to my colleague, Dr. Bernard G. Berenson, with whom I have shared many learning experiences, both in and out of therapy and its supervision. In addition, the graduate students who have shared counseling seminars with me and who have conducted their own relevant and meaningful research have been a constant source of stimulation. In this regard, I am particularly grateful to Dr. William Anthony, Dr. John Cannon. Dr. Ted Friel, Dr. B. Todd Holder, Dr. Dan Kratochvil, and Dr. Richard Pierce. I wish also to acknowledge the diligent effort of Dr. Raphael Vitalo in preparing the systematic desensitization manual that appears in Appendix B.

Finally, I am in greatest debt to the person who, devoid of all role characteristics, has provided me with nourishment and support in all of her roles as helper and helpee, boss and worker—my wife Bernice, without whom this work would not have been possible.

R.R.C.

Springfield, Massachusetts
March 1969

CONTENTS

Helping and
Human Relations

PART ONE

Introduction

PART ONE of this text introduces the literature on the differential effectiveness of lay and professional training and treatment. Briefly, the available evidence indicates that lay training programs have been more effective in demonstrating change on indexes that measure constructive helpee change. In addition, the evidence indicates that with or without training and/or supervision lay helpers function as effectively or more effectively than professionals in the helping role. The potential sources of these effects are explored: trainee personnel; selection procedures; training personnel; training programs; and treatment programs.

1

THE DIFFERENTIAL EFFECTIVENESS
OF LAY AND PROFESSIONAL HELPERS[1]

A number of programs involving (1) short-term accelerated training for professional counselors (such as the institutes set up under the National Defense Education Act, NDEA, and Counselor-Advisor University Summer Education, CAUSE), and (2) the employment of nonprofessional practitioners have been proposed and implemented to meet ever-growing social service needs. Concern over the development of these programs has taken two principal directions: First, speaking for many in the helping professions, some writers have warned of the dangers of lowering professional standards and have recommended the employment of lay persons *only* as aides and assistants to free professional counselors from clerical and other more menial duties (Odgers, 1964; Patterson, 1965; Rosenbaum, 1966; Schlossberg, 1967). Second, another group has emphasized the direct counseling contributions that lay persons can make and has explored the unique advantages of using selected subprofessionals (Carkhuff, 1966; Gordon, 1965; Holzberg, 1963; Reiff, 1966; Reiff & Riessman, 1965; Riessman & National Institute of Labor Education, 1964). The development of these "lower-level" programs has, in addition, become a concern of the major national associations involved with guidance, counseling, and therapeutic activities. The American Personnel and Guidance Association (1964) and Kennedy and Strowig (1967) have acknowledged the limited contributions (at maximum, short-term interviewing; at minimum, clerical assistance) of subprofessionals and have noted that these persons be encouraged to continue further professional

[1] Based upon an article that first appeared in the *Journal of Counseling Psychology*, 1968, 15, 117–126, as "The Differential Functioning of Lay and Professional Helpers." Reprinted with permission from the American Psychological Association.

study. The American Psychological Association (Hoch, Ross, & Winder, 1965) has, in turn, with some apparent ambivalence, assumed a relatively open stance, suggesting that "psychology ought to keep an open mind, letting the results speak for themselves" (p. 51).

Partly because they are concerned with protecting the public from potentially harmful practices, professionals have assessed the processes and outcomes of lay training and treatment. The following sections, which summarize the research that has been done on lay training and treatment programs (Carkhuff, 1967), are presented in the hope of letting the results speak for themselves. In these summaries the results of subprofessional training and treatment programs are contrasted with those of professional training and treatment. It is hoped that the summary nature of the propositions that follow will lay the groundwork for generating a series of tentative hypotheses concerning the differential processes and outcomes of lay and professional training and treatment.

EFFECTIVENESS OF TRAINING

While a number of lay as well as professional training programs have been implemented, only a few studies have systematically assessed their effects in terms of process variables related in previous research to a variety of indexes of constructive client outcome. Those that have assessed dimensions such as the counselor's communication of empathy, warmth, regard or respect, and genuineness or congruence and, to a lesser degree, such dimensions as concreteness or specificity of expression, self-disclosure, and openness (the outcome research is summarized in Carkhuff & Berenson, 1967, and Truax & Carkhuff, 1967) have yielded the following conclusions:

1. Extensive evidence indicates that lay persons can be trained to function at minimally facilitative levels of conditions related to constructive client change over relatively short periods of time. Both carefully screened college graduates interested in school guidance activities and unselected volunteers from the school, hospital, and community at large demonstrate change in the direction of more facilitative functioning on dimensions related to constructive client change or gain in training periods ranging from 20 hours to one year (Berenson, Carkhuff, & Myrus, 1966; Carkhuff & Truax, 1965a; Demos, 1964; Demos & Zuwaylif, 1963; Gunning, Holmes, Johnson, & Rife, 1965; Hansen & Barker, 1964; Jones, 1963; Kratochvil, 1969; Martin & Carkhuff, 1968; Munger & Johnson, 1960; Pierce, Carkhuff, & Berenson, 1967; Webb & Harris, 1963; Wrightsman, Richard, & Noble, 1966).

2. There is little evidence to indicate that persons in professional trainee programs are being trained to function effectively on any dimensions related to constructive client change over very long periods of training. The evidence on the communication of facilitative dimensions related to constructive client change (Bergin & Soloman, 1963; Carkhuff, Kratochvil, & Friel, 1968), as well as of the ability to judge the personality characteristics of others (Arnhoff, 1954; Kelly & Fiske, 1950; Taft, 1955; Weiss, 1963), to graduate trainees who were screened primarily on intellective indexes was negative over periods ranging from four years upward. Although the results in one intermediate-type professional two-year rehabilitation-counselor training program were positive (Anthony & Carkhuff, 1969), the initial level of trainee functioning was so low that the final level of trainee functioning was still lower than the initial level of most professional trainees in other programs. Thus, the results, while statistically significant, should be interpreted cautiously.

3. Comparative statistics indicate that lay and lower-level guidance training programs are more effective in eliciting constructive trainee change on those conditions related to constructive client change. While there are few directly comparable studies, in general, following training, on both identical and converted indexes lay trainees function at levels essentially as high or higher (never significantly lower) and engage clients in counseling process movement at levels as high or higher than professional trainees (Anthony & Carkhuff, 1969; Berenson *et al.*, 1966; Bergin & Soloman, 1963; Carkhuff, Kratochvil, & Friel, 1968; Carkhuff & Truax, 1965a; Martin & Carkhuff, 1968; Pierce *et al.*, 1967).

Of course, the fact that one program can demonstrate the movement of its trainees on indexes (even those related in previous research to constructive client change) while another can give no evidence of any significant movement (even on indexes unrelated to any meaningful criteria) does not necessarily translate immediately and directly to client benefits in favor of the former group. In order to break free of possible circularity in our efforts, we must assess the effects of the consequent treatment engaged in by the trainees of both groups.

EFFECTIVENESS OF TREATMENT

Again, although ongoing treatment programs, lay as well as professional, are of necessity much more numerous than the training programs, few studies have systematically assessed their effects. However, where the varied assessments of the efficacy of the helper's treatment offering

have included those made by outside experts—the helper's supervisors
and co-workers, the patient's ward attendants, and significant others—
as well as reports by the patient himself, and where the client outcome
criteria have included hospital discharge and recidivism rates, assessments of psychological functioning and total adjustment, social-interpersonal behavior, communication and cooperation, self-care and mo-
bility, reaction time and verbal fluency, and indexes of sexual-marital and
educational-vocational functioning, as well as the more traditional testing indexes, the following conclusions emerge:

1. It appears that lay persons can effect significant constructive
changes in the clients whom they see. Extensive evidence indicates that
hospitalized neuropsychiatric patients (Anker & Walsh, 1961; Appleby,
1963; Beck, Kantor, & Gelineau, 1963; Carkhuff & Truax, 1965b; Colarelli
& Siegel, 1963; Glasser, 1965; Greenblatt & Kantor, 1962; Holzberg &
Knapp, 1965; Kantor & Greenblatt, 1962; Korson & Hayes, 1966; Poser,
1966; Siegel & Colarelli, 1964; Tudor, 1952; Warme, 1965), outpatient
neuropsychiatric patients (Magoon & Golann, 1966; Mendel & Rapport,
1963; Rioch, Elkes, Flint, Usdansky, Newman, & Silber, 1963), normals
situationally distressed or otherwise (Brown, 1965; Harvey, 1964; Zunker
& Brown, 1966), and children (Guerney, 1964; Guerney, Guerney, &
Andronico, 1966; Wahler, Winkel, Peterson, & Morrison, 1965) demonstrate significant constructive changes as a consequence of their contacts
with lay persons.
2. Professional graduate programs have not yet demonstrated the relevant evidence for the translation of their training efforts to client benefits. The lack of empirical demonstration of the positive effects of professional graduate programs is perhaps due not so much to the inability
to do so as to the universal reluctance of these programs to make enlightened and systematic inquiries into their training efforts. Ironically,
that benefits do accrue to patients treated by professional helpers can
be inferred from the data of Eysenck (1965), Levitt (1963), and Lewis
(1965). These data, while indicating no average differences between
treatment and control groups of adult and child patients, also indicate
that approximately two thirds of patients improve over a one- to two-
year period. The fact is that constructive change does occur in both
treatment and control groups. Perhaps we must devote more attention
to studying the control group members who, although not assigned to
professional helpers, may have found nonprofessional helpers.
3. In directly comparable studies selected lay persons with or without
training and/or supervision have patients who demonstrate change as
great or greater than the patients of professional practitioners. While

the number of comparable studies is limited, with both outpatients and inpatients lay persons effect changes on the indexes assessed that are at least as great or, all too frequently, greater (never significantly less), than professionals (Anker & Walsh, 1961; Harvey, 1964; Magoon & Golann, 1966; Mendel & Rapport, 1963; Poser, 1966; Rioch *et al.*, 1963).

QUESTIONS AND EXPLORATIONS

The results raise a number of unanswered questions. Are the results, for example, attributable to differences in (1) the trainees themselves, (2) the selection processes, (3) the training personnel, (4) the training programs proper, (5) the treatment procedures, or to (6) several or all of the above? In order to shed more light on these results, we will explore what evidence there is in all of these areas.

Trainee Personnel

Indications are that, in general, lay counselors are less intelligent, as measured by traditional intellective indexes, less educated, and from lower socioeconomic classes than professional counselors and therapists, who by virtue of education and vocation are upper class. In addition, it would appear that lay persons are motivated to help by other than the overdetermined needs of the professional to find in the helping role position, status, prestige, money, and perhaps some "handles" on his own psychological difficulties. Perhaps the lay person is motivated to help simply because he is most in contact with the need for help, for himself and for others. How do these differences translate to the helping process? Here, interestingly, extensive base rate data exists which indicates that the typical professional trainee at the beginning of training is functioning at significantly higher levels of those dimensions related to constructive client change than is the typical lay person (summarized in Carkhuff & Berenson, 1967). The fact that the professional trainee is functioning at higher levels prior to training and at lower levels following training, both in relation to lay trainees and himself (Bergin & Soloman, 1963; Carkhuff, Kratochvil, & Friel, 1968), implies that something deleterious to his level of functioning on those indexes related to client change may happen to him over the course of training. In summary, we can conclude that both the means and the intentions of prospective lay helpers are more humble and direct, or honest, at the beginning of training than the means and intentions of prospective professional helpers.

Trainee Selection

While the process of professional trainee selection is quite stable, the methods of selecting candidates for lay training programs vary widely, ranging from cases in which trainees are virtually self-selected volunteers from an unselected population to those in which helpers are very carefully selected. However, although the selection procedures of at least one lay program (Rioch *et al.*, 1963) closely paralleled those of graduate programs, the screening efforts by the promulgators of most lay programs are typified by the work of Harvey (1964) and his colleagues, who made an intensified attempt to select "persons who exhibit a sincere regard for others, tolerance and ability to accept people with values different from one's own, a healthy regard for the self, a warmth and sensitivity in dealing with others, and a capacity for empathy" (p. 349). The professional training programs, in turn, are dominated by highly intellective indexes of selection, primarily grade-point average (GPA), complemented by Graduate Record Examination performance. Even though the professional trainees' higher levels of functioning on facilitative dimensions suggest a relation between intellective indexes and level of functioning, within the range of levels of functioning of candidates for graduate school, there is little or no relation to GPA (Allen, 1967; Carkhuff, Piaget, & Pierce, 1968). This finding is consistent with that of Holland and Richards (1965), indicating that academic performance is independent of real-life indexes of achievement. Further, within graduate school there are tentative indications of a slightly negative relation between GPA and the levels of trainee functioning on indexes relevant to constructive client change (Bergin & Soloman, 1963). Thus, while professional selection indexes at best appear irrelevant to effective counseling and therapeutic functioning, it can be concluded that lay trainees, ranging from self-selected volunteers to carefully selected psychologically healthy persons, are able to employ effectively the training experiences that are provided them. With the thought in mind that there is no necessary reason why high levels of intellectual functioning should present a handicap to the acquisition of improved interpersonal skills (Berenson *et al.*, 1966; Carkhuff & Truax, 1965a), we turn to a consideration of the training programs and their promulgators.

Training Personnel

Base rate data indicate that experienced practitioners, including those conducting professional training programs, are functioning at less than minimally facilitative levels. Indeed, they are functioning at levels equal to or lower than professional trainees at the beginning of graduate training (summarized in Carkhuff & Berenson, 1967). Further, evidence indicates that just as clients converge on the level of functioning of their counselors (Pagell, Carkhuff, & Berenson, 1967), so do trainees converge on the level of functioning of their trainers (Pierce *et al.*, 1967). The trainees of trainers who are functioning at high levels demonstrate uniformly positive change; those of trainers who are functioning at moderate or low levels demonstrate little, no, or deteriorative change. It can be inferred that the level of functioning of the professional trainer may account in large part for the negative results in studies of graduate training. While the work of Hansen (1965) suggested that NDEA guidance institute trainers may be functioning at levels higher than the pretraining expectations of trainees (and this suggestion has implications for either the high level of functioning of these trainers or the low level of expectations of the trainees), there is little direct evidence concerning the level of functioning of the lay trainer.

Training Programs

Lay training programs are, by and large, simple, rather homogeneous programs geared to producing counselors who can effectively relate to persons in need of help and facilitate their positive movement. In the limited time available these programs appear to focus on two areas: (1) sensitivity training or the teaching of interpersonal skills and (2) inducing change in the personality and the attitudes of the trainee himself. These programs are thus built around such conditions as understanding, regard, and genuineness, both in their didactic teaching for the helping role and in the experiential base provided the trainee. By contrast, the professional training programs are highly complex, and heterogeneous; they are often apparently self-neutralizing admixtures of science and art and research and practice and frequently offer little to bridge the gap between the two.

While the results of lay programs exhibit trainee gains on those dimensions related to client change, the professional programs exhibit a drop in the level of trainee functioning over the course of graduate training, with the largest drop seeming to occur between the first and the second year (Carkhuff, 1968; Carkhuff, Kratochvil, & Friel, 1968; Carkhuff, Piaget, & Pierce, 1968). Although with experience practitioners appear to recoup some of their losses in functioning, there are direct suggestions that many may never again function at the level at which they did when they entered graduate school (Carkhuff & Berenson, 1967). Two follow-up evaluation studies indicate that those who drop out of professional training tend to be functioning at higher levels of facilitative conditions than those who stay in. There is, however, evidence to indicate improvement in the ability of graduate trainees to discriminate the levels of conditions offered by other counselors (Carkhuff, Kratochvil, & Friel, 1968). While there is no evidence to relate discrimination to client change, the direct implication is that the main effects of graduate training are related to the development of discriminators rather than communicators in a world that is in need of communicators. It can be concluded, then, that lay training programs attempt to use the little time they have available to effect as great trainee changes as they can on indexes related to counselee and trainee change. Professional programs, in turn, appear to use the great amount of time they have available to them to effect trainee change on indexes unrelated to counselee or trainee change. Simply stated, lay programs try to prepare people to help people. While graduate training sets for itself many different objectives, it apparently does not prepare individuals to help others.

Treatment

While professional programs have failed to produce tangible evidence of their translation to client benefits, or, indeed, evidence that they are concerned with researching their training efforts, assessments of lay counselor programs have yielded positive results. In treating his client the professional practitioner all too often focuses upon highly elaborate, highly cognitive systems. His efforts are role dominated, and it is frequently his theories and techniques that are on the line in counseling rather than himself, the counselor. By contrast, the lay counselor has less expertise; he is more in contact with his uncertainty, less sure and less formulative; he has only himself (and sometimes his supervisor) to rely upon, and often he tries only to stay with and "be with" the client. The lay counselor is also unencumbered by the professional role conflicts that disallow his full and intense involvement and entry into the life activities of another person. He thus enjoys several distinctive advantages over his professional counterpart: He appears to have a greater ability (1) to enter the milieu of the distressed; (2) to establish peer-like relations with persons needing help; (3) to take an active part in the client's total life situation; (4) to empathize more effectively with the client's style of life; (5) to teach the client, within the client's own frame of reference more successful actions; and (6) to provide the client with an effective transition to higher levels of functioning within the social system. In short, the lay counselor when appropriately employed can be the human link between society and the person in need of help —a necessary link that professionals are not now adequately filling. Here there is some evidence concerning the differential effects in help- ing of both race and social class (Banks, Berenson, & Carkhuff, 1967; Carkhuff & Pierce, 1967). That is, helpers who are most different from their helpees in race and social class have the greatest difficulty effecting constructive helpee changes, while those helpers who are most similar to their helpees in these respects have the greatest facility for doing so.

EXTENSIONS AND IMPLICATIONS

The helping professions have raised critical questions concerning the effectiveness of lay training and treatment programs. A review of these programs indicates that (1) lay persons can be trained to function at minimally facilitative levels of conditions related to constructive client change in relatively short periods of time and (2) lay counselors can effect significant constructive change in clients. One implication, then, is that the process of one individual attempting to help another is not the exclusive province of professional helpers. In fact, the lack of signifi- cant differences between treated and untreated groups in the Eysenck- Levitt-Lewis data may be accounted for by the possibility that some of the patients in the "untreated" control groups sought the help of un- trained lay persons. This is not to say, of course, that any form of psychological treatment is significantly more effective in eliciting con- structive client movement than other forms of activities. In order to resolve this question, studies are needed that incorporate treatment control groups of patients who meet for the same amount of time for activities other than the treatment procedures being assessed. (Anker & Walsh, 1961).

Perhaps the main value of lay counseling research is to point up the need for similar research of professional training and treatment programs. While many people, in defense of their programs, particularly those in psychology, have stated that they are not engaged in training people to help people, this position does not appear to be tenable. If these individuals are primarily training researchers, then at a minimum the first order of investigation should be to assess the translation of pro- fessional training to treatment benefits. We can no longer afford the luxury of assuming the effectiveness of professional treatment.

For the present it appears that both the trainees and the trainers, the procedures by which they are selected, and the training and treatment procedures are all potential sources of the differential results of lay and professional programs. However, there is no reason why professional programs cannot be effective in enabling their trainees to function at higher levels of those conditions related to client change; in fact, evidence from at least one one-semester program indicates that graduate students can do very well indeed (Carkhuff & Truax, 1965a).

Interestingly, whereas it is traditional to look upward to the next higher rung in the status hierarchy in order to emulate its modes and, hopefully, to achieve its successes, the highest rung—the medical profession and, particularly, psychiatry—is already seriously considering the extensive employment of lay personnel (Coggeshall, 1965; Creech, 1966; Joint Commission on Mental Illness and Health, 1961; Lief, 1966). It is imperative that the professional programs in guidance, counseling, and clinical psychology, as well as those in psychiatry and social work, not only look downward to the "lower-level" programs for their own distinctive contributions but also that they incorporate the simple emphasis upon core conditions conducive to facilitative human experiences and the simple procedures for training people in discriminative and communicative skills. Such an approach would be congruent with the client's perception of what is helpful to him in counseling (Deane & Ansbacher, 1962; Lorr, 1965; Matarazzo, 1965; Miller, 1965; Spiegel & Spiegel, 1967).

All of this is not to say that there are no problems associated with lay counseling. Of the programs reviewed here, at least one treatment program assessing unselected and untrained hospital attendants (Sines, Silver, & Lucero, 1961) yielded no positive results. In addition, there are problems involved in recruiting lay helpers as well as in implementing lay programs (Weiner & Brand, 1965), including those involving consultation and role definition (Warme, 1965). Finally, there are problems having to do with assessing the long-term effects of short-term programs. For one thing, the trainee products frequently return to an environment that does not support and reinforce their activities (Meadow & Tillem, 1963; Munger, Myers, & Brown, 1963). Lay counseling training and treatment activities may run counter to many of the prevailing traditional forces in the helping profession as well as in the community at large. Reluctant approval may give way to unconscious undermining as lay counseling becomes a real possibility. Already, for example, the critics of programs demonstrating the greater effectiveness of lay helpers over professionals on indexes selected by professionals are saying that with time the effectiveness of the lay persons will wear off (Rioch, 1966; Rosenbaum, 1966). With the question, "What happens to the professional counselor over time?" we encourage these critics to research the long-term effectiveness of both lay and professional helpers.

Further examples of problems associated with lay counseling revolve around the question of employing lay persons as clerical assistants in order to free counselors for counseling duties. While this practice seems to make sense when the counselors are effective, it appears premature. There is not now available any reliable measure of counselor effectiveness. Even if the counselors were freed of their administrative responsibilities—most of which are of dubious value in the first place—to engage in more counseling activities—which appears unlikely in the second place—the result would merely be the perpetuation of more of the same practices—which are of unknown or questionable efficacy in the third place. Such an approach would not foster new learning in a profession that needs to learn a great deal about itself.

The dangers of professionalization, in part as we have described them in our explorations of professional programs, but much more extensive in terms of professional concerns for image, status, and spheres of influence, will beset the potent practitioner, lay and otherwise. On the one hand, those who have acquired master's and doctoral degrees will feel that their positions are being threatened. On the other hand, some people are already arguing for a master's program in lay counseling for college graduates. Indeed, there may come a day when there will be proposals for doctoral programs in lay counseling.

Finally, while the results of lay programs point upward to the need to explore and, if necessary, reconstruct our professional programs, they also point downward to indigenous personnel within the populations of persons receiving help. This approach represents the helper therapy principle by which persons in need of help may be selected and trained to offer help. At a minimum there is evidence to suggest that indigenous persons giving help demonstrate constructive change themselves as a consequence of being cast in the helping role (Holzberg, Gewirtz, & Ebner, 1964; Holzberg, Whiting, & Lowy, 1964; Knapp & Holzberg, 1964; Riessman, 1965).

REFERENCES

Allen, T. W. The effectiveness of counselor trainees as a function of psychological openness. *Journal of Counseling Psychology*, 1967, **14**, 35–40.

American Personnel and Guidance Association, Professional Preparation and Standards Committee. *The relationship of short-term and specialized programs to the A.P.G.A. policy statement, "The counselor: Professional preparation and role."* Washington, D.C.: American Personnel and Guidance Association, 1964.

Anker, J. M., & Walsh, R. P. Group psychotherapy: A special activity program and group structure in the treatment of chronic schizophrenics. *Journal of Consulting Psychology*, 1961, **25**, 476–481.

Anthony, W., & Carkhuff, R. R. The effects of professional training in rehabilitation counseling. *Journal of Counseling Psychology, in press.*

Appleby, L. Evaluation of treatment methods for chronic schizophrenia. *Archives of General Psychiatry,* 1963, **8,** 8–21.

Arnhoff, F. N. Some factors influencing the unreliability of clinical judgments. *Journal of Clinical Psychology,* 1954, **10,** 272–275.

Banks, G., Berenson, B. G., & Carkhuff, R. R. The effects of counselor race and training upon Negro clients in initial interviews. *Journal of Clinical Psychology,* 1967, **23,** 70–72.

Beck, J. C., Kantor, D., & Gelineau, V. A. Follow-up study of chronic psychotic patients "treated" by college case-aide volunteers. *American Journal of Psychiatry,* 1963, **120,** 269–271.

Berenson, B. G., Carkhuff, R. R., & Myrus, P. The interpersonal functioning and training of college students. *Journal of Counseling Psychology,* 1966, **13,** 441–446.

Bergin, A., & Soloman, S. Personality and performance correlates of empathic understanding in psychotherapy. *American Psychologist,* 1963, **18,** 393.

Brown, W. F. Student-to-student counseling for academic adjustment. *Personnel and Guidance Journal,* 1965, **43,** 811–817.

Carkhuff, R. R. Training in the counseling and therapeutic processes: Requiem or reveille? *Journal of Counseling Psychology,* 1966, **13,** 360–367.

Carkhuff, R. R. The effects of lay counseling: Evaluation and implications. Paper presented at a conference on innovations in rehabilitation counseling. State University of New York at Buffalo, March 1967.

Carkhuff, R. R. A nontraditional assessment of traditional programs. *Counselor Education and Supervision,* 1968, **7,** 252–261; 393–394.

Carkhuff, R. R., & Berenson, B. G. *Beyond counseling and therapy.* New York: Holt, Rinehart and Winston, Inc., 1967.

Carkhuff, R. R., Kratochvil, D., & Friel, T. The effects of graduate training. *Journal of Counseling Psychology,* 1968, **15,** 68–74.

Carkhuff, R. R., Piaget, G., & Pierce, R. The development of skills in interpersonal functioning. *Counselor Education and Supervision,* 1968, **7,** 102–106.

Carkhuff, R. R., & Pierce, R. The differential effects of therapist race and social class upon patient depth of self-exploration in the initial clinical interview. *Journal of Consulting Psychology,* 1967, **31,** 632–634.

Carkhuff, R. R., & Truax, C. B. Training in counseling and psychotherapy: An evaluation of an integrated didactic and experiential approach. *Journal of Consulting Psychology,* 1965, **29,** 333–336. (a)

Carkhuff, R. R., & Truax, C. B. Lay mental health counseling: The effects of lay group counseling. *Journal of Consulting Psychology,* 1965, **29,** 426–432. (b)

Coggeshall, L. T. *Planning for medical progress through education.* Evanston, Ill.: Association of American Medical Colleges, 1965.

Colarelli, N. J., & Siegel, S. M. A re-evaluation of the role of the psychiatric aide. Progress Report, 1963, Project Grant OM-770, National Institute of Mental Health.

Creech, O. Medical practice in 1990. *Bulletin of the Tulane University of Louisiana Medical Faculty*, 1966, **25**, 229–238.

Deane, W. N., & Ansbacher, H. L. Attendant-patient commonality as a psychotherapeutic factor. *Journal of Individual Psychology*, 1962, **18**, 157–167.

Demos, G. D. The application of certain principles of client-centered therapy to short-term vocational counseling. *Journal of Counseling Psychology*, 1964, **11**, 280–284.

Demos, G. D., & Zuwaylif, F. H. Counselor movement as a result of an intensive six-week training program in counseling. *Personnel and Guidance Journal*, 1963, **42**, 125–128.

Eysenck, H. J. The effects of psychotherapy. *International Journal of Psychiatry*, 1965, **1**, 99–178.

Glasser, W. *Reality therapy: A new approach to psychiatry.* New York: Harper & Row, Publishers, Inc., 1965.

Gordon, J. E. Project CAUSE, the federal anti-poverty program, and some implications of subprofessional training. *American Psychologist*, 1965, **20**, 334–343.

Greenblatt, M., & Kantor, D. Student volunteer movement and the manpower shortage. *American Journal of Psychiatry*, 1962, **118**, 809–814.

Guerney, B. Filial therapy: Description and rationale. *Journal of Consulting Psychology*, 1964, **28**, 304–310.

Guerney, B., Guerney, L. F., & Andronico, M. P. Filial therapy. *Yale Scientific Magazine*, 1966, **40**, 6–14.

Gunning, T. J., Holmes, J. E., Johnson, P. W., & Rife, S. M. Process in a short-term NDEA counseling and guidance institute. *Counselor Education and Supervision*, 1965, **4**, 81–88.

Hansen, J. C. Trainees' expectations of supervision in the counseling practicum. *Counselor Education and Supervision*, 1965, 4, 75–80.

Hansen, J. C., & Barker, E. N. Experiencing and the supervisory relationship. *Journal of Counseling Psychology*, 1964, **11**, 107–111.

Harvey, L. V. The use of nonprofessional auxiliary counselors in staffing a counseling service. *Journal of Counseling Psychology*, 1964, **11**, 348–351.

Hoch, E. L., Ross, A. O., & Winder, C. L. Conference on the professional preparation of clinical psychologists. *American Psychologist*, 1965, **21**, 42–51.

Holland, J. L., & Richards, J. M. Academic and nonacademic accomplishment: Correlated or uncorrelated? *Journal of Educational Psychology*, 1965, **56**, 165–174.

Holzberg, J. D. The companion program: Implementing the manpower recommendations of the Joint Commission on Mental Illness and Health. *American Psychologist*, 1963, **18**, 224–226.

Holzberg, J. D., Gewirtz, H., & Ebner, E. Changes in self-acceptance and moral judgments in college students as a function of companionship with hospitalized patients. *Journal of Consulting Psychology*, 1964, **28**, 299–303.

Holzberg, J. D., & Knapp, R. H. The social interaction of college students and chronically ill patients. *American Journal of Orthopsychiatry*, 1965, **35**, 487–492.

Holzberg, J. D., Whiting, H. S., & Lowy, D. G. Chronic patients and a college companion program. *Mental Hospitals*, 1964, **15**, 152–158.

Joint Commission on Mental Illness and Health. *Action for mental health*. New York: Basic Books, Inc., 1961.

Jones, V. Attitude changes in an N.D.E.A. institute. *Personnel and Guidance Journal*, 1963, **42**, 387–389.

Kantor, D., & Greenblatt, M. (eds.). *College students in a mental hospital*. New York: Grune & Stratton, Inc., 1962.

Kelly, E. L., & Fiske, D. W. The prediction of success in the VA training program in clinical psychology. *American Psychologist*, 1950, **5**, 395–406.

Kennedy, E. G., & Strowig, R. W. Support personnel for the counselor: Their technical and nontechnical roles and preparation. *Personnel and Guidance Journal*, 1967, **45**, 857–861.

Knapp, R. H., & Holzberg, J. D. Characteristics of college students volunteering for service to mental patients. *Journal of Consulting Psychology*, 1964, **28**, 82–85.

Korson, S., & Hayes, W. Empathic relationship therapy utilizing student nurses: A 5-year pilot study. *American Journal of Psychiatry*, 1966, **123**, 213–218.

Kratochvil, D. Changes in values and interpersonal functioning of nurses in counselor training. *Counselor Education and Supervision*, 1969, 8, 104–107.

Levitt, E. E. Psychotherapy with children: A further evaluation. *Behavior Research and Therapy*, 1963, **1**, 45–51.

Lewis, W. W. Continuity and intervention in emotional disturbance: A review. *Exceptional Children*, 1965, **31**, 465–475.

Lief, H. I. Subprofessional training in mental health. *Archives of General Psychiatry*, 1966, **15**, 660–664.

Lorr, M. Client perceptions of therapists: A study of therapeutic relations. *Journal of Consulting Psychology*, 1965, **29**, 146–149.

Magoon, T. M., & Golann, S. E. Nontraditionally trained women as mental health counselors-psychotherapists. *Personnel and Guidance Journal*, 1966, **44**, 788–793.

Martin, J. C., & Carkhuff, R. R. The effects of training upon trainee personality and behavior. *Journal of Clinical Psychology*, 1968, **24**, 109–110.

Matarazzo, J. D. Psychotherapeutic processes. *Annual Review of Psychology*, 1965, **16**, 181–224.

Meadow, L., & Tillem, K. Evaluating the effectiveness of a workshop rehabilitation program. *Personnel and Guidance Journal*, 1963, **42**, 541–545.

Mendel, W. M., & Rapport, S. Outpatient treatment for chronic schizophrenic patients: Therapeutic consequences of an existential view. *Archives of General Psychiatry*, 1963, **8**, 190–196.

Miller, T. K. Characteristics of perceived helpers. *Personnel and Guidance Journal*, 1965, **12**, 353–358.

Munger, P. F., & Johnson, C. A. Changes in attitudes associated with an

N.D.E.A. counseling and guidance institute. *Personnel and Guidance Journal*, 1960, **38**, 751–753.

Munger, P. F., Myers, R. A., & Brown, D. F. Guidance institutes and the persistence of attitudes. *Personnel and Guidance Journal*, 1963, **41**, 415–419.

Odgers, J. C. Cause for concern. *Counselor Education and Supervision*, 1964, **4**, 17–20.

Pagell, W., Carkhuff, R. R. & Berenson, B. G. The predicted differential effects of the level of counselor functioning upon the level of functioning of out-patients. *Journal of Clinial Psychology*, 1967, **23**, 510–512.

Patterson, C. H. Subprofessional functions and short-term training. *Counselor Education and Supervision*, 1965, **4**, 144–146.

Pierce, R., Carkhuff, R. R., & Berenson, B. G. The differential effects of high and moderate level functioning counselors upon counselors-in-training. *Journal of Clinical Psychology*, 1967, **23**, 212–215.

Poser, E. G. The effect of therapists' training on group therapeutic outcome. *Journal of Consulting Psychology*, 1966, **30**, 283–289.

Reiff, R. Mental health manpower and institutional change. *American Psychologist*, 1966, **21**, 540–548.

Reiff, R., & Riessman, F. The indigenous non-professional. *Community Mental Health Journal*, 1965, No. 1.

Riessman, F. The "helper" therapy principle. *Social Work*, 1965, **10**, 27–32.

Riessman, F., & National Institute of Labor Education. New approaches to mental health treatment for labor and low income groups. Report No. 2, 1964, National Institute of Labor Education, Mental Health Program, New York.

Rioch, M. J. Changing concept in the training of therapists. *Journal of Consulting Psychology*, 1966, **30**, 290–292.

Rioch, M. J., Elkes, E., Flint, A. A., Usdansky, B. S., Newman, B. G., & Silber, E. NIMH pilot study in training mental health counselors. *American Journal of Orthopsychiatry*, 1963, **33**, 678–689.

Rosenbaum, M. Some comments on the use of untrained therapists. *Journal of Consulting Psychology*, 1966, **30**, 292–294.

Schlossberg, N. K. Sub-professionals: To be or not to be. *Counselor Education and Supervision*, 1967, **6**, 108–113.

Siegel, S. M., & Colarelli, N. J. Gaining more from research experience. *Mental Hospitals*, 1964, **15**, 666–670.

Sines, L. K., Silver, R. J., & Lucero, R. J. The effect of therapeutic intervention by untrained therapists. *Journal of Clinical Psychology*, 1961, **17**, 394–396.

Spiegel, P. K., & Spiegel, D. E. Perceived helpfulness of others as a function of compatible intelligence levels. *Journal of Counseling Psychology*, 1967, **14**, 61–62.

Taft, R. The ability to judge people. *Psychological Bulletin*, 1955, **52**, 1–23.

Truax, C. B., & Carkhuff, R. R. *Toward effective counseling and psychotherapy: Training and practice*. Chicago. Aldine Publishing Company, 1967.

Tudor, G. A socio-psychiatric nursing approach to intervention in problems of mutual withdrawal on a mental hospital ward. *Psychiatry*, 1952, **15**, 193–217.

Wahler, R. G., Winkel, G. H., Peterson, R. F., & Morrison, D. C. Mothers as behavior therapists for their own children. *Behavior Research and Therapy*, 1965, **3**, 113–124.

Warme, G. E. Consulting with aide-therapists. *Archives of General Psychiatry*, 1965, **13**, 432–438.

Webb, A. J., & Harris, J. T. A semantic differential study of counselors in an N.D.E.A. institute. *Personnel and Guidance Journal*, 1963, **42**, 260–263.

Weiner, H. J., & Brand, M. S. Involving a labor union in the rehabilitation of the mentally ill. *American Journal of Orthopsychiatry*, 1965, **35**, 598–600.

Weiss, J. H. The effect of professional training and amount and accuracy of information on behavioral prediction. *Journal of Consulting Psychology*, 1963, **27**, 257–262.

Wrightsman, L. S., Richard, W. C., & Noble, F. Attitude changes of guidance institute participants. *Counselor Education and Supervision*, 1966, **5**, 212–220.

Zunker, V. G., & Brown, W. F. Comparative effectiveness of student and professional counselors. *Personnel and Guidance Journal*, 1966, **44**, 738–743.

PART TWO

Toward Effective Helping

PART TWO PRESENTS a model for the development of human functioning and dysfunctioning and examines the treatment of the latter (Chapter 2). One critical conclusion which emerges is that there is a need for the further development of models of functioning and dysfunctioning that incorporate all relevant parties and variables. The succeeding chapters do so. The facilitative and action-oriented dimensions offered by the first person or helper to the second person or helpee are described (Chapter 3). Insofar as the helper variables do not have an effect independent of helpee variables, the helpee variables are explored in order to determine those that are most relevant. The evidence points toward indexes of (1) initial level of helpee functioning and (2) helpee involvement in the helping process as those variables that are most promising for understanding the process leading to the constructive change of the helpee (Chapter 4). Finally, since neither helper nor helpee variables interact independent of context and environment, these variables are assessed, with special attention given to the potentially modifying effects of the people who comprise the environment (Chapter 5).

2

A MODEL FOR DYSFUNCTIONING
AND TREATMENT

Several significant lines of evidence flow from the basic assumption that counseling and psychotherapy are aspects of interpersonal learning and relearning processes or, more briefly, of human relations in general. First, there is extensive evidence to indicate that significant human encounters may have constructive or deteriorative consequences, that is, counseling and therapy may be "for better or for worse." Second, evidence indicates that all effective interpersonal processes share a common set of conditions that are conducive to facilitative human experiences. For example, clients of counselors who offer high levels of the facilitative conditions of empathy, respect, and concreteness as well as the more action- and activity-oriented conditions of genuineness and self-disclosure and confrontation and immediacy improve while those of counselors who offer low levels of these conditions deteriorate. Thus, we can account for a great part of the counselor's effectiveness independent of his orientation and technique by assessing the level of facilitative and action-oriented conditions offered by the counselor (summarized in Berenson & Carkhuff, 1967; Berenson & Mitchell, 1968; Carkhuff & Berenson, 1967; Rogers, Gendlin, Keisler, & Truax, 1967; Truax & Carkhuff, 1967).

The proposition that all human learning or relearning processes may have constructive or deteriorative consequences leads quite readily to a model for effective and ineffective functioning, or psychopathology. At each critical encounter between those persons designated by society as more knowing (parents, teachers, counselors) and those designated as less knowing (children, students, clients), the effects upon the less knowing and, indeed, upon the more knowing person may be for better or for worse. That is, the less knowing person, or the individual being "helped," may be retarded or facilitated in his physical, emotional, or intellectual growth (summarized in Carkhuff & Berenson, 1967). Personal growth or deterioration, then, as demonstrated through positive or negative movement at the crisis points in an individual's life can be illustrated diagrammatically, as in Figure 2-1.[1] The severely deteriorated person who is not functioning effectively in any realm (level 1) may be seen as a product of a series of retarding relationships, some of which perhaps promised hope but all of which delivered failure experiences. Similarly, at the other extreme the person functioning at very high levels in many realms (above level 3) may be seen as a product of a series of facilitative relationships. *Between these extremes most individuals (around level 2) may be viewed as products of a series of mixed relationships, often neither constructive nor deteriorative, although all too frequently they are the latter. Such persons are functioning yet not fulfilling, living yet not alive, dying yet not yet dead. These are the people who populate our everyday world—counselors as well as patients, students as well as teachers—searching for help yet rejecting it, seeking light yet preferring darkness, crying for life yet choosing death.*

Each significant encounter, then, between more knowing and less knowing persons may be considered a crisis in the lives of both groups. Whether an individual grows or deteriorates is dependent in large part upon the interaction of the activities of both the more knowing and the less knowing persons. With respect to the more knowing persons, there is extensive evidence to relate the offering of high levels of facilitative and action-oriented conditions by parents, teachers, counselors, and therapists to constructive change or gain on the part of their children, students, and clients on both emotional and intellective indexes. Similarly, the initiation of low levels of facilitative and action-oriented dimensions has been related to the deterioration of children, students, and clients on emotional and intellective indexes (the literature is summarized in Aspy, 1969; Aspy, Carkhuff, & Douds, 1968; Berenson & Carkhuff, 1967; Berenson & Mitchell, 1968; Carkhuff & Berenson, 1967; Carkhuff & Truax, 1966; Kratochvil & Carkhuff, 1969; Rogers, 1967; Truax & Carkhuff, 1967).

All of this is not to say, of course, that there are not inherent differences in resources and predispositions of the individuals involved.[1] Nor is it to say, for example, that more physically or chemically oriented

---

[1] The point of origin in Figure 2-1 may be conceived of in a third dimension in order to avoid making assumptions concerning the inherent resources and constructive or destructive predispositions of the individual involved. A description of this model appears in Chapters 2 and 3 of *Beyond Counseling and Therapy* (Carkhuff & Berenson, 1967).

treatment cannot contribute to the constructive change of a distressed individual. In this area, however, the treatment of one individual by another can make a significant difference in the lives of either or both. We do know that an individual's basic directionality depends a great deal upon what happens at each critical stage in his development. Thus, it is possible to make a constructive difference at a crisis point in a person's life.

GROWTH AND DETERIORATION IN FUNCTIONING

A number of propositions and derivative corollaries flow from the basic findings that (1) all interpersonal learning or relearning processes may

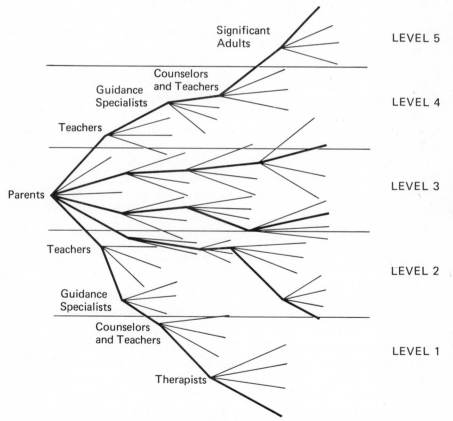

Figure 2-1. Systematic representation of levels of functioning as a consequence of a series of facilitative and retarding relationships. (Carkhuff & Berenson, 1967)

be for better or for worse and (2) constructive or destructive results can be accounted for by the level of facilitative and action-oriented dimensions offered by the more knowing person, for example, the parent, the teacher, or the counselor. Together these propositions constitute the beginnings of a model for understanding the development of human functioning and dysfunctioning as well for the effective treatment of the latter.

Proposition I. Growth and deterioration are physical, emotional, and intellectual.

Growth or deterioration is measured on physical, emotional, and intellectual indexes. The physical, emotional, and intellectual dimensions are inextricably related in both the healthy and the unhealthy person. The persons in between these extremes may for a moment in time appear to be functioning at higher levels on one of these dimensions than on another, but ultimately the respective dimensions will move in one direction or another. While growth may be reflected most rapidly and deterioration least rapidly in the physical realm, the physical dimension is given the least attention in the literature and research. Similarly, in developmental studies retardation in the physical realm is the most difficult dimension to deal with because of inherent physical growth trends. These statements raise related questions of concomitant or concurrent learning. In most studies of learning we select one achievement index or the other. In so doing we are neglecting the great multitude of relevant indexes that reflect concurrent growth or deterioration on other meaningful dimensions.

A number of corollaries flow directly from this central proposition.

Corollary I. Growth is reflected in the actualization of the individual's physical, emotional, and intellectual resources.

The actualization of resources is dependent upon the developmental stage of an individual. Growth is reflected in the individual's *increasing ability* (1) to understand his physical, emotional, and intellectual worlds and (2) to act upon these worlds, both internally, or within himself, and externally, or in his environment.

Corollary II. Deterioration (retardation) is reflected in the deterioration (retarded development) of the individual's physical, emotional, and intellectual resources.

Again, the deterioration or retardation of resources is dependent upon the individual's stage of development and is reflected in the individual's *decreasing ability* (1) to understand his physical, emotional, and intellectual worlds and (2) to act upon these worlds.

Corollary III. The conditions of effective helping are physical, emotional, and intellectual.

Effective facilitative and/or therapeutic processes cannot concentrate upon any one of the physical, emotional, or intellectual dimensions to the exclusion of the others. All must be integrated in a whole and growing person and in the helping process which he is conducting so that the person being helped can grow toward wholeness.

Corollary IV. The goals of all helping processes involve (1) understanding the physical, emotional, and intellectual worlds and (2) being able to act upon these worlds.

The growth of an individual depends not only upon his sensitivity to his internal and external world but also upon his ability to act upon the discriminations he makes. Only then is a person involved in a constructive growth process.

Proposition II. Physical, emotional, and intellectual growth or deterioration is dependent upon first person, second person, and contextual and environmental variables.

The growth or deterioration of the less knowing as well as the more knowing person is contingent upon *first person* (parents, teachers, counselors), *second person* (children, students, clients), and *contextual* (primarily the conditions of the setting) and *environmental* variables (in large part the conditions offered by others in the individual's environment), alone and in their various interactions. Thus, we must understand all variables potentially relevant to the constructive gain or loss of either or both parties. The effects of one variable may modify the effects of another, and different interactions of the variables may yield different results.

These statements warrant further exploration in corollary form.

Corollary I. The level of functioning of the first person has a potentially critical effect upon the level of functioning of both the first and second persons in a relationship.

The level of facilitative and action-oriented conditions offered by the more knowing person has a critical effect upon the sensitivity and responsiveness of the second person to his physical, emotional, and intellectual worlds. Too, the level of functioning with which the first person enters the relationship is influential in determining the degree to which he gains from his relationship with the second person.

Corollary II. The level of functioning of the second person has a potentially critical effect upon the level of functioning of both the first and second persons in the relationship.

Growth or deterioration is dependent upon an individual's level of development when he experiences threats to his physical and/or psychological survival. Persons with sufficient resources can discriminate and respond appropriately to the demands of the significant figures in their environment; those whose resources are inadequate or inadequately developed are either overwhelmed or develop very rigid cosmologies which are functional only in very limited spheres, and then only for a limited period of time.

Corollary III. The level of conditions offered by the environment and the context within which the helping relationship takes place has a potentially critical effect upon the level of functioning of both the first and second persons in the relationship.

It is sometimes difficult in the face of the extensive attention given to physical and socioeconomic factors to remember that the *environment is people,* that is, the significant others who relate to the first and second persons in the relationship and to whom these persons return following all of their important interactions. The significant others who can facilitate or retard gains or losses can, in turn, be facilitated or retarded by the first and second persons.

Corollary IV. The growth or deterioration of all parties involved is dependent upon the interaction of all relevant first person, second person, and contextual and environmental variables.

Only persons who are functioning at higher levels can enable persons functioning at lower levels raise their level of functioning; similarly, persons who are functioning at lower levels elicit lower levels of functioning from low-level functioning persons. The latter, in turn, work upon the first person to bring him to function at still lower levels. The persons in an individual's environments can have facilitating or neutralizing effects which are analogous to these changes.

Proposition III. The physical, emotional, and intellectual effects of facilitative or retarding experiences at crisis points are cumulative.

Growth or deteriorative processes take place at crisis points in an individual's life. These points occur when there is conflict over whether the threats to the person's physical and/or psychological survival are stronger than his physical, emotional, and intellectual resources. The response the individual makes at the crisis point increases the probability of his responding in a similar manner at the next crisis point— the more constructively a person is able to respond, the greater the probability that he will respond constructively at the next crisis point; the more destructively he responds, the greater the probability that he will respond destructively at the next crisis point.

A number of related corollaries follow from this proposition.

Corollary I. The more retarding experiences an individual has had, the less he is able to employ constructive experiences and the more vulnerable he is to destructive experiences.

As an individual deteriorates his discriminations become increasingly faulty and the less able he is to act upon them. To an increasing extent he allows destructive persons to enter his world and influence his life.

Corollary II. The more facilitative experiences an individual has had, the more he is able to employ constructive experiences and the less vulnerable he is to destructive experiences.

As an individual grows his discriminations become more accurate and the more able he is to act upon them. He increasingly allows only constructive persons to enter his world and influence his life.

Corollary III. The change in the level of functioning of the physical, emotional, or intellectual dimensions will influence the level of functioning of the other dimensions in the same direction.

Physical growth or deterioration has a facilitative or retarding effect upon growth in the emotional and intellectual spheres. The same is true of the emotional and intellectual dimensions, with a change in the level of each dimension acting to influence the other dimensions in the same direction.

Corollary IV. The change in one problem area of functioning will influence the change in the functioning of other areas in the same direction.

An increased level of functioning in, for example, the educational-vocational sphere will influence the individual to function at higher levels in the sexual-marital, child-rearing, and social-interpersonal areas; similarly, a deterioration in the sexual-marital area may influence the individual to function at lower levels in the other spheres.

CONCLUSIONS AND DIRECTIONS

The need in counseling and psychotherapy and, indeed, in all human relations is for a model that is comprehensive in scope and effective in its translation to human benefits. In this regard the present model for functioning and dysfunctioning, even in the broad outlines with which it is presented, has a number of important characteristics, which will be considered in detail in later chapters. The further development of such a comprehensive model offers several distinct advantages.

Conclusion I. There is a need for the further development of models of functioning and dysfunctioning that have direct implications for treatment.

Traditional models of psychopathology have had little or no translation to treatment benefits. Traditional diagnoses do make a difference.

Conclusion II. There is a need for the further development of models of functioning and dysfunctioning that incorporate the effects of all relevant parties and variables.

First person, second person, and contextual and environmental variables, alone and in their various interactions, are all potentially critical sources of deficits as well as benefits, both within and outside treatment.

Conclusion III.   There is a need for the further development of models of functioning and dysfunctioning that incorporate a wide variety of dimensions as well as problem areas of functioning.

It is essential that physical dimensions, and to a lesser degree intellectual dimensions, be reintroduced for consideration along with the more traditional concerns for emotional learning and relearning. The physical, emotional, and intellectual dimensions, in turn, cut across the problem areas of functioning such as social-interpersonal, educational-vocational, sexual-marital, and child-rearing.

Conclusion IV.   There is a need for the further development of models of functioning and dysfunctioning that can be tested both experimentally and experientially.

It is essential that the models which are developed allow us to generate and check out our predictions in both clinical experience and research.

Conclusion V.   There is a need for the further development of models of functioning and dysfunctioning that allow us to reintegrate the whole human being.

Artificial and detrimental divisions have developed between the physical, emotional, and intellectual dimensions. Only when we think in terms of the whole person, both as means and ends will it be possible to integrate all of the dimensions of human functioning.

We seek, then, to develop a comprehensive model that accounts for growth and deterioration in human functioning. This objective must be further extended and refined in appropriate theory-building processes. The inductive function of theory building allows us to generalize to the level of laws from the stable body of phenomena (facts) concerning what facilitative and action-oriented conditions relate specifically to differential changes in different populations: (1) high levels of facilitative and action-oriented conditions lead to physical, emotional, and mental growth; (2) low levels of facilitative and action-oriented conditions lead to physical, emotional, and mental deterioration. While a number of lower-order hypothetical constructs may account for these laws,[2] at this point in time it is perhaps most meaningful to consider

[2] The lower-order hypothetical constructs that account for the operation of the laws are examined in Chapter 3.

the functions of higher-order theory building.[3] At higher levels man's basic objectives in life are survival and growth, with the latter dominating only when the former is assured. The conditions of survival and growth are physical (the need for food, shelter, and so on), emotional or psychological (the need for understanding, respect, love, and so on), and intellectual (the need for an effective working cosmology, or a functional assumptive world, and so on). When these needs have been filled to a sufficient degree the individual moves to levels where he makes and acts upon his sensitive discriminations of his internal and external physical, emotional, and intellectual worlds. Threats to survival and/or growth, in turn, make it impossible for the individual to make such discriminations in the physical, emotional, and/or intellectual realms. The threats may, depending upon the level of development of the individual's resources, cause physical, emotional, and intellectual retardation or deterioration. The rehabilitation process, then, involves those physical (sleep, exercise, diet), emotional/psychological (warmth and understanding), and intellectual (a functional and rewarding cosmology) conditions that enable the individual once again, if he ever did, to understand and act upon his physical, emotional, and intellectual environment, both internal and external.

The deductive function of theory building makes it possible, in turn, to generate and assess predictions concerning the change in the individuals who seek to be helped in the physical, emotional, and intellectual spheres of functioning. Thus, depending upon the level of functioning of both the more knowing and the less knowing person in the relevant spheres, as well as upon the type of treatment offered, we may generate predictions concerning the potential gains of the less knowing person. By employing the schematic representation of the consequences of facilitative and retarding relationships, we may estimate how much a child, student, or client may gain in a prolonged relationship with a parent, teacher, or counselor. As Table 2-1 indicates, only those helpees who are functioning at level 3 or below are included, since these are the people who seek out helping relationships. Individuals who function at higher levels are not only more rare in our world but they are also self-sustaining persons who, on their own or in interaction with intimate friends who are themselves functioning at high levels, work through their own difficulties and act on their own new learnings (Carkhuff & Berenson, 1967). As the table also indicates, only helpers who are functioning above level 3 can offer uniformly positive

---

[3] The function of theory will be examined in detail in Volume II on practice and research.

Table 2-1. Predicted Differential Levels of Helpee Gain Based upon Initial Levels of Helper and Helpee Functioning

Levels of Functioning		
Helper	*Helpee*	*Helpee changes*
1	1	0
	2	−1
	3	−2
2	1	+1
	2	0
	3	−1
3	1	+2
	2	+1
	3	0
4	1	+3
	2	+2
	3	+1
5	1	+4
	2	+3
	3	+2

gains in levels of functioning to the persons seeking help from them. Of course, such predictions are not unqualified.[4] What is presented here, however, are general guidelines for determining what constitutes effective training and treatment in the helping processes.

We know that one individual can make a contribution in the lives of others if he himself is growing toward wholeness and if he is not only willing but committed to employing all of the means available to him in the helping process. *In a real sense, then, the helping process is a process of rehabilitation as well as a process of personal emergence and/or re-emergence. It is a process in which each barrier looms higher than the last but one in which the rewarding experiences of surmounting previous hurdles increases the probability of future successes. If the helper is not committed to his own physical, emotional, and intellectual development, he cannot enable another to find fulfillment in any or all of these realms of functioning.*

[4] For a more comprehensive description of the development of the dimensions that are incorporated within such a model see Chapters 2 and 3 of *Beyond Counseling and Therapy* (Carkhuff & Berenson, 1967).

REFERENCES

For a more detailed discussion of the issues considered in this chapter see the asterisked readings and the references upon which the readings are based.

Aspy, D. The differential effects of high and low functioning teachers upon student achievement. *Florida Journal of Educational Research*, in press.

Aspy, D., Carkhuff, R. R., & Douds, J. Counseling and real life. In *The counselor's contribution to facilitative processes* (R. R. Carkhuff, ed.). Mimeographed manuscript, State University of New York at Buffalo, 1968.

Berenson, B. G., & Carkhuff, R. R. *The sources of gain in counseling and psychotherapy.* New York: Holt, Rinehart and Winston, Inc., 1967.

Berenson, B. G., & Mitchell, K. *Confrontation in counseling and life.* Mimeographed manuscript, American International College, Springfield, Mass., 1968.

Bierman, R. *Counseling and child-rearing.* Mimeographed manuscript, University of Waterloo, Canada, 1968.

*Carkhuff, R. R., & Berenson, B. G. *Beyond counseling and therapy.* New York: Holt, Rinehart and Winston, Inc., 1967.

*Carkhuff, R. R., & Truax, C. B. Toward explaining success or failure in interpersonal learning processes. *Personnel and Guidance Journal*, 1966, **46**, 723–728.

Kratochvil, D., & Carkhuff, R. R. The cumulative effects of parent- and teacher-offered levels of facilitative conditions upon indexes of student physical, emotional and intellectual functioning. *Journal of Educational Research*, in press, 1969.

Rogers, C. R., Gendlin, E., Kiesler, D., & Truax, C. B. (eds.). *The therapeutic relationship and its impact: A study of psychotherapy with schizophrenics.* Madison, Wisc.: University of Wisconsin Press, 1967.

*Truax, C. B., & Carkhuff, R. R. *Toward effective counseling and psychotherapy.* Chicago: Aldine Publishing Company, 1967.

3

THE HELPER'S CONTRIBUTION TO
HELPING PROCESSES

The need to expand existing models that account for constructive client or helpee change has become imperative. The already considerable evidence relating the level of facilitative conditions offered by the helper to indexes of constructive helpee change or gain (Berenson & Carkhuff, 1967; Carkhuff & Berenson, 1967; Truax & Carkhuff, 1967) must be complemented by additional dimensions if we are ever to account for a significant degree of truly effective helping processes. Thus, the more receptive and responsive helper offerings of warmth and understanding must be complemented by more active, assertive offerings involving direction, confrontation, and more action-oriented activities. Although some of the facilitative dimensions such as counselor genuineness and self-disclosure appear to be related to more action-oriented dimensions, this characteristic of the helping process has not been made explicit in past formulations. To be sure, while in many respects the traditional facilitative dimensions of warmth and understanding may in fact appear independent of the action-oriented dimensions involved in most processes leading to constructive change or gain, with the highest-level practitioners these conditions also appear to fuse in a highly interrelated offering.

At another level if we equate the sensitive and responsive components with the feminine dimension, the facilitative conditions may be viewed as the essential offerings of a healthy female—or mother. If we equate the active and assertive components with the masculine dimension, the action-oriented dimensions may be seen as the essential offering of the healthy male—or father. In effective helping processes both the male and female components are present to varying degrees, depending upon the needs of the person being helped. *The effective helper is both mother and father. The whole person has incorporated both the responsive and assertive components. He (or she) can understand his internal and external physical, emotional, and intellectual world with sensitivity and can act upon these worlds with responsibility.*

With these thoughts in mind we will consider a number of assumptions that we must make in order to develop comprehensive models for the helping processes.

Assumption I. Any comprehensive model of helping processes must include relevant dimensions concerning the helping person.

All too frequently upon the failure of a given helping process we look to certain helpee and other variables to discover the cause of the failure. For example, there are counselors whose clients terminate treatment following an initial contact, or, if they return, request a different counselor; or grammar school teachers who develop seven stutterers per year without fail. Do we study the helpers? The situation is similar for success cases. Success or failure of the helping process is no doubt a function of the interaction of helper, helpee, and other variables. Our logical beginning point, nonetheless, is to understand the helper's contribution, since at least initially this is the variable that can most easily be controlled.

Assumption II. Any comprehensive model of helping processes must relate helper variables to indexes of helpee change.

The helper variables that we study must not function independently of the helpees who are seen by the helpers. They must not have functional autonomy. The helper serves for the helpee's purposes. Accordingly, we must relate the helper-offered conditions to criteria of helpee change or gain. The helper variables must be relevant and functional for the helpee's purposes.

Assumption III. Any comprehensive model of helping processes must relate helper variables to differential treatment approaches.

The helper variables must be related not only to indexes of helpee change but also to different approaches for achieving different goals on the helpee's behalf. That is, we do not have precisely the same goals for all helpees. We must be able to relate the helper variables to the particular objectives we are seeking to attain.

Most of the work on the helping processes has focused upon the helper's contribution. This chapter will serve only to introduce these variables. Later sections of these volumes on training and treatment will present a detailed exposition of these dimensions.

RESPONSIVENESS AND INITIATIVE

Effective helping processes, then, may be broken down broadly into the components of understanding and action. We may view the facilitative dimensions as those offered *in response to* the expressions of the person being helped while the action-oriented dimensions are *initiated* by the helper. The potential sources of learning for the person seeking help are multiple. In regard to both a more responsive understanding and an active confrontation of life, the helpee may benefit from each or all of the following sources when present at high levels: (1) in the physical world in particular, modeling or imitative processes will serve to increase the helpee's behavioral response repertoire; (2) in the emotional world the helpee's experiential base of both understanding and action will free him to further experience and experiment with himself; (3) in the intellectual world direct teaching or shaping may enable the trainee to develop a functional and fulfilling cosmology of life. It is to be noted in the following explorations that some of the dimensions, such as concreteness and genuineness, are "swing" dimensions that may, according to the developmental phases of helping, be either responsive or initiative. Thus, with both outpatient neurotic and inpatient psychotic populations as well as with more "normal" populations two dominant propositions emerge which lead to a number of corollaries.

Proposition I. The degree to which the helping person offers high levels of facilitative conditions in response to the expressions of the person seeking help is related directly to the degree to which the person seeking help engages in processes leading to constructive change or gain.

Of necessity this proposition refers directly to the helping person. For example, to the degree that the helping person is himself open to a wide range of experiences in himself, to that degree can he be open to a wide range of experiences in another person, and, in turn, enable the other person to become open to a wide range of experiences in himself. The degree to which the helper understands and accepts himself is related to the degree to which he understands and accepts others.

The sources of learning, again, are modeling, the experiential base of understanding and action, and direct teaching. All of these sources must be integrated in a whole process conducted by a whole person. Only when the helper is sensitively responsive to, and acceptant and respectful of, the feelings and experiences that dominate the helpee's world may he involve the helpee in a process leading to a sensitive responsiveness to his world.

A number of related corollaries flow from this basic proposition.

Corollary I. The degree to which the helping person offers high levels of empathic understanding of the helpee's world is related directly to the degree to which the helpee is able to understand himself and others.

When the first person's responses *add significantly* to the expressions of the second person in such a way as to express accurately feelings several levels below what the second person was able to express, or in the event of ongoing deep self-exploration on the part of the second person, when the first person is fully with him in his deepest moments (Carkhuff, 1968; Carkhuff & Berenson, 1967; Truax & Carkhuff, 1967), then the second person can learn through the significant sources of learning to respond sensitively to his own world and those of others.

Corollary II. The degree to which the helping person communicates high levels of respect and warmth for the helpee and his world is related to the degree to which the helpee is able to respect and direct warm feelings toward himself and others.

Although in many ways the actively assertive dimension of genuineness communicates the most respect when one person refuses to be less than he can be with another, it has been traditional to incorporate respect within a more passively receptive and warm context. Nevertheless, we must emphasize that we are not speaking of "unconditional positive regards," "nonpossessive warmth," or "nonretaliatory permissiveness." Thus, when the first person communicates the very deepest respect for the second person's worth as a person and his potentials as a free individual (Carkhuff, 1968; Carkhuff & Berenson, 1967; Pierce, 1968; Truax & Carkhuff, 1967), then the second person can learn through the significant sources of learning to respect his own world and those of others.

Corollary III.   The degree to which the helper is helpful in guiding the exploration to specific feelings and content is related directly to the degree to which the helpee is able to make concrete his own problem areas.

Again, while this dimension may also be effectively implemented in an active and assertive manner, especially during the latter phases of helping, it is effective in a passively facilitative mode in which concreteness serves to complement the accuracy of communications of empathy. In either context the helper's ability to enable the helpee to discuss fluently, directly, and completely specific feelings and experiences will enable the helpee to experience and articulate specifically his own life experiences (Carkhuff, 1968; Carkhuff & Berenson, 1967; Truax & Carkhuff, 1967).

Corollary IV.   The degree to which the helper is responsively genuine in his relationship with the helpee is related to the degree to which the helpee is able to be responsively genuine in his relationship with himself and others.

To be sure, the genuineness dimension, particularly during latter phases of helping, may also be an initiative dimension in the sense that the source of its active expression is the helper's experience. Here, however, the emphasis is upon being genuinely responsive or responsively genuine in response to the helpee's experience. With the helpee's experience as the locus during the earlier phases of helping, the emphasis is not so much upon the helper's free and spontaneous expression of his own feelings as it is upon not being inauthentic (Carkhuff, 1968; Carkhuff & Berenson, 1967).

Proposition II.   The degree to which the helping person initiates action-oriented dimensions in a helping relationship is directly related to the degree to which the person seeking help engages in processes that lead to constructive change or gain.

The helpee must learn not only to make fine and sensitive discriminations in his internal and external world but also to act upon these discriminations. Hopefully, the action will be accomplished in the context of high levels of facilitative conditions involving sensitive understanding. Frequently, however, it is necessary for the person to act in the absence of understanding—*often sensitive understanding can only follow action.* The following conditions represent the highest level of translation of understanding to action-orientation *within* the helping process. Thus, the helper must be equipped with the potential for directive action as well as nondirective understanding. Again, the sources of learning described previously dominate.

Corollary I. The degree to which the helper can be freely, spontaneously, and deeply himself, including the disclosing of significant information about himself when appropriate, is directly related to the degree to which the helpee is able to be genuine and self-disclosing in appropriate relationships.

As we have just noted, genuineness can be an active and assertive expression of the helper's experience in the moment, or it can be more passive and responsive to the helpee's experience. In particular, through the effects of modeling, but also through the helpee's experience of genuineness and self-disclosure from a more knowing person, the helpee learns that he can be freely, spontaneously, and deeply himself and that he can disclose information about himself in a constructive fashion (Carkhuff, 1968; Carkhuff & Berenson, 1967; Truax & Carkhuff, 1967).

Corollary II. The degree to which the helper actively confronts the helpee and himself is directly related to the degree to which the helpee is able to confront himself and others.

In the context of high levels of facilitative conditions the helper's ability to confront the helpee with discrepancies between (1) the helpee's expression of who or what he wishes to be and how he actually experiences himself, (2) the helpee's verbal expression of his awareness of himself and his observable or reported behavior, and (3) how the helper experiences the helpee and the helpee's expression of his own experience enable the helpee to confront both himself and others in a constructive manner (Berenson & Mitchell, 1968; Carkhuff & Berenson, 1967).

Corollary III. The degree to which the helper both acts and directs the actions of the helpee immediately in the present to the relationship between helper and helpee is related to the helpee's ability to act with immediacy and later to direct the actions of others.

Both through modeling and the direction of action the helpee learns to act with immediacy (Berenson & Mitchell, 1968; Bierman,

1968; Cannon & Carkhuff, 1968). Again, the extensive repertoire of the helper behaviors serve to increase the restrictive repertoire of helpee behaviors. The helper teaches the helpee (1) that he can act with immediacy and (2) how to act with immediacy by relating the helpee's verbal or behavioral expressions to what is currently going on between helper and helpee.

Corollary IV. The degree to which the helper can make concrete a course of constructive action is related to the degree to which the helpee can go on to make concrete courses of action for himself and others.

Again, concreteness can be a dimension of initiative as well as responsiveness, particularly during the late phases of helping. Following all else in the helping process, the advantages and disadvantages of alternative courses of action must be specified and considered. The "who, what, why, when, where, and how's" must be concretized in developing and implementing a constructive course of action for the helpee (Carkhuff, 1968; Carkhuff & Berenson, 1967).

CONCLUSIONS AND DIRECTIONS

If we are ever to account for a significant degree of effective helping processes, then we must expand our existing models to incorporate the helper-initiated or traditional masculine dimension as well as the helper-responsive or traditionally feminine dimension. As we have seen, some dimensions, such as concreteness and genuineness, are not exclusively one or the other. The differential employment of these dimensions will, of course, be most effective in interaction with relevant client dimensions. For example, depending upon the background and experience of the helpee, it may be most effective at one point in time to be responsive or motherlike and at a later point to be assertive or fatherlike, or vice versa. Obviously, at many points both dimensions will be appropriate. In any event, a number of conclusions concerning models for helping processes are warranted.

Conclusion I. Any comprehensive model of helping processes must include both actively assertive as well as passively responsive components.

Although these different dimensions may operate at different points in time within the helping process, they do not need to operate to the exclusion of each other. They are independent in a statistical sense and not mutually exclusive.

Conclusion II. Both the passive responsive and the active initiative components must be integrated in both the helping process and the helping person.

Except in exceptional cases the helping process cannot be effective if it does not incorporate both components. Similarly, both ingredients must be integrated in the helping person or they cannot be incorporated in the helping process.

Conclusion III. The passive responsive and the active initiative components constitute both the means and the ends of effective helping processes.

The incorporation and integration of the responsive and assertive components constitute not only the means but the goals of helping, that is, an individual who has integrated the responsive and initiative components and can make the necessary discriminations concerning when it is appropriate to employ either or both.

The facilitative and action-oriented dimensions serve complementary functions in the process leading to constructive helpee change or gain. As Figure 3-1 shows, the offering of a high level of facilitative and action-oriented dimensions by the helper leads directly to a process in which the helpee explores and experiences himself at deeper and deeper levels. In turn, the helper's increasingly higher levels of understanding enables the helpee to understand himself, first at minimally effective levels and later at higher or deeper levels. Following this phase the helpee is directly encouraged through all sources of learning to act upon his increasingly fine discriminations and his growing understanding. Finally, the helpee engages in that action, goal, or conflict resolution which we label the outcome criterion, a single index or multiple indexes of constructive helpee change or gain. Of course, the process may be reversed in some instances. When appropriate the process may initially emphasize action or behavior change and then concentrate on the understanding of the resultant feedback from the action or the change.

The offering of low levels of facilitative and action-oriented dimensions by the helper leads in a similar manner to negative helpee change. Thus, the helpee is unable to explore himself in the relevant areas to a sufficient degree. Consequently, he never achieves an accurate level of self-understanding, and the distortions that result from this kind of helping relationship disallow any constructive action or change on the part of the helpee.

The part played by the facilitative and action-oriented dimensions in aiding the helpee to achieve his goals become clearer if we conceive of all helping processes as involving primarily two phases, the downward or inward phase and the upward phase or the period of emergent directionality (Carkhuff & Berenson, 1967).

Phase 1 of Helping

The first phase of the helping process involves the helpee's inward probing to explore and experience his innermost depths. During this phase the helper does everything he can to enable the helpee to examine himself in order that during a later phase together they might find some effective direction for the helpee's life. In this context the dynamic functions of the facilitative dimensions may be seen in several meaningful ways.

Proposition I. High levels of facilitative conditions serve as a stimulus complex to elicit a depth of self-exploration and immediacy of experiencing necessary for positive change or gain; the self-exploration, in

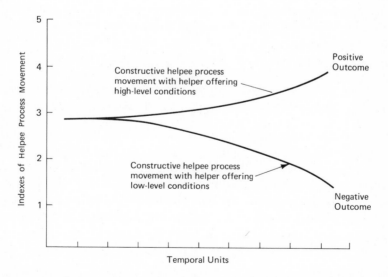

Figure 3-1. Schematic representation of helpee process movement with helpers offering high- and low-level conditions.

turn, is positively reinforced in areas that were negatively reinforced previously.

The facilitative conditions serve as both stimulus and reinforcer for the helpee's response. The experiences that have been responsible for past difficulties are elicited and the helpee's attendant anxiety is reduced (Carkhuff & Berenson, 1967).

Proposition II.   High levels of facilitative conditions enable the helpee to lower his defenses and share more meaningful material.

With a more psychodynamic approach using the impulse-defense paradigm, the decreased need for defenses increases the probability that the helpee will share material he previously viewed as forbidden. Again, the expression of these impulses in a context in which the helpee is not punished is rewarding or reinforcing.

Proposition III.   High levels of facilitative conditions enable the helper to understand the helpee and the helpee to experience the feeling of being understood.

Not only do high levels of facilitative conditions enable the helper to understand who the helpee is and at what level of development he is functioning but they also give the helpee the experience of being or having been understood. Both ingredients are keys to establishing a relationship that might lead to further growth and development on the part of the helpee.

Proposition IV.   High levels of facilitative conditions elicit positive results just as low levels of facilitative conditions elicit negative results.

Through the principle of reciprocal affect high levels of facilitative conditions elicit positive feelings on the part of the helpee toward himself and the expression of positive feelings toward others. This positive result, in turn, increases the probability that the helpee will be the recipient of expressions of positive feelings by others (Truax & Carkhuff, 1967). Thus, a new and progressively constructive cycle is established.

Phase 2 of Helping

After the helpee has explored himself in depth and experienced with immediacy a wide range of problem areas the helping relationship enters its second phase, the upward phase or the period of emergent directionality (Carkhuff & Berenson, 1967). Having delved into himself, the distressed person experiences a need to come up and out of himself in a manner that is much more effective and functional than his previous style of life. That is, he desires to live and act upon his world in a manner that is constructive for both himself and others. It is the helper's task to give the helping process the direction that flows from the exploration of phase 1. Indeed, *the helper guides the process most effectively in the context of having established his offering of high levels of facilitative conditions.*

Proposition V.   Together the facilitative and action-oriented dimensions enable the helper to establish himself as a potent reinforcer of the helpee's behavior so that he may direct the helpee's constructive actions.

The helper, through his depth of understanding and his ability to act upon his sensitive discriminations, becomes a significant figure in the helpee's world, one who can extinguish destructive behavior and reinforce constructive patterns of life (Carkhuff & Berenson, 1967).

Proposition VI.   Together the facilitative and action-oriented dimensions enable the helper to discern, dictate, and implement the preferred modes of treatment necessary for the helpee's recovery.

The self-exploration of phase 1 makes possible the discrimination of alternate courses of treatment and action, including their advantages and disadvantages. During the second phase of helping the helper acts upon his discrimination of the course of action most beneficial to the distressed person. In this context the helper also encourages and directs the helpee to act in his own life.

Proposition VII.   Together the facilitative and action-oriented dimensions enable the helper to implement a process involving labeling, insight giving, and other learning activities.

Having established the experiential base in phase 1, the helper is better able to teach didactically discrimination and other forms of learning that will increase the helpee's perceptual base and repertoire of responses. At higher levels the helper may actively push the helpee toward activities of a creative nature.

PHASES 1 AND 2.   The two phases of helping are not always distinctive and sequential. In particular, the phases are modified by helpee variables. In some cases, for example, phase 2 may appear to precede phase 1—that is, action may precede insight. *Helping is in fact a highly interactional and, hopefully, a lifelong process involving both phases in different problem areas.* Sensitive discriminations lead to the most constructive actions at a given developmental level. In turn, the actions lead to deeper insights and finer discriminations, which lead to more personally rewarding actions. In some cases the helping process must be initiated at phase 2; that is, the helper directs the activities of those who cannot initiate either meaningful communication or action on their own. The facilitative and action-oriented dimensions converge to make the total helping process effective.

Proposition VIII.   Together the facilitative and action-oriented dimensions are the dimensions of effective functioning and improvement in functioning.

Again, understanding and action are both the means and the ends of effective helping processes in and perhaps well beyond our culture.

Proposition IX.   Together the facilitative and action-oriented dimensions constitute the inverse of the conditions that led to the development of the problem or the dysfunctioning in the first place.

The environmental history of the individual in need of help indicates a lack of sufficient amounts or degrees of either the facilitative or action-oriented dimensions or both. As a consequence, the distressed individual finds himself unable to make sensitive discriminations and/or to act upon these discriminations. The presence of high levels of either the facilitative or the action-oriented dimensions dictates, of course, further consideration of differential treatment (Carkhuff & Berenson, 1967).

Proposition X.   Together the facilitative and action-oriented dimensions work to break down the distressed person's experiences of isolation and hopelessness.

Only when another individual can enter the distressed person's world without being intimidated by it, and only when he can act in concert with or even for the distressed person, only then can the person in need of help know that he is not alone and that there is hope.

Proposition XI.   Together the facilitative and action-oriented dimensions when offered at high levels by the helper establish the helper as a person who has something the distressed person wants.

In some respects this is the most critical aspect of all effective help-ing processes. *If the helper cannot establish himself as a person who is himself living at more effective levels than the distressed person, if the helper cannot establish that given the same circumstances he could bring about a more effective resolution, there is no meaningful basis for helping.*

Proposition XII.   Together the facilitative and action-oriented dimen-sions establish the helper as a model for effective living.

Perhaps the point on which to conclude a consideration of the coun-selor's contribution to helping processes is the point at which all effec-tive helping begins, that is, with an integrated and growing person, one who is personally productive and creative, one whose life is domi-nated by personal meaning and fulfillment. Without such persons in the helping role there is no hope in the world or for the world.

REFERENCES

For a more detailed discussion of the issues considered in this chapter see the asterisked readings and the references upon which the readings are based.

*Berenson, B. G., & Carkhuff, R. R. *The sources of gain in counseling and therapy.* New York: Holt, Rinehart and Winston, Inc., 1967.

Berenson, B. G., & Mitchell, K. *Confrontation in counseling and life.* Mimeo-graphed book, American International College, Springfield, Mass., 1968.

Bierman, R. Counseling and child-rearing. In *The counselor's contribution to facilitative processes.* Mimeographed book, State University of New York at Buffalo, 1968.

Cannon, J., & Carkhuff, R. R. *The experimental manipulation of therapeutic process variables.* Mimeographed manuscript, State University of New York at Buffalo, 1968.

Carkhuff, R. R. *The counselor's contribution to facilitative processes.* Mimeo-graphed book, State University of New York at Buffalo, 1968.

*Carkhuff, R. R. & Berenson, B. G. *Beyond counseling and therapy.* New York: Holt, Rinehart and Winston, Inc., 1967.

Pierce, R. Counselor respect. In *The counselor's contribution to facilitative processes.* Mimeographed book, State University of New York at Buffalo, 1968.

*Truax, C. B., & Carkhuff, R. R. *Toward effective counseling and psycho-therapy.* Chicago: Aldine Publishing Company, 1967.

4

THE HELPEE'S CONTRIBUTION TO HELPING PROCESSES

How the helpee becomes involved in the helping process and the degree to which he does so may have both immediate and long-term effects upon the helpee and whether or not the helping process leads to a constructive change or gain in his behavior. The facilitative and action-oriented dimensions offered by the helper must, then, be considered in relation to the relevant dimensions contributed by the helpee. Thus, we can understand the effect of helper variables only when we have learned something about the characteristics the helpee brings to the helping process as well as those that emerge over the course of the process. Unfortunately, the literature that gives attention to helpee dimensions, while abundant, is unsystematic and by and large unrelated to meaningful indexes of helpee change or gain. Nevertheless, there are a number of assumptions which any comprehensive model of effective helping processes must make concerning these dimensions.

Assumption I. Any comprehensive model of helping processes must include relevant dimensions concerning the distressed person.

A comprehensive model must take into consideration both helper and helpee variables, alone and in interaction with each other. There must be particular emphasis upon the effects of the helpee variables upon what the helpee brings with him to the helping process, how the helpee reacts within the helping process, and, finally, what changes the helping process has brought about in the helpee.

Assumption II. Any comprehensive model of helping processes must relate helpee variables to indexes of helpee change.

By definition the helping process is calculated to help the helpee with difficulties he might not otherwise be able to handle. Whether the process involves a concentration upon learning or relearning, it is dedicated to ameliorating, modifying, or eliminating problems which prevent the helpee from functioning effectively.

Assumption III.   Any comprehensive model of helping processes must relate helpee variables to differential treatment.

Since all counseling and therapeutic activities begin with the helpee, if helpee characteristics do indeed make a difference in treatment, then we must relate differential treatment to these different characteristics. We must be able to determine and set in motion the course of action that will lead to permanent and constructive change in the helpee.

With these assumptions in mind we will explore what the literature has to say concerning the distressed person seeking help.[1] At the outset we must divide helpee variables into two broad categories: (1) the characteristics the distressed person brings with him to the helping process and (2) the characteristics of the helpee that emerge within the helping process.

WHAT THE HELPEE BRINGS WITH HIM

The characteristics the helpee brings with him to the helping process may be further subdivided into (1) the demographic or actuarial characteristics of helpee populations and (2) the levels of functioning of helpee populations, including traditional diagnostic categories. Other personality and motivational characteristics, including the helpee's mental set and expectations for counseling, may fall into a category incorporating both what the helpee brings with him and what he does within the helping process. At this point we turn to an examination of the relevant literature in order to determine whether any of these characteristics affect or are affected by differential treatment.

[1] The propositions presented in Chapters 4 and 5 are integrative and creative summary statements resulting from an exhaustive review of articles too numerous to enumerate in the following psychological, psychiatric, social work, and educational journals: *Counselor Education and Supervision; Journal of Abnormal Psychology; Journal of Abnormal and Social Psychology; Journal of Clinical Psychology; Journal of Consulting Psychology; Journal of Counseling Psychology; Journal of Personality and Social Psychology; Journal of Social Work; Personnel and Guidance Journal; Psychiatric Quarterly; Psychiatry; Psychological Abstracts; Rehabilitation Journal; Social Service Review.*

Demographic Characteristics

Demographic characteristics describe helpee populations in terms of age, sex, race, socioeconomic class, or other characteristics. A review of the literature relevant to helpee characteristics yields a number of propositions of dubious significance. First, while traditional psychological folklore has it that helpee demographic characteristics are related to therapeutic prognosis, there is little or no research relating helpee demographic characteristics to differential treatment. The typical work suggests instead a relation between demographic characteristics and other indexes of the helpee's level of functioning and other kinds of personality variables. The only variables that receive minimal support are social class variables—and even these often do not hold up under many describable conditions, no doubt for a variety of reasons. What evidence there is in this area is not particularly meaningful.

Proposition I. The evidence suggests, in general, that some helpee demographic variables are related to whether the helpee begins and continues in treatment or terminates it.

At this point in time we simply do not know whether it is beneficial for a helpee to begin or continue in most treatment programs. Even if the helpee does change in the direction of his helper, we most often do not know whether the change is beneficial to the helpee or not. A number of related corollaries flow from the interaction of helper and helpee variables.

Corollary I. The effects of demographic helpee variables reflect the biases of helpers in selecting helpees.

Counselors, therapists, and other helpers tend to select for treatment and to continue in treatment helpees who are much like themselves in demographic description. Like begets like. Indeed, it is likely in inpatient settings that therapists select for treatment those patients who for a variety of reasons are likely to be discharged anyway and within the immediate future.

Corollary II. Helpers who find themselves working with helpees whose characteristics do not meet their prejudices and needs do not under ordinary circumstances function as effectively in offering the kinds of conditions that lead to constructive change in the helpee.

If for some reason the helper finds himself working with helpees who are not attractive to him, he will ordinarily function at lower levels, make poorer prognoses, and terminate the processes earlier than he would with helpees who are attractive to him. The helper who functions at a lower level tends to function at an even lower level with helpees whom he does not want to see. This statement, however, is not without qualification.

Proposition II.   There is evidence to indicate that helpees who are seen by motivated helpers have an opportunity for constructive change that is independent of their demographic characteristics.

Evidence indicates that therapists who know each other well feel under pressure to continue with the hospitalized patients assigned to them at random in research projects (Rogers, Gendlin, Kiesler, & Truax, 1967; Truax & Carkhuff, 1967). Under these circumstances no demographic characteristics can be related to successful or unsuccessful treatment. An important corollary, then, may be derived from this statement.

Corollary I.   Helpees with seemingly poor characteristics for successful treatment when seen by motivated helpers have as much chance to improve as those with seemingly good characteristics for treatment.

For example, elderly persons from lower socioeconomic classes with poor educational backgrounds and premorbid adjustments demonstrate as much ability to make constructive gains as young, privileged, and previously resourceful persons under appropriate conditions. To be sure, however, the change is relative to the helpee's initial level of functioning, and helpers may still have to make decisions concerning efficiency, that is, which helpees can make maximum use of the helper's minimum investment.

Corollary II.   Helpers who discharge their full commitment to helpees with seemingly poor demographic characteristics are effective according to the level at which they are functioning.

If the helper is functioning at high levels, the results he obtains with his seemingly poor helpees are positive, just as they are with his seemingly good helpees (Pagell, Carkhuff, & Berenson, 1967; Pierce, Carkhuff, & Berenson, 1967). If the helper is functioning at low levels, the results he obtains are negative with both categories of helpees.

Corollary III.   A helpee who is functioning at a low level may not gain as much relatively nor function at as high a level as rapidly as a helpee who is functioning at a higher level initially.

With longer-term treatment, though, a low-level functioning helpee may gain as much and function at as high a level as an individual who is functioning at a higher level initially but who is seen for a briefer duration. This corollary leads, then, to a consideration of helpee levels of functioning.

Helpee Levels of Functioning

Helpee levels of functioning are measured in terms of his level of functioning in such areas as the emotional, intellectual, social-interpersonal, and vocational. Included in the assessment are specific diagnoses of the initial degree of disturbance, the severity of the difficulty, and premorbid adjustment. In general, a review of the literature relevant to helpee levels of functioning reveals that, while therapy *may be* an aid in changing an individual's undesirable personality characteristics as judged by himself or others, there is little evidence to indicate that traditional assessments of levels of functioning are related to differential treatment. *Traditional diagnosis does not make a difference.* The vast amount of research in this area suggests that helpee variables are largely unrelated to differential treatment and outcome.

Proposition I.   Much of the evidence relates one index of helpee levels of functioning to another index of helpee levels of functioning.

Unfortunately, none of the helpee's responses are relevant to differential treatment. Indeed, the research may reflect the stability of test-taking responses more than anything else.

Corollary I.   The more deviant a helpee is on one dimension, the more deviant he is on other dimensions.

Marginal people are marginal people! However, this tells us nothing about the need for or the effects of treatment.

Corollary II. The more "abnormal" a helpee is on one dimension, the more he differs from "normals" on a variety of indexes.

The fact that "abnormals" differ from "normals" on a variety of indexes raises critical questions concerning the meaningfulness of the research in this area.

Proposition II. The few studies of differential treatment offer only very limited treatment alternatives.

Most of the literature simply does not deal with the differential effects of the traditional psychoanalytic, client-centered, existential, behavioristic, and trait-and-factor approaches (Carkhuff & Berenson, 1967). Practitioners, generally, are not concerned with differential treatment, primarily because they offer only one form of treatment *independent of relevant helpee variables.*

Corollary I. When differential treatment is offered, the alternate modes of treatment are most often drugs, activity therapy, or group therapy.

Drugs are most often employed with individuals who do not meet the helper's biases. Activity therapy such as occupational therapy, in turn, is probably used as an alternate approach because the helper is active in some significant way that traditional therapists are not. (In the few studies of cases in which this method has been employed as an alternative treatment it has been demonstrated to be more effective than therapeutic treatment.) Finally, group therapy may be an effective alternate treatment because it makes available, hypothetically at least, a number of potential helpers rather than only one therapist and, conceivably, one such helper may be functioning in relation to a particular helpee at a higher level than might be the case with the single, traditional helper.

Corollary II. The principal differential treatment involves whether or not the potential helpee begins treatment.

Indeed, much of the evidence indicates that, aside from the helpees seen by the top 10 or so percent of the counselors, the helpees may be better off in a control group, that is, *not subject* to the single approach the therapist has to offer.

Corollary III. Whether or not the helpee begins and continues in treatment depends upon his conformity or marginality in functioning.

Those helpees who are most deviant from the helper and/or those who are functioning most marginally in terms of the helper's biases are likely not to be seen for treatment or, if they are, are likely to receive the lowest levels of treatment conditions relevant to constructive helpee change. *Ironically, or perhaps purposefully, in the traditional selection process the best as well as the worst prospects may be eliminated.*

WHAT THE HELPEE DOES WITHIN COUNSELING

What the helpee does within counseling may include the "set" and other motivational characteristics elicited in the helping process, as well as (1) those variables that describe what the successful helpee does during helping and (2) indexes of helpee outcome, that is, changes that occur in more stable helpee characteristics as a consequence of the helping process. The emphasis here is also upon whether or not any of these characteristics affect or are affected by differential treatment.

Helpee Set, Expectancies, and Motivation

Helpees have different levels of sets and expectancies concerning helping which potentially influence motivation and thus the helping process and its outcome. Set and expectancies, as well as the other motivational variables, may be gleaned from experiences prior to the helping process or they may be elicited by the helper or setting within counseling. A review of the growing literature on set and expectancies, especially as they relate to motivational variables, while it yields highly variable results which are not directly related to differential treatment, indicates that these variables are at least potentially critical to constructive client change.

Proposition I. Helpee set, expectancies, and motivation change over time and with counseling.

The changing interaction of helper and helpee variables influences the changes in these helpee variables.

Corollary I. Basically what the helpee expects and, indeed, needs are a high level of understanding and direction in his life.

The assumption made here is that the helpee's need for understanding and direction runs deep, cutting below both the helpee's expectancies gleaned from prior experiences and the influences of the helper upon these expectancies.

Corollary II. Generally the helper attempts to convert the helpee to the helper's own set for one treatment approach.

Usually the helper tries to get the helpee to acquire a liking for the kind of treatment the helper has to offer. Those helpees who do not oblige terminate treatment on their own or on the suggestion of the helper.

Corollary III. Usually the helper does not meet either the helpee's original or changed expectancies.

Unfortunately, while the distortions in interpersonal functioning inherent in the helpee's makeup prohibit his making accurate discriminations concerning the level of facilitative and action-oriented conditions at which his helper is functioning, the helper is most often functioning at a level that disallows meeting any of the helpee's basic expectancies or needs for experiencing understanding and finding direction in his life.

Helpee Process Variables

Helpee process variables include dimensions such as the degree of helpee self-exploration, the immediacy of experiencing and the immediacy of the relationship, the range of problem expression, and the significance of the person discussed within and over the course of the counseling or therapeutic sessions. While there is little research to relate process variables to differential treatment, the literature converges on what it is that successful helpees do in general within counseling and psychotherapy.

Proposition I. Helpee involvement in the therapeutic process is essential to constructive helpee change or gain.

Helpees with a prospect of changing constructively involve themselves in the helping process in such a way as to see all relevant, ongoing experiences in order (1) to reorganize the assumptive base from which they operate and (2) to act upon the meaningful discriminations that base affords (Carkhuff & Berenson, 1967). Conversely, helpees who resist or are unable to, either with or without the counselor's help, engage in self-exploration and immediacy of experiencing are poor prospects for effective treatment.

Corollary I. The degree to which the helpee can explore himself within the helping process is related to the degree to which he changes constructively.

When the helpee actively and spontaneously engages in an inward probing to newly discover feelings or experiences about himself and his world, then he has the opportunity to reorganize and reassess previous distorted perceptions of himself and his world (Carkhuff & Berenson, 1967; Truax & Carkhuff, 1967).

Corollary II. The degree to which the helpee focuses upon his immediate experiences is directly related to the degree to which he changes constructively.

When the helpee focuses upon his here and now relationships, particularly that between himself and his helper, then he has an opportunity to work through and comprehend his feelings and experiences involving himself and others in a direct and constructive manner. (Berenson & Mitchell, 1968; Carkhuff & Berenson, 1967).

Proposition II. Helpee action as a consequence of the helping process is essential to helpee change or gain.

In order to translate the therapeutic process the helpee must act, both within and without counseling, upon his increased understanding and discriminations. Sometimes, to be sure, he must act before he can accomplish any new and significant learning (Carkhuff & Berenson, 1967).

Corollary I. Initially the helpee may act at the behest of the helper.

Both in terms of the helper's direct influence upon the direction and content of counseling as well as in terms of the "homework" assigned the helpee, the helpee learns that it is possible to act for himself and upon his world.

Corollary II. Ultimately the helpee must develop the capacity to act with autonomy.

In the end the helpee must be able to act under his own direction and control or treatment has not been successful. Here again the effects of modeling are critical not only to an increased repertoire of behavioral responses but also to the possibility of independent action.

Helpee Outcome

Helpee outcome indexes include a variety of potential goals of counseling such as improvement reflected in reports by the helpee himself, by experts, and by significant others; in objective and projective tests; in ward behavior ratings; and in whether or not the individual has remained in or out of an institution. It is apparent that different methods of assessing outcome yield different results. There is, then, some highly tentative evidence to support the case for differential treatment.

Proposition I.   Inferential evidence indicates that different kinds of treatment affect different outcome indexes.

For example, the client-centered mode of treatment may affect changes between the real and the ideal self as measured by Q-sorts while the trait-and-factor approach may affect satisfaction as reflected in inventory statements and the behavioristic, specific symptom reduction as indicated in behavioral change or self-reports. Unfortunately, some of this evidence is inferential and may be in part an artifact of the research methodology employed.

Corollary I.   The outcome indexes employed are related to the treatment process.

In many cases the measures applied might more properly be considered process measures for the treatment procedures. The techniques dictated attend directly and primarily to changes on the specific indexes which they employ to assess their efficacy. In many ways the changes are analogous to those on intelligence tests produced by teaching children the answers to the questions posed by the tests but unrelated to criteria having to do with independent change. To be sure, depending upon the goals involved, *all effective helping processes involve step-by-step procedures that lead to particular goals, and in that sense the goals are dependent upon the process.* Indeed, rather than limit these procedures we should increase them in order to make possible the achievement of all of the goals having to do with surmounting the difficulties associated with daily living. However, these problems raise questions concerning concomitant indexes of change, or changes that take place on other indexes (in positive or negative directions) along with those being assessed on a specific index.

Corollary II. Concurrent or concomitant indexes must be employed in order to pin down differential treatment effects.

In all learning or relearning processes a variety of indexes beyond those dictated by current theory, practice, and research (Thorne, 1967) must be employed in order to ferret out the differential effects of the treatment or education process. It is conceivable, for example, that an individual might change constructively with treatment on one index of emotional adjustment while changing negatively on several other indexes of emotional adjustment as well as on physical and intellectual indexes. Similarly, a student may demonstrate positive gain on the one intellectual index assessed while exhibiting negative change on other intellectual, physical, and emotional indexes.

CONCLUSIONS AND DIRECTIONS

Usually the distressed person is dominated by two tendencies. First, he distorts all experiences in order to fit them into his limited and rigid cosmology, or the set of assumptions he has developed in order to make some sense out of incoming stimuli and delimit their threat to him. Second, the individual is unable to act either for himself or upon his world. Succinctly, he is impotent.

In order to develop a more expansive cosmology, one that is open yet has direction, the distressed individual must look at himself and his world. Hopefully, he will ultimately be able not only to look at but to see himself and his world clearly, lucidly, and with a minimum of distortion. In order to act upon this world, the distressed individual must begin by acting in small ways, both in and out of the counseling relationship. What happens within the helping relationship is critical since it is often only in such a protective environment that the individual can first act without fear of retaliation—although later when the helper has established himself as a potent reinforcer and has become conditional in his attitude toward the helpee there may be a distinct possibility of retaliation. What happens outside the relationship is even more critical, because if the helping process does not translate to outside events, then the helping program has failed.

In developing a comprehensive model incorporating the helpee's contribution to effective helping processes a number of conclusions emerge.

Conclusion I. A comprehensive model for helping processes must account for improved helpee capacities for both understanding and action.

The more traditional approaches such as the psychoanalytic, the client-centered, and the existential have stressed improvement in discrimination (greater insight, awareness, and so on) to the exclusion of action. Some of the newer behavioristic approaches, perhaps largely in reaction to the more traditional methods, have emphasized action and direction (assertive behavior, symptom reduction, and so on) independent of insight. A high level of functioning in both discrimination and action are essential for a productive and fulfilled person in our society.

Conclusion II. A comprehensive model for helping processes must relate treatment procedures leading to improved helpee capacities for understanding and action to helpee characteristics before and during treatment.

In some way relevant and distinctive helpee characteristics must be related to differential treatment. Thus, we must be able to specify the potential changes that might take place for a helpee working with a helper functioning at a given level who is implementing a particular orientation with specifiable techniques in a particular environment. We may, for example, be able to say that the client-centered mode with a helper functioning at minimally facilitative levels in a college-type setting is a preferred mode of treatment for a college student for whom a finer congruence between his real and ideal self is critical. We may be able to dictate a treatment such as this even though the desired changes may or may not be independent of other meaningful indexes of real life functioning.

Conclusion III. A comprehensive model for helping processes must consider helpee movement toward improved capacities for understanding and action in interaction with relevant responsive and initiative helper variables.

Just as the helper variables cannot be considered independently of the helpee variables, the helpee variables cannot be considered apart from the helper variables. Thus, the helpee's movement toward exploration, understanding, and action must be considered in interaction with relevant helper variables. Accordingly, the response dispositions character-

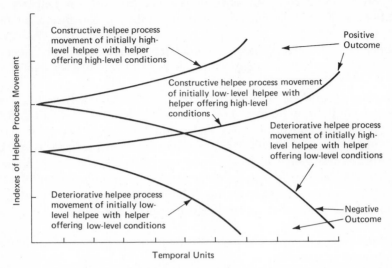

Figure 4-1. Schematic representation of helpee process movement of helpers and helpees functioning at high and low levels.

istic of the helpee will be modified in conjunction with the level of facilitative and action-oriented dimensions offered by the helper.

As Figure 4-1 indicates, the helpee may have initial response dispositions toward process movement within helping that may be characterized as high or low. Indeed, a number of investigations indicate, for example, that persons who are functioning at the highest levels of facilitative and action-oriented conditions in the helping role also have a response disposition toward exploring themselves at the deepest levels initially. We can see, however, that two helpees may enter the helping process at identical levels and, in interaction with helpers functioning at different levels of facilitative and action-oriented conditions, demonstrate very different outcomes. Thus, the high-level helpee in interaction with a high-level helper demonstrates positive movement and change while the high-level helpee in interaction with a low-level helper demonstrates negative movement and change. Similarly, two helpees with initially low dispositions toward process movement and change may be affected differently, depending on the levels at which their helpers are functioning. In summary, in interaction with a high-level helper both high- and low-level helpees may change constructively. To be sure, while the relative changes may be related, the final level of helpee functioning will tend to be significantly higher for the initially high-level helpee as compared with the initially low-level helpee over similar time periods. In addition, in interaction with a low-level helper both high-and low-level helpees may change negatively. Here too while the relative changes may be related, the final level of helpee functioning will tend to be significantly higher for the initially high-level helpee as compared with the initially low-level helpee over similar time periods. Figure 4-1 also indicates that, with extended duration of treatment, the initially low-level helpee may ultimately achieve the level of functioning of the initially high-level helpee in interaction with the high-level helper. Similarly, with extended duration of treatment the initially high-level helpee may ultimately deteriorate to the level of functioning of the initially low-level helpee in interaction with the low-level helper.

In this context we will explore further some directions for future research into helpee variables in the helping processes.

Proposition I.   If helpees are treated who would not ordinarily be treated because of certain demographic characteristics, they will have as good a chance of changing as those whom helpers would ordinarily prefer to treat.

Can the practitioner be freed from demographic helpee variables or is he tied to them just as the helpee is? This question has implications for increasing the number of available therapeutic agents as well as for improving the quality of the treatment they offer. While raising the question makes for a more honest confrontation of the issues involved, it does not, however, avoid the responsibility for determining what individuals are going to receive therapeutic help. Here the minimum-maximum principle must dominate: those persons who will respond with a maximum amount of progress as a function of a minimum investment on the part of the helper will receive treatment. This system will allow the most people to receive the greatest treatment benefits. Similarly, the discriminating helpee should *choose* the helpers who offer him the greatest return for his investment (Carkhuff, 1968; Spiegel & Spiegel, 1967).

Proposition II.   Helpees who function at different levels require different forms of treatment.

Both helpees and helpers can be assessed in terms of their functioning on the same dimensions (the communication of facilitative and action-oriented dimensions) and in the same physical, emotional, and intellectual areas. Differential treatment procedures can be generated from the proposition that persons who are functioning at lower levels can gain from persons who are functioning at higher levels: (1) With persons functioning at the lowest level (level 1), those who have lost contact with reality, the preferred goals and treatment procedures involve re-establishing effective communication and interaction with the world; (2) the outpatient neurotic's (level 2) errors in his assumptive world require, in turn, a process and outcome that will help him in modifying his distortions and in establishing or re-establishing an effective working cosmology; (3) With relatively well-functioning but situationally distressed clients (level 3), often a viable communication process may be assumed, and more cognitive decision-making and problem-solving processes may be incorporated into the helping process. These gross differentiations may be further defined and acted upon in treatment (Carkhuff & Berenson, 1967).

Proposition III.   High- and low-level functioning helpers differentially affect the helpee's set, expectancies, and motivation.

It is difficult to assess the effects of the helpee's set, expectancies, and motivation in the absence of knowledge of the level of functioning of the helper and the cycle that he is part of. Counselors who are functioning at high levels have high expectancies based upon success experiences; these experiences, in turn, result from the high-level functioning of the individuals. Conversely, counselors who are functioning at low levels have low expectancies based upon failure experiences; these experiences, in turn, are based upon the low-level functioning of the individuals. This circular process may be broken only by empirical research studying the interaction of both helper and helpee on (1) level of functioning and (2) level of expectancy.

High- and low-level functioning helpers differentially affect the helpee's set, expectancies, and motivation. While the high-level helper understands the distortions in the helpee's perceptions, he takes the helpee's phenomenology into consideration in setting the highest possible individual helpee goals—that is, he will elicit helpee expectations for higher and higher levels of functioning. An increasing convergence of the expectancies of helper and helpee will occur as the helpee has success experiences in his movement to higher levels of functioning. The low-level helper will not, on the other hand, understand the helpee's distortions and will not take the helpee's phenomenology into consideration in setting up expectations for the helpee's accepting his lot in life as he, the helper, has done. Over time, then, the low-level helper will elicit helpee expectations for lower levels of functioning. In a sense, his "success" cases are really failures because they have setttled for lower terms.

In summary, the differential results are accounted for by the fact that (1) a healthy person takes his helpee into consideration and (2) an unhealthy person does not really take his helpee into consideration.

Proposition IV.   Helping is a mutual shaping process between helper and helpee.

There is a great need to study the reciprocal effects of the helper-helpee interaction. Thus, just as the level of specifiable facilitative and action-oriented dimensions affect helpee process variables of exploration and experiencing, helpee dimensions affect helper variables. Although we tend to emphasize the helper's acceptance of the helpee, it is just as critical to study the helpee's acceptance of the helper. The helpee has to know, for example, that, given his circumstances, the helper could have resolved his conflicts more effectively than the helpee has been able to do. Similarly, just as helpee self-exploration is an indication of helpee progress, so may increasing levels of counselor self-disclosure be an indication of the increasing reciprocal and equalitarian interaction of an effective counseling process. Further study of the effect of helper and helpee strategies upon each other will, hopefully, yield the ingredients of a helping process to be conducted on the terms of the healthier party in the relationship.

Proposition V.   We must study those high-level functioning helpers who have the largest repertoire of responses and who effect the greatest changes on the most outcome indexes.

In a very real sense *outcome indexes are really cut-off process measures.* That is, successful helpees explore themselves, communicate at high levels, and act upon their fine discriminations in regard to their world. These characteristics may be considered outcome as well as process measures of effective helping and should, hopefully, translate to improvement on a variety of more traditional outcome indexes. In addition, we must develop step-by-step procedures to goals that are specific to the helpee involved, and we must develop as many of these goals as are necessary to enable the helpee to surmount the obstacles that occur in his daily living. In studying these indexes we should employ multiple measures in order to determine what treatment affects what indexes, particularly those indexes that are reflected in real life. In this regard we may be wasting our time trying to understand the vast number of mediocre helpers who do not make a difference in the lives of others anyway, and who surely do not employ differential treatment. We should, instead, study those high-level functioning helpers who have the largest repertoire of responses because they have the largest number of differential treatment procedures available to them and thus the greatest opportunity to effect significant changes on the most helpee indexes— *that is, if they are motivated to do so.*

In summary, we must understand how the helpee can come to *look now,* in the hope that he might *see in the future,* to *act now* in the hope that he might *act in the future.* The helper's task is thus to serve as a guide on the helpee's journey toward finding himself and acting upon who he is. *Through the helper's eyes and ears the helpee can come to see and hear the sights and sounds of life; with the helper's hands he can learn to touch and to act; through the helper's life he can come to find his own life.*

REFERENCES

For a more detailed discussion of the issues considered in this chapter see the asterisked readings and the references upon which the readings are based.

Berenson, B. G., & Mitchell, K. *Confrontation in counseling and life.* Mimeographed book, American International College, Springfield, Mass., 1968.

Carkhuff, R. R. The differential functioning of lay and professional helpers. *Journal of Counseling Psychology,* 1968, **15,** 117–126.

*Carkhuff, R. R., & Berenson, B. G. *Beyond counseling and therapy.* New York: Holt, Rinehart and Winston, Inc., 1967.

Pagell, W. A., Carkhuff, R. R., & Berenson, B. G. The predicted differential effects of the level of counselor functioning upon the level of functioning of outpatients. *Journal of Clinical Psychology,* 1967, **23,** 510–512.

Pierce, R., Carkhuff, R. R., & Berenson, B. G. The differential effects of high and low functioning counselors upon counselors-in-training. *Journal of Clinical Psychology,* 1967, **23,** 212–215.

Rogers, C. R., Gendlin, E. Kiesler, D., & Truax, C. B. (eds.). *The therapeutic relationship and its impact: A study of psychotherapy with schizophrenics.* Madison, Wisc.: University of Wisconsin Press, 1967.

Spiegel, Patricia K., & Spiegel, D. E. Perceived helpfulness of others as a function of compatible intelligence. *Journal of Counseling Psychology,* 1967, **14,** 61–62.

*Thorne, F. C. The etiological equation. Appendix A in R. R. Carkhuff & B. G. Berenson. *Beyond counseling and therapy.* New York: Holt, Rinehart and Winston, Inc., 1967.

*Truax, C. B., & Carkhuff, R. R. *Toward effective counseling and psychotherapy.* Chicago: Aldine Publishing Company, 1967.

5

THE CONTRIBUTION OF CONTEXTUAL
AND ENVIRONMENTAL INFLUENCES

In developing any comprehensive model to account for the effectiveness of the helping processes we must incorporate the potentially modifying effects of contextual and environmental factors (Carkhuff, 1966; Carkhuff & Berenson, 1967). That is, the helper and the helpee do not interact in a vacuum. The setting within which the helping process takes place may modify or qualify the effects of the process in significant ways. In addition, following helping the helpee must return to an environment that also incorporates potentially critical variables (Goffman, 1956, 1961; Jones, 1953; Rappoport, 1960; Scheff, 1966, 1967; Shibutani, 1961; Smelser & Smelser, 1963; Wesseu, 1964), including in particular the people to whom the helpee must relate upon his return to the real world. Although the potential effects of contextual and environmental variables have received some theoretical treatment in the literature, few systematic investigations have been conducted in this area. Again, any comprehensive model of effective helping processes must make a number of assumptions concerning these variables.

Assumption I. A comprehensive model of helping processes must include relevant contextual and environmental dimensions.

Helper and helpee variables cannot be considered independently of (1) the setting in which the helping process takes place and (2) the environment from which the helpee comes and to which he returns.

Assumption II. A comprehensive model of helping processes must relate the contextual and environmental variables to indexes of helpee change.

63

Since constructive helpee change or gain is the only rationale for help-ing, the effects of the contextual and environmental variables upon mean-ingful indexes of helpee change must be ascertained.

Assumption III. A comprehensive model of helping processes must relate contextual and environmental variables to differential treatment.

We must be able to determine the relation between the contextual and environmental variables and the appropriate treatment approach to the helpee's needs at a given point in time.

With these assumptions in mind, then, we will explore what the litera-ture has to say concerning the effects of the context and the environ-ment upon the person seeking help.

THE CONTEXT OF HELPING

Contextual variables refer to immediate or proximal setting variables, or variables that represent critical aspects of the context within which the helping process takes place. Environmental variables refer to the setting or settings from which the helpee comes and to which he returns after each helping session and after termination of the helping process. A simple relation exists between contextual and environmental variables. Although there may be vast differences between the context in which the helping process takes place and the individual's environment, the same physical and social-psychological dimensions operate within both the helping context and the environment to which the helpee returns.

Both contextual and environmental variables, then, may be further subdivided into two predominant categories: (1) those involving physi-cal dimensions and (2) those involving personal or people-oriented dimensions. In all instances the critical question is, Do the dimensions involved, whether physical or personal, facilitate or retard the construc-tive effects of the helping process? Put another way, Are the physical and personal characteristics of both the immediate setting and the envi-ronment helpful or harmful?

The immediate context thus refers to all aspects of the setting within which the helping process takes place. Although there are a multitude of potentially influential physical and personal contextual variables, we will enumerate only a few of those that are most prominent. Thus, within the larger category of physical contextual variables there are those variables that have to do with (1) physical location and appearance and those that are (2) immediate or proximal setting variables. The first group of variables describe the location of the helping setting within

the community at large, including the internal and external characteristics of the setting as well as such factors as whether the individual
is in inpatient or outpatient treatment (Caudill, 1958). More relevant to
the helping process is the second category of variables, which has to do
with the characteristics of the actual setting within which the process
takes place: the furniture, a factor which includes the relative positioning of helper and helpee; lighting; decor and art; music; the presence or absence of tape recorders and other devices; and a variety of
other factors that might be varied with differential effects upon helpee
functioning.

The personal variables, in turn, may be broken down into those that
have to do with (1) people; (2) the arrangements surrounding the
treatment program; and (3) the availability of different kinds of treatment. The people variables involve the helpee's experiences with all of
the persons associated directly or indirectly with the helping agency.
More tangential but nevertheless potentially influential are the arrangement variables, which are often set during the prehelping phase: fees
and terms of payment; financial arragements; appointment schedules; and
other factors involved in the waiting experience, including the experiences that take place in the waiting room itself. Finally, the variables
that have to do with the availability of a variety of modes of treatment
or of a particular treatment within the setting as well as the availability
of the necessary duration of treatment are critical to constructive helpee
changes.

Contextual variables, then, may have a potentially critical modifying
effect upon the effects of the helper-helpee interactions. Although the
evidence is often more experiential than experimental, we will summarize the effects of these contextual variables in propositional form for
both physical and personal dimensions.

*Proposition I. Physical dimensions of the helping setting are related to
whether the helpee initiates and invests himself in the helping process.*

Both the external and internal characteristics of the helping setting
are potentially influential in determining whether or not the helpee seeks
out and is serviced by the helping agency.

*Corollary I. Location and appearance variables are related to
whether the helpee gets to the helping agency in the first place.*

The clientele of a helping agency is to a large degree a function
of the location and appearance of the agency. If the agency is not
comfortably available to a distressed person, he is not likely to

seek its help or to continue to seek its help if he does make the initial contact. Similarly, the outward and inward appearance of the helping agency may have differential effects in encouraging or deterring the initiation of the helping process.

Corollary II. Immediate or proximal variables are related to whether the helpee invests himself in a process leading to his constructive change.

The physical characteristics of the very room within which helping takes place may directly influence the helpee's involvement in the helping process. A number of examples may be cited: The helper's positioning himself on a higher, swivel chair with many degrees of freedom may contrast with the helpee's experience of rigidity and subordinacy in a lower, straight-backed chair. The helper's employment of his physical surroundings to influence the ambiguity or distinctiveness of his appearance may influence the degree to which the helpee is able to trust him. The presence of a tape recorder may influence the helpee to disclose more or less material about himself—depending upon the ability of the helper to handle this minor crisis—that may be critical to the helping process.

Proposition II. Personal dimensions of the helping setting are related to whether the helpee remains in and is helped by the helping process.

Having initiated contact with a helping agency, the helpee is influenced by people and people-oriented dimensions operating within the setting.

Corollary I. People variables are related to whether the helpee remains in the helping process.

The helpee's experiences with people in and around the helping agency are particularly critical. Thus, for example, the helpee's experiences with the receptionist, the interviewer, or the test examiner or the staff conversations he overhears may have constructive or destructive effects upon his motivation to continue in the helping process. In addition, group treatment experiences introduce significant others who may have an impact upon the helpee.

Corollary II. Arrangement variables are related to whether the helpee remains in the helping process.

Having made the initial contact, the helpee may be influenced by certain arrangement variables. Do the financial arrangements deter or motivate him? Does the scheduling offer him the prospect of help with minimal negative disruption of other necessary aspects of his life? Does the very process of making arrangements, including the period of time he must wait to begin the helping process as well as his experience in the waiting room, influence him positively or negatively? In summary, do the people making the arrangements for the helpee tune in on the helpee's needs?

Corollary III.   The variables that have to do with the availability of different approaches to treatment relate to whether or not the helper can be helped.

The presence or absence of a preferred mode of treatment offered by the helpers in a given setting which is necessary for the helpee's development, as well as the question of whether or not the duration of treatment available is sufficient to ameliorate the helpee's condition are two contextual variables that influence whether, in fact, the helping agency has anything to offer the helpee (Carkhuff & Berenson, 1967). Temporal, or time, variables are integrally related to the outcome assessments of the helping process (Paul, 1967). That is, the period of time intervening between initial and final contacts will influence the outcome of helping.

THE ENVIRONMENT

The setting within which helping takes place is no more critical than the environment, both immediate and remote, from which the helpee has come and to which he must return when treatment is terminated. The effectiveness of the helping process must be judged by the functioning of the individual in the old environment to which he returns or the new environment he searches out or develops. As with the contextual variables, physical and personal dimensions cut across the environmental factors. The physical environmental variables may be broken down as follows: (1) those that relate to physical nourishment and (2) those that have to do with physical support. The personal environmental variables, in turn, may be broken down into (1) significant reference groups and (2) the work and/or school environment.

The physical nourishment variables involve the availability of adequate shelter, food, and conditions for rest, comfort, and security. The variables that have to do with aiding in the helpee's growth efforts include the community facilities that nourish and support the helpee. Of the personal environmental variables, significant reference groups include family members, friends, and neighbor reference groups who have the potential for exerting a constructive or destructive impact upon the helpee. Finally, in a similar vein, those significant persons of the helpee's work and/or educational environment who might have facilitative or retarding effects in relation to the helpee must be considered. Again the evidence, which is largely experiential and theoretical, may be summarized in propositional form.

Proposition I.   Physical environmental variables are related to the degree to which the helpee's involvement and gains are made possible and supported.

The physical environment must support the activities of the helpee in an effective helping process. Not only must the helpee be adequately nourished but he must have available to him the facilities of an actively supportive environment.

Corollary I.   Physical nourishment variables are related to the degree to which the helpee's involvement and gains are made possible.

Survival must be assured before growth is possible. Adequate food, shelter, sanitation, exposure to the outdoors, activity, and rest are essential to the helpee's effective employment of the helping experience. Indeed, deficits in these areas may account for more difficulties in functioning than intellectual and other handicaps. High levels of physical nourishment are requisites for high levels of helpee functioning.

Corollary II.   Physical support variables are related to the degree to which the helpee's involvement and gains are supported.

The helpee must have available to him the active support of the facilities of an open and receptive environment. Physical facilities that offer possibilities for physical, emotional, and intellectual growth are essentially ancillary ingredients of an effective helping process.

Proposition II.   Personal environmental variables are related to the degree to which the helpee can effectively utilize and complement the learning experiences derived in the helping process.

We often forget that critical aspects of an individual's environment involve people. Just as the helper can affect the helpee for better or for worse, so also can other significant persons in the helpee's environment. If the environment is reinforcing, the probability that the helpee will retain improved levels of functioning is very high.

Corollary I. Significant reference groups are related to the degree to which the helpee can effectively utilize the learning experiences derived in the helping process.

The reference groups of family, friends, and neighbors not only provide the helpee with role models that may interact with the effects of the helping process but also with levels of emotional and intellectual nourishment that may have facilitative or retarding effects upon the helpee's effective utilization of his helping experiences.

Corollary II. Vocational and/or educational environmental variables are related to the degree to which the helpee can effectively complement his learning experiences and solidify his gains.

Significant persons in dominant peer and subordinate relationships at work and/or school may or may not offer learnings that complement or subtract from the essential learnings derived in the helping process. To the degree that these individuals complement the helpee's learnings, they help to solidify his gains. To the degree that they do not, they contribute to his deterioration.

CONCLUSIONS AND DIRECTIONS

The rationale for helping is that *what the helpee learns to do within the context of the helping relationship can be generalized to other significant areas of his life.* Thus, hopefully, what happens within the context of the helping process will generalize to the individual's functioning in his environment. It is apparent that some kind of working relation must be established between the contextual and environmental variables.

In this regard the contextual variables, although more directly under the control of the helper, are less familiar to the helpee and thus potentially threatening. The contextual variables that we consider, then, while more subtle than the gross environmental variables, nevertheless have the potential for being more intensely experienced in the moment by the helpee. Little things that the helpee might ordinarily disregard in his everyday environment he may exprience intensely in the context of the helping process. On the other hand, just as the helpee may be threatened by the setting provided by the helper, so may the helper be threatened by the environment of the helpee. In summary, the contextual variables must be employed in such a way as to smooth the transition from the helping process to real life.

Several conclusions may be drawn concerning the influence of contextual and environmental variables on the helping process.

Conclusion I. Contextual and environmental variables are primarily modifiers of the effects of the helper-helpee interaction.

This conclusion does not imply, however, that contextual and environmental variables do not effect significant changes themselves. Indeed, the distressed individual frequently seeks help because of inadequate and/or inappropriate environmental experiences, both of a physical and a personal nature. Nevertheless, in terms of our emphasis these variables must be considered potential modifiers of the effects of helping—modifiers that, to be sure, must be viewed as integral parts of a comprehensive helping process.

Conclusion II. Contextual variables can be controlled in such a way as to maximize the constructive effect of both the helping experience and the environment.

The appropriate employment of contextual variables may not only affect the helping process directly but may also facilitate the helpee's future environmental experiences. The latter can be accomplished by approximating as closely as possible the significant conditions of the helpee's environment in order to facilitate generalization of the learning experiences. Carried to its extreme, this conclusion is a good argument for treating some individuals within the actual setting and community in which they live. Here too, however, we must be sensitive to individual needs. While some helpees wish to function more effectively in their old communities, the very crisis that brings others to seek help involves their searching out new communities. In our eagerness to help we cannot tie down those who would move on.

Conclusion III. Environmental variables can be influenced in such a way as to constitute an effective source of treatment.

The direct influence of the helpee's environment, including in particular the significant persons in the helpee's life, must be considered an integral part of treatment. Treatment is incomplete until these potentially modifying variables are dealt with. We must exercise as much control as possible over the environment the helpee enters or re-enters. For example, we must involve significant others in the helping process or, at a minimum, prepare them for changes in the helpee by "programing" some of their responses—that is, giving them a "set" to make helpful responses where they might once have made harmful responses.

Conclusion IV. Together contextual and environmental variables constitute a significant source of differential treatment.

Relevant contextual and environmental variables may be manipulated on an individualized basis so that they constitute preferred modes of treatment and maximize the helpee's opportunity to gain constructively in and out of the helping process. A total treatment program involves consideration and manipulation of the helpee's total setting and environment.

Obviously one condition may be more effective than another. Most often the helping context is more effective than the environment to which the helpee returns, although this situation could conceivably be reversed. Most frequently, however, some factors in the environment are negative and in this sense are handicapping to the helpee.

As Figure 5-1 shows, three helpees who had experienced effective helping processes and demonstrated essentially similar movement from relatively low levels of functioning to relatively high levels may have differential experiences upon returning to their environments. Thus, the first helpee may return to a very positive environment. Perhaps the helper did what he could to influence this helpee's environment, either involving significant persons and institutions in the helping process and/or preparing them for the helpee. The helpee's progress continues. The environment, with a mixture of positive and negative forces canceling each other out, may act upon the helpee in a manner that neutralizes the helpee's basic directionality. Finally, the environment may be comprised of totally negative forces which, at best, do not support the helpee's emergence or, at worst, counteract his return to real life. In this case the consequences are often disastrous.

Of course, the helper can do much to counteract negative or destructive forces, even without attempting to influence the helpee's environment. Although the helpee's chances for gain are greatest when both helper and helpee can exert some control over the environment, a constructive helping relationship under the direction of a strong helper may successfully overcome the handicap of a poor environment. Under these conditions the helper must prepare the helpee for the difficulties he will encounter. Behavioristic techniques involving ideational, role playing, and finally lifelike approximations of the difficulties may help a great deal in this area. In addition, if the helpee has been able to internalize his new learning, he can encounter his environment with a sense of inner direction—as an individual who can influence his environment as well as one who is open to being influenced by what is constructive in it. Finally, a poor helper may also counteract to some degree the effects of a healthy environment, as for example, a destructive teacher's impact upon a child from an otherwise positive environment.

It may be noted that while Figure 5-1 concentrates upon portraying the differential effects of the environment upon helpees who have demonstrated positive movement in the helping process, the segment of life during and following helping may be put back in the context of the total life process as portrayed schematically in Figure 2-1. Thus, the process of the individual in interaction with his environment, and particularly with the people in it, continues with differential consequences. Depending in large part upon the effectiveness of the persons involved in the interaction, the consequences may continue to be for better or for worse.

Several propositions point up possible future directions in this area.

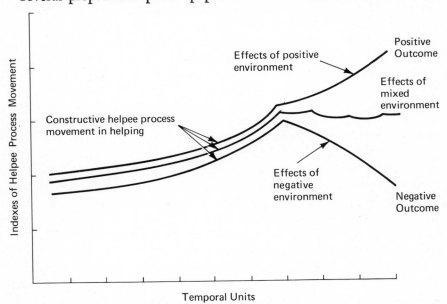

Figure 5-1. Schematic representation of differential process movement in helpee's life during and following helping.

Proposition I.   Contextual and environmental variables must be taken into consideration in planning for helping communities as well as individuals.

Since these variables are related to whether prospective helpees seek, find, enter, and remain in treatment as well as whether any gains they make are nourished, supported, complemented, and solidified, they constitute in part the ingredients of community helping programs. What influences the individual influences the community, and vice versa, for individuals make up communities. The viability of a community is a function of the effectiveness of the people and the institutions that comprise the community. At the same time the emergence of an individual is a function of the effectiveness of the total community or communities in which he lives.

Proposition II.   The sources of the effectiveness and ineffectiveness of all contextual and environmental phenomena must be analyzed.

We must find within our social institutions those people and other sources who make a constructive difference in as well as those who have a destructive impact upon the lives of the people with whom they interact. The individuals who have a constructive effect must be placed in positions of responsibility, while those whose effect on others is negative must be assigned subordinate positions.

Proposition III.   Effective helping processes must be capable of actively manipulating and controlling both contextual and environmental variables.

While we have demonstrated an aversion in the past to controlled environments, the kind of environmental manipulation that is geared to the helpee's needs is an effective source of constructive change or gain. Beyond assuring the necessary physical conditions of survival, this approach means developing and maximizing the levels and sources of nourishment available in the environment and at the same time minimizing or eliminating the destructive factors. It may mean, in addition, manipulating the environment to fit the individual, and vice versa. The characteristics of both institutions and individuals must be matched and/or changed *for the maximum benefit of both.*

Proposition IV.   A constructive society must make maximum use of the potential contribution of contextual and environmental variables.

If we are going to effect and sustain constructive changes in individuals, we must also make constructive changes in the environments in which they function. We need not only to study the conditions that nourish an individual but also to maximize those that are sources of nourishment. We must not only analyze, plan, and manipulate but we must also reorganize and, where appropriate, retrain, for we know a great deal more about effective living than we have been willing to acknowledge thus far. The increasing number and intensity of personal and social crises press us, and we no longer have the luxury of delay in putting our knowledge into practice. Finally, in implementing our plan we must allow for those who in addition to adapting effectively to their environment may also contribute to shaping their environment in a manner constructive for all concerned. *We must not be bound to our past knowledge except insofar as it leads us to sources of new learnings.*

In summary, we could all obtain a firsthand feeling for the critical nature of both the contextual and the environmental variables by changing places with our associates. If we slept in their beds, ate at their tables, worked at their jobs, we might come to understand how crucial these variables are in the lives of human beings. If we could put ourselves in another's place, we might not take as much for granted as we do.

In effect we are suggesting the possibility of a helping or helper society in which those who are capable of making a constructive difference in the lives of other people are selected, trained, and placed in positions responsible for the total environment. In a sense we are suggesting a society in which we begin a chain reaction by working initially with those individuals who are best equipped to utilize and transmit their experience. In turn, these people would select and work with other people in a similar manner. Only through this approach can we close the growing gap between human needs and the availability of social services.

REFERENCES

For a more detailed discussion of the issues considered in this chapter see the asterisked readings and the references upon which the readings are based.

°Carkhuff, R. R. Counseling research, theory and practice—1965. *Journal of Counseling Psychology*, 1966, **13**, 467–480.

°Carkhuff, R. R., & Berenson, B. G. *Beyond counseling and therapy.* New York: Holt, Rinehart and Winston, Inc., 1967.

Caudill, W. *The psychiatric hospital as a small society.* Cambridge, Mass.: Harvard University Press, 1958.

Goffman, E. *The presentation of self in everyday life.* Edinburgh: University of Edinburgh, Social Sciences Research Centre, 1956.

Goffman, E. *Encounters: Two studies in the sociology of interaction.* New York: The Bobbs-Merrill Company, Inc., 1961.

Jones, M. *The Therapeutic Community.* New York: Basic Books, Inc., 1953.

Paul, G. L. Outcome research in psychotherapy. *Journal of Consulting Psychology,* 1967, **31**, 109–118.

Rapaport, R. N. *The community as a doctor.* Chicago: Charles C Thomas, Publisher, 1960.

Scheff, T. S. *Being mentally ill: A sociological theory.* Chicago: Aldine Publishing Company, 1966.

Scheff, T. S. *Mental illness and social processes.* New York: Harper & Row, Publishers, Inc., 1967.

*Shibutani, T. *Society and personality: An interactional approach to social psychology.* Englewood Cliffs, N.J.: Prentice-Hall, Inc., 1961.

Smelser, N. J., & Smelser, W. T. (eds.). *Personality and social systems.* New York: John Wiley & Sons, Inc., 1963.

Wesseu, A. F. *The psychiatric hospital as a social system.* Chicago: Charles C Thomas, Publisher, 1964.

Toward Effective Selection

PART THREE introduces the literature on the selection of helpers. Chapter 6 describes the lack of validity of our traditional indexes and explores more functional indexes of communication and discrimination. The positive evidence on communication based upon the responses of prospective helpers to helpee stimulus expressions crossing helpee affect and problem areas is presented in Chapter 7. The less promising and more equivocal evidence on discrimination based upon the prospective helper's discriminations of helper's responses to the helpee expressions is considered in Chapter 8. Finally, Chapter 9 examines the applications of effective selection procedures.

6

THE DEVELOPMENT OF VALID
SELECTION PROCEDURES

Unless we make the assumption that all persons are capable of being trained and, ultimately, of functioning effectively in the helping role (Carkhuff & Berenson, 1967)—and the increasing number of persons who need help makes this assumption a difficult one—we must develop selection indexes that are relevant, meaningful, and valid for purposes of helping. Unfortunately, beyond the exploration of a variety of intellective criteria, which has yielded disappointing results, the effort dedicated to the selection of both professional and nonprofessional helpers has been both sparse and limited, no doubt reflecting the general reluctance on the part of the helping professions to make enlightened and systematic inquires into either their treatment or training programs. Indeed, the conclusions of this limited work on counselor characteristics and selection does not warrant detailed consideration and can be summarized for our purposes in propositional terms. In so doing we can begin where others (Carkhuff, 1966; Hill, 1966; Kelly & Fiske, 1950; Patterson, 1963, 1967; Wrenn, 1966) have ended, with the conclusion of inconclusiveness, and get on with the task at hand, that of developing the selection indexes that will discern those persons who are most capable of (1) making maximum utilization of the training programs and (2) offering maximum treatment benefits to the distressed persons seeking their help.

Proposition I. Traditional selection procedures have been primarily intellective in nature and have yielded essentially negative results in terms of the discrimination of effective helpers.

First, little or no attempt has been made to relate grade-point averages, graduate record examinations, and Miller analogies indexes to indexes

79

of real-life functioning in the helping role. There is no evidence to indicate that performance on traditional tests does anything but predict performance on traditional tests (Holland & Richards, 1965). In the few studies conducted intellective indexes are minimally and insignificantly related to those helping conditions related to constructive helpee change (Allen, 1967; Bergin & Soloman, 1963; Carkhuff, Piaget, & Pierce, 1967). The most that we can hope for from the now dominant mode of selection based upon ability and achievement is the establishment of some minimum level of intellectual functioning beyond which functioning in the helping role is unrelated to these more academic criteria.

Proposition II.   Studies of helper trainee characteristics suggest, in general, that helper trainees demonstrate more traditionally feminine response patterns.

The one consistent thread weaving through the otherwise highly variable results of testing by a wide variety of traditional instruments is that reflecting what would be considered to be a feminine response disposition on the part of counselors and therapists. That is, whether by self or institutional selection, helpers tend to get high scores on social service interests and nurturant inclinations as well as on indexes of restraint, friendliness, deference, intraception, affiliation, and other more traditionally feminine personality dispositions and low scores on more aggressive, assertive, and achievement-oriented traits (summarized in Farson, 1954; McClain, 1968; Patterson, 1967).

Proposition III.   Studies of selection and training suggest, in general, that the helper trainee's original response dispositions become more intensified over time and with training.

The more traditionally feminine characteristics discriminated by the implicit self and institutional selection processes are further reinforced over the course of training (Patterson, 1967). *The hypothesis that trainees learn to respond the way they are trained to respond* is reinforced by the trainers' promulgation of procedures that result in the selection of those persons most similar to the trainers, at best in the absence of evidence, at worst independent of evidence of the treatment efficacy of their selection process. Like begets like, independent of outcome.

Again the inconclusiveness of the research on the selection procedures and, insofar as they are relevant, on the effects of training upon these procedures, brings us to search out our own directions. One major conclusion sets the stage.

Conclusion I. Studies of helper characteristics must be related to functioning on indexes related to effectiveness in the helping role.

Little research on selection procedures has been conducted to indicate that persons functioning in the helping role are more effective than those who are not. Indeed, naturalistic studies of over-all effects which indicate that on the average treatment does not effect significantly more constructive change than no treatment provide us with inferential evidence suggesting that there are few, if any, functional differences between helpers and nonhelpers.

Corollary I. There are many helpers and helper trainees who do not exhibit the characteristics of the dominant grouping of helpers yet whose success rate is as good or better than that of the dominant grouping.

Patterson (1967) suggests that "there is some evidence that some counseling students do not appear to possess characteristics usually considered desirable in counselors." Could these persons be those with more traditionally masculine response dispositions, those who, under specifiable conditions, may indeed have more to offer a given helpee than those with more feminine response tendencies? Again, with the expressed concern for a helper with a repertoire of behaviors large enough to offer his helpee the possibility of differential treatment, let us hope that both the masculine and feminine response possibilities are incorporated and integrated in a fully functioning helper.

Corollary II. The characteristics of those helpers whose helpees improve on a variety of change indexes must be ,studied.

We must do intensified analyses of those few counselors who consistently obtain positive treatment results and disregard the large number of those who do not effect changes in other persons. From this group, at best, we can learn much about the behavior of ineffective helpers.

With the hope of relating the selection of helpers to the ultimate functioning of helpers, we turn to the development of relevant and meaningful means of selecting helpers.

DISCRIMINATION AND COMMUNICATION

An approach to helping that focuses upon the core of conditions shared by all helping processes, or, indeed, all human relations, complemented by a variety of potential preferred modes of treatment, leads readily to a consideration of discrimination and communication of these conditions. To be sure, the evidence for a relation between the helper's skill in communication and a variety of helpee outcome indexes is now quite considerable (Carkhuff & Berenson, 1967). Effective helping processes, of necessity, then, involve the discrimination and communication of both facilitative and action-oriented conditions. Sensitive discrimination allows the helper to (1) discern the helpee's areas of functioning and dysfunctioning and (2) during the latter phases of treatment to make accurate prescriptions and prognoses concerning which of the available alternate treatment modes might be most efficacious. Effective communication by the helper, in turn, enables the helpee to experience being understood and facilitates movement toward deeper levels of self-exploration and self-understanding. In addition, during the latter phases of treatment effective communication on the part of the helper aids the helpee in developing an awareness of the degree of effectiveness of the orientation and techniques that might be employed in his treatment. Thus, discrimination and communication serve necessarily complementary roles, with the helper's discriminations making possible communications that facilitate the helpee's improved discrimination and communication, not only within the treatment setting but outside it. *One of the major implicit, if not explicit, goals of treatment is the improved functioning of the helpee in both sensitive discrimination of what is going on in his internal and external worlds as well as effective communication with himself and his world.*

Although both high discrimination and communication on the part of the helper are necessary for accurate and directionful helping interactions, the evidence indicates that a high degree of relationship between discrimination and communication is not necessarily the case. Instead, the evidence suggests that among low-level functioning communicators discrimination and communication are unrelated (Anthony & Carkhuff, 1969; Antonuzzo & Kratochvil, 1968; Carkhuff, Kratochvil, & Friel, 1968; Greenbaum, 1968), or perhaps even negatively related, particularly when low-functioning helpers rate themselves (Burstein & Carkhuff, 1969). That is, within a restrictive range of functioning (approximately level 1 to 2 on communication) discrimination is as likely to be relatively high as it is to be relatively low. On the other hand, contrasting evidence indicates that among communicators rated as high level, discrimination scores are high (Carkhuff, Kratochvil, & Friel, 1968), suggesting that *discrimination is a necessary but not sufficient condition for communication.* In support of this evidence, the work of Cannon and Carkhuff (1969), addressing itself to the different rater selection, training, and rating methodologies dictated by the criteria of rigor and meaning, indicates that high-level communicators are the best discriminators of those conditions related to constructive client change or gain.

With the necessary view that the effects of all interpersonal learning or relearning processes are a function of the levels of functioning on relevant dimensions of both the more knowing and the less knowing person (Carkhuff, 1967; Carkhuff & Berenson, 1967), let us at this point summarize our discussion. In regard to (1) both discrimination and communication and (2) both training and treatment, the following proposition emerges.

Proposition I. The gains or deficits in the less knowing person's level of functioning are a function of the initial level of functioning of both the more knowing and the less knowing person.

Thus, in relation to communication as well as discrimination the initial level of communication (discrimination) of both trainer and trainee is critical to generating a later level of communication (discrimination). In this regard the direction of growth of the trainer (helper) over training (treatment) is as critical as his initial or absolute level of functioning. In this context two important corollaries may be derived.

Corollary I. Under specifiable conditions high-level communicators both learn and enable learners to function more effectively than low-level communicators.

Because a high level of discrimination is a prerequisite to high-level communication, the high-level communicator not only discriminates at higher levels and thus learns more about himself as well as others but also communicates effectively with those who must learn about and communicate with themselves and others. However, the fact that high-level communication necessarily incorporates high-level discrimination does not mean that high-level discrimination indicates high-level communication.

Since discrimination and communication have different relationships under different conditions, we must attempt to discern the relevant aspects of these variables. It is readily apparent that discrimination is a more passive phenomenon and communication a more active one. Thus, two separate activities appear to be involved —one that involves seeing and one that involves acting. Accordingly, while high-level communicators may both learn and enable learners to function effectively on both discrimination and communication, the only statement that we can make about high-level discriminators relates to their ability to discriminate over time.

Corollary II.   Under specifiable conditions high-level discriminators learn to discriminate more effectively than low-level discriminators.

Since discrimination does not relate to the ability of helpers to communicate, we can only hypothesize concerning their facility for learning and not teaching. Again, this is not to say that high-level discriminators will learn a communication task, but under the right conditions they will learn to discriminate a communication task well.

The complex relation that exists between discrimination and communication is not unrelated to the knotty problem in the helping process of the discrepancy between insight and action. We will be examining problems of this kind throughout these volumes. In summary, while high levels of discrimination are necessary for communication at high levels, high discrimination does not imply high communication.

These propositions and corollaries can be heuristically integrated with the training and treatment literature, yielding a number of derivative working assumptions.

SELECTION PROCEDURES: AN EXPLORATION

Not all persons, then, can be trained either to treat or to train others. Some may be trained, some may be treated, and, perhaps, some may neither be trained nor treated successfully. In addition, there is no evidence to indicate that individuals who are presently being trained or who are functioning in the helping role are more effective in treatment than those who are not being trained. Instead, most of the evidence, both experiential as well as empirical, points toward the level of communication of the helper, whether professional or nonprofessional, as the critical variable in effective helping processes. Effective communication, in turn, is made possible only by sensitive and accurate discrimination, a function that is necessary but not sufficient for high-level communication. Unfortunately or fortunately, as the case may be in regard to discrimination and communication, it appears that the rich get richer. The evidence suggests that those individuals who are functioning at the highest levels of both discrimination and communication are both the most effective trainers and trainees, the latter when they are learning in the context of a program conducted by a high-level trainer. Similarly, individuals who are functioning at the lowest levels of discrimination—and thus of necessity of communication—are most difficult to train or treat, although conditioning approaches that cannot easily be incorporated in training can be effectively employed in treatment for low discriminators.

Those who are concerned with selection, therefore, must develop relevant indexes that discern those prospective helpers who can most meaningfully employ their training experiences and most effectively discharge their treatment functions. This goal can best be accomplished by breaking down both training and treatment into their critical process variables and assessing the level of functioning of the prospective helpers on these dimensions. The most relevant indexes that emerge for both training and treatment, then, are those which assess the helper trainee's level of communication and discrimination as well as related dimensions, such as the ability to handle crises in treatment and the ability to invest oneself and gain from meaningful learning experiences. In our efforts to develop these selection indexes we are guided by one principle.

Proposition I. The principle of selection: The best index of a future criterion is a previous index of that criterion.

The development of selection indexes necessitates an analysis of a future criterion for which we intend to prepare our prospective helper. Thus, an analysis of the helper's contribution, as well as the concomitant contribution of the helpee, to the helpee's constructive change or gain is essential. The problems of whether we view helping as a process of direct manipulation and modification of helpee behavior (as the behaviorists do) or as a more indirect process through verbal interaction in an interview setting (as the more traditionally oriented therapists do) fade as we incorporate an analysis of both helper and helpee variables to include, hopefully, increasingly assertive actions as well as sensitive discriminations of both helper and helpee. The problems of whether our goals of helping are operational and finite or more global disappear as we incorporate multiple measures of outcome, which, again hopefully, are not totally independent of either treatment or each other. An open, eclectic stance allows us to explore any and all analogues of our future goals of training and helping as potential sources of effective selection procedures. To be sure, in order to avoid potential circularity in our systematizations, we must conduct periodic outcome and follow-up studies of both training and treatment.

A corollary of the principle of selection, then, may be stated simply:

Corollary I. If we want to predict effective helping, we need to obtain an index of the prospective helper trainee's level of functioning in the helping role.

Again, the best index of future functioning in the helping role is a previous index of functioning in the helping role. This proposition leads readily and directly to a number of potential selection indexes.

I. *Index of communication: The best index of future communicative functioning in the helper's role involves casting prospective helpers in the helping role in order to obtain a present index of communicative functioning in the helper's role.*

Casting persons in the helping role is a rather simple procedure in which the prospective helper is given a mental set "to be as helpful as you would ordinarily be if a distressed person came to you in a time of need." The helpee, in turn, might be either a real-life helpee or client (where precautions must be taken by the personnel supervising the assessment program) or, more frequently, a "standard helpee." The standard helpee most often is either a trained or an untrained person who is cast in the role of helpee, with the set "to discuss as fluently as you can, according to how facilitative your helper is, any areas of real concern to you, either in the present, the past or the future." In part the selection of helpees for assessment purposes depends upon whether the primary emphasis is upon training or treatment. The ideal, then, is to approximate as closely as possible a real-life helping process involving a helpee with real-life problems. Assessments can be made, then, of both the level of facilitative and action-oriented conditions offered by the helper as well as the degree to which the helpee invests himself in the treatment process. The procedure has been employed using real-life as well as standard helpees, although the latter method has, for a variety of reasons, been employed most frequently. The procedure has been found effective in assessments of training in rehabilitation counselor education (Anthony & Carkhuff, 1969), guidance counseling (Martin &

Carkhuff, 1968), and clinical psychology training (Carkhuff, Kratochvil, & Friel, 1968) as well as in evaluating dormitory counselors (Berenson, Carkhuff, & Myrus, 1966), nurses (Kratochvil, 1969), lay volunteers (Pierce, Carkhuff, & Berenson, 1967) and parents trained to help their own children (Carkhuff & Bierman, 1969). The results of all of these studies are consistent with the model being explicated, particularly with the emphasis upon the level of the trainer's communicative functioning as the critical ingredient in effective training. In general, the trainee's level of communication moves in the direction of the trainer's level of functioning; when the trainer is functioning at a high level the trainee gains significantly and rapidly; when the trainer is functioning at a low level the trainee does not gain or he deteriorates. Similarly, the procedure has been effectively employed in assessing the effects of treatment by counselors of counseling center clients, by therapists of neuropsychiatric patients (Pagell, Carkhuff, & Berenson, 1967), counseling interns of undergraduate students (Kratochvil, Aspy, & Carkhuff, 1967), and therapists of patients and their children (Carkhuff & Bierman, 1969; Donofrio, 1968). The results, in general, are very analogous to those obtained in studies of training: therapists functioning at high levels and moving toward higher levels have patients who come to function at higher levels.

II. *Index of discrimination: The best index of future discriminative functioning involves obtaining an index of the prospective helper's present discriminative functioning.*

A discrimination procedure involves presenting the prospective helper with varying examples of high, moderate, and low levels of helper-offered conditions, whether taped or in writing, such as those presented in Carkhuff and Berenson (1967), and asking the prospective helper to identify the levels at which the helpers in the respective excerpts are functioning. Those whose ratings agree closely with those of experts with demonstrated predictive validity of ratings are considered high discriminators; those whose ratings deviate greatly are considered low discriminators. Tapes of high, moderate, and low levels of both real-life and role-played counseling have been developed and effectively employed in assessing training programs (Anthony & Carkhuff, 1969; Carkhuff, 1969a, 1969b; Carkhuff, Collingwood, & Renz, 1969; Friel, Kratochvil, & Carkhuff, 1968; Carkhuff, Kratochvil, & Friel, 1968). In general, the results are similar to those obtained in studying communication. With the recognition that communication is independent of discrimination among low-level functioning communicators, it was found that the trainee's level of discrimination moved in the direction of the trainer's level of discrimination—when the trainer is functioning at a high level of discrimination, the trainee comes to function at higher levels; when the trainer is functioning at a low level, the trainee demonstrates little, no, or negative change in his level of discrimination.

III.   *Critical incident index: The best index of the helper's future ability to handle helpee crises effectively involves obtaining an index of the prospective helper's present ability to handle crises.*

Within the counseling session when the prospective helper is cast in the helping role, either with a real-life or a standard helpee, the helpee is likely to present the helper with a number of crises, both within and outside the counseling setting. In fact, the standard helpees can be "programed," or given a set to present the helper with real crises, whether verbally explicit or behaviorally implicit. This procedure has been effectively implemented in assessments of both treatment (Alexik & Carkhuff, 1967; Carkhuff & Alexik, 1967) and training (Friel, Kratochvil, & Carkhuff, 1968). The evidence suggests that high-level functioning helpers mobilize their energies to act forcefully and decisively at these points while low-level helpers are manipulated and, thus, helpless in the face of the crisis (Carkhuff & Berenson, 1967). All of this evidence has implications for the course of treatment and training over time. Persons functioning at high levels mobilize both their own resources and those of the helpee at crisis points and a constructive directionality emerges; over time and with repeated crises the process and outcome is positive. Persons functioning at low levels do not mobilize either their own resources or those of the helpee at crises points, if they acknowledge the crises at all; over time and with crises, whether acknowledged or not, a deterioration process ensues.

IV.   *Index of trainability: The best index of whether a helper trainee can effectively employ the training experience involves an index of the prospective helper's present ability to employ a training analogue.*

In particular, this procedure is directed at training, although it might be employed in a similar fashion using initial interviews with the helper to determine whether prospective helpees could effectively utilize a longer-term treatment program. The procedure simply involves presenting the prospective trainee with an analogue or representative aspect of the training program for which he is being considered and assessing the effects of the brief training by pre- and post-testing of his functioning on relevant indexes. For example, the analogue of training might focus upon a few hours' training in discriminative and communicative aspects of empathy, with pre- and post-training analogue assessments being made of the trainee's discrimination and communication of empathy. Those who demonstrate the greatest increments in learning are considered for further training. A major consideration with this procedure involves incorporating assessments of the level of functioning of the trainer in both the analogue and the training proper in order to control for the differential effects of high- and low-level trainers. This procedure has been employed in the assessment of human relations training programs (Carkhuff, 1969c), with the evidence indicating that those prospective trainees best able to gain from a brief training experience are also those best equipped to utilize a long-term experience.

V. *Index of self-exploration: The best index of the helper trainee's inclination to explore himself in training involves an index of the prospective helper's present inclination to explore himself.*

One of the most critical aspects of any personal learning or relearning processes involves the learner's exploration and experiencing of himself, in particular insofar as it relates to the creative and productive employment of the learning experience. That is, effective learning or relearning most often involves the development or reorganization of personal constructs and cosmologies reflecting the individual's uniqueness in relation to his world. The individuals who are most disposed toward exploring themselves in this manner, that is, *those persons who, while they live fully and with direction in the immediate moment, nevertheless view themselves and their world as tentative hypotheses, are the best candidates for training or, for that matter, treatment.* Those who are not so inclined are poor candidates. In general, based upon evidence relating functioning in the helper and helpee role, this procedure has been employed formally in assessing the effects of lay mental health counselor training (Carkhuff, 1969c). The results suggest that (1) higher-level functioning persons are also disposed to exploring themselves at higher levels and (2) persons disposed toward exploring themselves most highly gain the most from a training experience.

In summary, then, employing the criterion of relevance, we have developed indexes that assess the critical process variables of training and treatment: discrimination and communication, the disposition and ability to handle crises and learning experiences, for they are often one and the same. Employing the criterion of competence, we can, on the basis of these indexes, select those individuals, trainer as well as trainee, helper as well as helpee, who will discharge their training and treatment responsibilities. In the interest of efficacy and efficiency, *only those persons who can discharge their full responsibilities can be allowed to train or function in the helping role.*

REFERENCES

For a more detailed discussion of the issues considered in this chapter see the asterisked readings and the references upon which the readings are based.

Alexik, M., & Carkhuff, R. R. The effects of the manipulation of client self-exploration upon high and low functioning counselors. *Journal of Clinical Psychology*, 1967, **23**, 210–212.

Allen, T. W. The effectiveness of counselor trainees as a function of psychological openness. *Journal of Counseling Psychology*, 1967, **14**, 35–40.

Anthony, W., & Carkhuff, R. R. The effects of rehabilitation counselor training upon discrimination, communication and helping attitudes. *Journal of Counseling Psychology*, in press, 1969.

Antonuzzo, R., & Kratochvil, D. Level of functioning and written responses to written and verbal stimulus expressions. Unpublished research, State University of New York at Buffalo, 1968.

Berenson, B. G., Carkhuff, R. R., & Myrus, P. The interpersonal functioning and training of college students. *Journal of Counseling Psychology*, 1966, **13**, 441–446.

Bergin, A., & Soloman, S. Personality and performance correlates of empathic understanding in psychotherapy. *American Psychologist*, 1963, **18**, 393.

Burstein, J., & Carkhuff, R. R. Objective, client and therapist ratings of therapist-offered facilitative conditions of moderate to low functioning therapists. *Journal of Clinical Psychology*, in press, 1969.

Cannon, J., & Carkhuff, R. R. Effects of rater level of functioning and experience on the ability to discriminate counselors' levels of functioning. *Journal of Consulting Psychology*, in press, 1969.

*Carkhuff, R. R. Training in counseling and psychotherapy: Requiem or reveille? *Journal of Counseling Psychology*, 1966, **13**, 360–367.

Carkhuff, R. R. Toward a comprehensive model of facilitative interpersonal processes. *Journal of Counseling Psychology*, 1967, **14**, 67–72.

Carkhuff, R. R. The prediction of teacher level of functioning in child counseling from discrimination and communication indexes. *Counselor Education and Supervision*, in press, 1969. (a)

Carkhuff, R. R. The effectiveness of undergraduate volunteers in a patient companion program. Unpublished research, State University of New York at Buffalo, 1969. (b)

Carkhuff, R. R. The prediction of success in training lay mental health counselors. Unpublished research, American International College, Springfield, Mass., 1969. (c)

Carkhuff, R. R., & Alexik, M. The differential effects of the manipulation of client self-exploration upon high and low functioning counselors. *Journal of Counseling Psychology*, 1967, **14**, 350–355.

*Carkhuff, R. R., & Berenson, B. G. *Beyond counseling and therapy*. New York: Holt, Rinehart and Winston, Inc., 1967.

Carkhuff, R. R., & Bierman, R. Filial therapy: The effects of training parents to help their children. *Journal of Counseling Psychology*, in press, 1969.

Carkhuff, R. R., Collingwood, T., & Renz, L. The prediction of successful didactic training in counseling. *Journal of Clinical Psychology*, in press, 1969.

Carkhuff, R. R., Kratochvil, D., & Friel, T. The effects of professional training: The communication and discrimination of facilitative conditions. *Journal of Counseling Psychology*, 1968, **15**, 68–74.

Carkhuff, R. R., Piaget, G., & Pierce, R. The development of skills in interpersonal functioning. *Counselor Education and Supervision*, 1967, **7**, 102–106.

Donofrio, D. The effects of level of therapist-offered conditions upon parents in group therapy and their children. Doctoral dissertation, State University of New York at Buffalo, 1968.

Farson, R. E. The counselor is a woman. *Journal of Counseling Psychology*, 1954, **1**, 221–223.

Friel, T., Kratochvil, D., & Carkhuff, R. R. The effects of training and experience upon the manipulation of client conditions. *Journal of Clinical Psychology*, 1968, **24**, 247–249.

Greenbaum, S. Discrimination of helper responses by low level communicators. Unpublished research, State University of New York at Buffalo, 1968.

Hill, G. E. The selection of school counselors. *Personnel Guidance Journal*, 1966, **45**, 16–19.

Holland, J. L., & Richards, J. M. Academic and nonacademic accomplishment: Correlated or uncorrelated? *Journal of Educational Psychology*, 1965, **56**, 165–174.

Kelly, E. L., & Fiske, D. W. *Prediction of performance in clinical psychology*. Ann Arbor: University of Michigan Press, 1950.

Kratochvil, D. Changes in values and interpersonal functioning of counselors in training. *Counselor Education and Supervision*, **8**, 104–107.

Kratochvil, D., Aspy, D., & Carkhuff, R. R. The differential effects of absolute level and direction of growth in counselor functioning upon client functioning. *Journal of Clinical Psychology*, 1967, **23**, 216–218.

Martin, J. C., & Carkhuff, R. R. The effects of training upon changes in trainee personality and behavior. *Journal of Clinical Psychology*, 1968, **24**, 109–110.

McClain, E. W. Is the counselor a woman? *Personnel and Guidance Journal*, 1968, **46**, 444–448.

Pagell, W., Carkhuff, R. R., & Berenson, B. G. The predicted differential effects of the level of counselor functioning upon the level of functioning of outpatients. *Journal of Clinical Psychology*, 1967, **23**, 510–512.

Patterson, C. H. The selection of rehabilitation counseling students. *Personnel Guidance Journal*, 1963, **41**, 318–324.

*Patterson, C. H. The selection of counselors. Paper presented at the Conference on Research Problems in Counseling, Washington University, St. Louis, Mo., 1967.

Pierce, R., Carkhuff, R. R., & Berenson, B. G. The differential effects of high and low functioning counselors upon counselors-in-training. *Journal of Clinical Psychology*, 1967, **23**, 212–215.

Wrenn, C. G. The selection and education of student personnel workers. *Personnel Guidance Journal*, 1966, **44**, 738–743.

7

ASSESSING COMMUNICATION

The extensive evidence relating the level of helper-communicated conditions to indexes of constructive helpee change or gain (Carkhuff & Berenson, 1967) provides a base upon which to build valid selection indexes. Insofar as communication is a central ingredient in all human relations, selection indexes are needed that are applicable to communication. To this end the principle of selection is relevant: *the best index of successful training or treatment is a previous index of a critical aspect of that training or treatment.* Both the criteria for assessing communication and the selection indexes have been developed on this basis. Thus, the best single device for selecting individuals who will function effectively in the helping role is an index of the level of communication of these individuals. *Those who communicate at high levels are best equipped to help persons in need.* With the proper training such individuals can learn to communicate even more effectively.

Unfortunately, a major problem associated with selection procedures involves the wide variability and lack of standardization in the methods employed to assess communication and discrimination. The problem is particularly troublesome when, for example, there are wide differences in the interview and extra-interview behavior of the real-life helpees or standard helpees employed, both within and between projects. In this regard a corollary of the selection principle might meaningfully be stated: *the best index of a particular selection procedure is a brief, standardized index that represents all relevant aspects of that procedure.*

In an effort to standardize procedures various helpee "stimulus expressions" have been developed to assess levels of communication. At the same time standard helper responses have been devised which in conjunction with the helpee stimulus expressions allow us to assess discrimination. Although theoretically and experientially discrimination (being a necessary but not a sufficient condition of communication) may precede communication, the process must be reversed in the selection process if we are to have a basis for direct comparison on the same indexes. That is, employing the same helpee stimulus expressions in conjunction with the standard helper responses in order to obtain an index of discrimination, we must elicit the prospective helper's responses to the helpee stimulus expressions while the helpers are uncontaminated by a knowledge of potential responses that might be learned from the discrimination experience. The usual order of presentation, then, involves first presenting the prospective helper with the helpee expressions and then giving him a set to respond either verbally or in writing to these expressions.

I.   *Helpee stimulus expressions: The best index of communicative functioning is an assessment of the level of responses to standardized and representative helpee stimulus expressions.*

Brief helpee stimulus expressions have been developed to sample responses that cover a wide range of problem areas. The prospective helper is simply asked to respond in the manner he considers most appropriate and helpful. The helpee stimulus expressions may be administered by means of audio tape, the usual method, or in written form. Similarly, the prospective helper may respond verbally or in writing, with the latter method allowing for group testing. The prospective helper's levels of functioning are obtained by rating his levels of responses to the helpee's expressions. Thus, the following set of instructions and helpee stimulus expressions may be presented the prospective helper trainee.

A DESCRIPTION OF HELPER STIMULUS EXPRESSIONS: AN INDEX OF COMMUNICATION

Introduction and Instructions

The following excerpts represent 16 helpee stimulus expressions; that is, expressions by a helpee of feeling and content in different problem areas. In this case the same helpee is involved in all instances.

You may conceive of this helpee not necessarily as a formal client but simply as a person who has come to you in a time of need. The helpee, for example, may be a student from one of your classes. We would like you to respond as you would if someone came to you seeking assistance in a time of distress.

In formulating your responses keep in mind those that the helpee can use effectively in his own life.

Frequently we may play the excerpt over; if you hear something differently each time you hear the excerpt and if you can formulate a different kind of response, please do so. In addition, following each excerpt it would be helpful to us if you wrote down the content of the helpee's discussion or the problem expressed and also the emotional feeling that dominates the helpee's expression. Finally, note those excerpts that have been most difficult for you to respond to.

In summary, formulate responses to the person who has come to you for help. The following range of helpee expressions can easily come in the first contact or first few contacts; however, do not attempt to relate any one expression to a previous expression. Simply try to formulate a meaningful response to the helpee's immediate expression.

Excerpt 1

HELPEE: I don't know if I am right or wrong feeling the way I do. But I find myself withdrawing from people. I don't seem to socialize and play their stupid little games any more. I get upset and come home depressed and have headaches. It seems all so superficial. There was a time when I used to get along with everybody. Everybody said, "Isn't she wonderful. She gets along with everybody. Everybody likes her." I used to think that was something to be really proud of, but that was who I was at that time. I had no depth. I was what the crowd wanted me to be—the particular group I was with.

Excerpt 2

HELPEE: I love my children and my husband and I like doing most household things. They get boring at times but on the whole I think it can be a very rewarding thing at times. I don't miss working, going to the office every day. Most women complain of being just a housewife and just a mother. But then, again, I wonder if there is more for me. Others say there has to be. I really don't know.

Excerpt 3

HELPEE: Sometimes I question my adequacy of raising three boys, especially the baby. I call him the baby—well, he is the last. I can't have any more. So I know I kept him a baby longer than the others. He won't let anyone else do things for him. If someone else opens the door he says he wants Mommy to do it. If he closes the door, I have to open it. I encourage this. I do it. I don't know if this is right or wrong. He insists on sleeping with me every night and I allow it. And he says when he grows up he won't do it any more. Right now he is my baby and I don't discourage this much. I don't know if this comes out of my needs or if I'm making too much out of the situation or if this will handicap him when he goes to school—breaking away from Mamma. Is it going to be a traumatic experience for him? Is it something I'm creating for him? I do worry more about my children than I think most mothers do.

Excerpt 4

HELPEE: It's not an easy thing to talk about. I guess the heart of the problem is sort of a sexual problem. I never thought I would have this sort of problem. But I find myself not getting the fulfillment I used to. It's not as enjoyable—for my husband either, although we don't discuss it. I used to enjoy and look forward to making love. I used to have an orgasm but I don't any more. I can't remember the last time I was satisfied. I find myself being attracted to other men and wondering what it would be like to go to bed with them. I don't know what this means. Is this symptomatic of our whole relationship as a marriage? Is something wrong with me or us?

Excerpt 5

HELPEE: Gee, those people! Who do they think they are? I just can't stand interacting with them any more. Just a bunch of phonies. They leave me so frustrated. They make me so anxious, I get angry at myself. I don't even want to be bothered with them any more. I just wish I could be honest with them and tell them all to go to hell! But I guess I just can't do it.

Excerpt 6

HELPEE: They wave that degree up like it's a pot of gold at the end of the rainbow. I used to think that, too, until I tried it. I'm happy being a housewife; I don't care to get a degree. But the people I associate with, the first thing they ask is where did you get your degree. I answer, "I don't have a degree." Christ, they look at you like you are some sort of a freak, some backwoodsman your husband picked up along the way. They actually believe that people with degrees are better. In fact, I think they are worse. I've found a lot of people without degrees that are a hell of a lot smarter than these people. They think that just because they have degrees they are something special. These poor kids that think they have to go to college or they are ruined. It seems that we are trying to perpetrate a fraud on these kids. If no degree, they think they will end up digging ditches the rest of their lives. They are looked down upon. That makes me sick.

Excerpt 7

HELPEE: I get so frustrated and furious with my daughter. I just don't know what to do with her. She is bright and sensitive, but damn, she has some characteristics that make me so on edge. I can't handle it sometimes. She just—I feel myself getting more and more angry! She won't do what you tell her to. She tests limits like mad. I scream and yell and lose control and think there is something wrong with me—I'm not an understanding mother or something. Damn! What potential! What she could do with what she has. There are times she doesn't need what she's got. She gets by too cheaply. I just don't know what to do with her. Then she can be so nice and then, boy, she can be as ornery as she can be. And then I scream and yell and I'm about ready to slam her across the room. I don't like to feel this way. I don't know what to do with it.

Excerpt 8

HELPEE: He is ridiculous! Everything has to be done when he wants to do it. The way he wants it done. It's as if nobody else exists. It's everything he wants to do. There is a range of things I have to do. Not just be a housewife and take care of the kids. Oh no, I have to do his typing for him, errands for him. If I don't do it right away, I'm stupid—I'm not a good wife or something stupid like that. I have an identity of my own and I'm not going to have it wrapped up in him. It makes me—it infuriates me! I want to punch him right in the mouth. What am I going to do? Who does he think he is, anyway?

Excerpt 9

HELPEE: I finally found somebody I can really get along with. There is no pretentiousness about them at all. They are real and they understand me. I can be myself with them. I don't have to worry about what I say and that they might take me wrong, because I do sometimes say things that don't come out the way that I want them to. I don't have to worry that they are going to criticize me. They are just marvelous people! I just can't wait to be with them. For once I actually enjoy going out and interacting. I didn't think I could ever find people like this again. I can really be myself. It's such a wonderful feeling not to have people criticizing you for everything you say that doesn't agree with them. They are warm and understanding and I just love them! It's just marvelous.

Excerpt 10

HELPEE: I'm really excited! We are going to California. I'm going to have a second lease on life. I found a marvelous job. It's great! It's so great, I can't believe it's true—it's so great! I have a secretarial job. I can be a mother and can have a part time job which I think I will enjoy very much. I can be home when the kids get home from school. It's too good to be true. It's so exciting. New horizons are unfolding. I just can't wait to get started. It's great!

Excerpt 11

HELPEE: I'm so pleased with the kids. They are doing just marvelously. They have done so well at school and at home; they get along together. It's amazing. I never thought they would. They seem a little older. They play together better and they enjoy each other and I enjoy them. Life has become so much easier. It's really a joy to raise three boys. I didn't think it would be. I'm just so pleased and hopeful for the future. For them and for us. It's just great! I can't believe it. It's marvelous.

Excerpt 12

HELPEE: I'm really excited the way things are going at home with my husband. It's just amazing. We get along great together now. Sexually, I didn't know we could be that happy. I didn't know anyone could be that happy. It's just marvelous! I'm just so pleased, I don't know what else to say.

Excerpt 13

HELPEE: I'm so thrilled to have found a counselor like you. I didn't know any existed. You seem to understand me so well. It's just great! I feel like I'm coming alive again. I have not felt like this in so long.

Excerpt 14

HELPEE: *Silence.* (*Moving about in chair*)

Excerpt 15

HELPEE: Gee, I'm so disappointed. I thought we could get along together and you could help me. We don't seem to be getting anywhere. You don't understand me. You don't know I'm here. I don't even think you care for me. You don't hear me when I talk. You seem to be somewhere else. Your responses are independent of anything I have to say. I don't know where to turn. I'm just so—doggone it—

I don't know what I'm going to do, but I know you can't help me. There just is no hope.

Excerpt 16

HELPEE: Who do you think you are? You call yourself a therapist! Damn, here I am spilling my guts out and all you do is look at the clock. You don't hear what I say. Your responses are not attuned to what I'm saying. I never heard of such therapy. You are supposed to be helping me. You are so wrapped up in your world you don't hear a thing I'm saying. You don't give me the time. The minute the hour is up you push me out the door whether I have something important to say or not. I—ah—it makes me so God damn mad!

Stop! If the reader is administering or being administered the standardized helpee stimulus expressions in order to assess level of communication, he should proceed no further until all relevant persons have responded in accordance with instructions.

COMMUNICATION ASSESSMENTS: BASE RATE DATA

The standard communication assessment procedure is designed to assess the level of communication in prospective helpers. The design of the helpee stimulus expressions is calculated to cross different helpee expressions of feeling with different helpee problem areas (see Table 7-1). Thus, the affective expressions of the different feelings of (1) depression-distress, (2) anger-hostility, and (3) elation-excitement cut across the different problems expressed by the helpee: (1) social-interpersonal,

Table 7-1. Communication: Design of Helpee Stimulus Expressions Index

	Affect		
Problem Areas	*Depression-Distress*	*Anger-Hostility*	*Elation-Excitement*
Social-interpersonal	Excerpt 1	Excerpt 2	Excerpt 3
Educational-vocational	Excerpt 4	Excerpt 5	Excerpt 6
Child-rearing	Excerpt 7	Excerpt 8	Excerpt 9
Sexual-marital	Excerpt 10	Excerpt 11	Excerpt 12
Confrontation of helper	Excerpt 15	Excerpt 16	Excerpt 13
Silence		Excerpt 14	

(2) educational-vocational, (3) child-rearing, (4) sexual-marital, (5) confrontation of helper. In addition, there is a silence to which the prospective helpers are requested to respond. Although helpee confrontation of helper may not be conceived of as the kind of problem that brings a helpee to seek help, it involves difficulties that the helpee has with the helper within the counseling process while offering the additional benefit of presenting the helper with a crisis situation. Similarly, silence does not denote a specific helpee problem area; however, the helpee may during a period of silence be working on problems that are very real for him. The silence excerpt has the additional benefit of presenting the prospective helper with a minor crisis.[1]

The over-all base rate data appear in Table 7-2. While the levels of functioning of the general population and undergraduate students are very similar, the data indicate that level of communication is a function of experience or training or both. There is a progression of ratings for the first response from approximately level 1.5 to level 3.0 for the experienced and systematically trained counselors.

The differences obtained in communication level according to affect and content, while statistically significant due to the large number of subjects involved, were not functionally meaningful. Rather, level of communication *appeared to be characteristic of the individual respondent, relatively independent of affect and content.* What this means in practice is that persons who were communicating at relatively low levels (either below level 3.0 or 2.5) over-all did not tend to emit high-level responses to any particular item while those functioning at relatively high levels (either above level 3.0 or 2.5) did not tend to emit any low-level responses.

In addition, at five different levels, groups involved with helping the prospective helpers were given a set to respond to as many times as they could, and the helpee stimulus expressions were played until the helpers acknowledged that they had exhausted their response repertoires. The base rate data appear in Table 7-3. It was found that response frequency was largely a function of systematic training on the conditions involved. Over-all, all groups emitted the lowest frequency of responses to the following categories: (1) the silence item (approximately one response fewer than the mean number of responses over-all); (2) elation-affect (approximately one-half response less than the mean number of responses over-all); and (3) confrontation-content (approximately one-half response less than the mean number of responses for all groups

---

[1] While the order of presentation of the first 12 excerpts has not been randomized, no effects of order have been found. However, the order may be randomized or the last four excerpts may be employed if this becomes a major concern.

Table 7-2. Communication: Ratings of Facilitative Conditions and Response Repertoire of Helper Responses to Helpee Stimulus Expressions[a]

Populations (Levels)	N (No. of subjects)	Level of Communication (Ratings of helper responses on 5-point scales)	
		Mean	Standard Deviation
1. *General population*			
Outpatients	10	1.5	0.4
Parents	20	1.5	0.5
Military	10	1.6	0.5
2. *College students*			
Freshman	330	1.6	0.5
Upperclass philosophy	30	1.5	0.5
Student leaders	30	1.5	0.5
Volunteer helpers	30	1.5	0.2
Senior psychology	30	1.6	0.5
3. *Lay personnel*			
Lay teachers	50	1.6	0.5
Lay counselors	50	1.6	0.4
4. *Professionals*			
Teachers	20	1.8	0.6
Beginning psychology graduate students	10	1.9	0.5
Experienced counselors (not systematically trained)	20	2.2	0.5
Experienced counselors (systematically trained)	10	3.0	0.4

[a] Carkhuff, 1969a.

except the beginning graduate students who equaled their over-all mean levels). While almost all groups exhibited the largest repertoire of responses to social-interpersonal content, there was a division according to age in response frequency to affect: the older groups (the teachers and the experienced counselors) demonstrated the largest repertoire of responses to depression while the younger respondents offered the highest frequency of responses to anger.

However, response frequency was not necessarily related to commu-

Table 7-3. Communication: Repertoire of Helper Responses to Helpee Stimulus Expressions[a]

Populations	N (No. of Subjects)	Repertoire of Responses (Response frequency upon repeated administration)	
		Mean	Standard Deviation
Senior psychology students	30	2.1	0.4
Professional teachers	20	1.9	0.8
Beginning psychology graduate students	10	2.5	1.2
Experienced counselors (not systematically trained)	20	2.3	1.1
Experienced counselors (systematically trained)	10	3.0	1.7

[a] Carkhuff, 1969a.

nication level. Indeed, while elation-affect expressions elicited the fewest responses, the communication levels demonstrated nonsignificant trends toward higher communication ratings; on the other hand, while confrontation-content expressions elicited the fewest responses, they demonstrated nonsignificant trends toward lower communication ratings. Again, although the response repertoire was in part a function of affect and content, the level of communication was characteristic of the individual respondent.

Finally, it is noteworthy that with the exception of the experienced groups the mean levels of functioning of all groups grew systematically lower on repeated administrations of the helpee stimulus expressions. That is, on successive administrations the respondents communicated at lower levels. Thus, the groups involved dropped as follows over four administrations: senior psychology students from 1.6 to 1.3; teachers from 1.8 to 1.5; and beginning graduate trainees from 1.9 to 1.5. These data are qualified, of course, by the fact that the number of respondents in each group also decreased systematically on successive administrations. The results contrast with those of the experienced (whether systematically trained or not) groups, which maintained a high level of consistency (between 2.9 and 3.0 for the trained and between 2.0 and 2.2 for the untrained, experienced) across administrations.

Factor analyses of the communication responses indicate a principle factor accounting for approximately two thirds of the variability in the indexes. Since all variables load significantly on the factor, the direct suggestion is that all of the tests are essentially measuring the same variable 16 times. This is true independent of both affect and content and independent of experience level. This is not true independent of level of functioning. Multivariate analyses for high-, moderate-, and low-functioning groups indicate significant differences not only in group means but also in group dispersions. However, again the essential finding is that within any level of functioning the differences are so slight between affects and problem areas that they are not meaningful.

Further exploration of the communication process was accomplished by a content analysis of the response tendencies of the groups assessed. Discriminations were made concerning whether the subpopulations tended in their responses to helpee stimulus expressions to emphasize the following: (1) content, affect, or both; (2) the helpee, themselves, or significant others; (3) the past, present, or future; (4) responsiveness, interpretation, or other styles; (5) directive, nondirective, or other modes of responding. In general, respondents who were inexperienced or low functioning or both (on both communication and discrimination) tended to respond to content almost exclusively while respondents who were experienced or moderate functioning or both tended to respond to affect about as frequently as content, with respondents who were experienced and trained or high functioning, or both, tending to respond to both affect and content simultaneously. Both experienced as well as high- and low-functioning respondents demonstrated strong tendencies to respond to the present rather than to the past or future. Similarly, all groups tended to respond to the helpee rather than themselves (the helpers), with respondents who were experienced and trained or high functioning, or both, demonstrating an increasing tendency to respond to the interaction between helper and helpee. The experienced and high-functioning respondents tended to respond experientially, although not to the exclusion of didactic responses, while the inexperienced and low-functioning respondents emphasized didactic responses but not to the exclusion of the experiential and other responses. The directive-nondirective discriminations were more complex, with experienced, low-functioning practitioners tending to be either directive or to ask questions (often irrelevant if not stupid questions), while experienced, high-functioning practitioners demonstrated a more even balance between directiveness and nondirectiveness. On the other hand, however, among the inexperienced respondents the high-functioning respondents tended to be more directive—apparently trying to *do* something about the helpee's problems—and the low-functioning respondents more nondirective.

In general, then, the results indicate increasingly higher communication and response frequency with training and experience. While the trend with experience was somewhat linear, the differences were small in the absence of the systematically trained helpers. There was a great jump in response frequency and communication level from experienced counselors who were not systematically trained to those who were. The results all suggest the necessity for training programs built systematically around the kinds of conditions assessed in this study. Indeed, the level of functioning of experienced, nonsystematically trained counselors, while higher than that of all other groups assessed, was significantly less than minimally facilitative. In this regard it is noteworthy that the levels of communication established here are essentially replications of previous data obtained in standard interviews.[2] Thus, the data establish not only the construct validity of the instruments employed but also the stability of the findings.

In relation to content and affect the major findings are twofold. First, the helper response repertoire is in part a function of helpee affect and content. Second, helper communication level is largely independent of helpee affect and content. Regarding the first finding it is noteworthy that all groups consistently had the fewest responses available for elation-affect and confrontation content, with each perhaps suggesting social psychological and personal phenomena related to the aspects of inter-personal functioning that are most difficult for helpers. Concerning the second finding, although the helper's response repertoire is related to the helpee's problem area, the helpee nevertheless tends to receive the highest levels of communication and the largest repertoire of responses from those helpers who are most experienced or systematically trained or both. To be sure, *a central occurrence in effective helping may involve a helper functioning at a relatively high level enabling a helpee functioning at a low level to function at a high level while concurrently enabling the helpee to increase his response repertoire and thus his degrees of freedom in different problem areas.*

STUDIES OF OUTCOME

A number of studies relating helpee stimulus expressions to meaningful indexes of training outcome have been conducted. Before proceeding further, however, it will be worthwhile to explore briefly some of the training and treatment studies of communication that have employed assessment devices based upon casting the helper in the helping role, since these studies laid the basis for many of the designs that

[2] See Carkhuff & Berenson, 1967, Table 1, p. 9.

followed. While early studies of training and treatment employed real patients for posttesting purposes (Carkhuff & Truax, 1965a, 1965b), the potential dangers for the patients in pretesting and the great differences among patients led to the employment of standard helpees. Usually the standard helpees were trained graduate students rather than under-graduate students. While the standard helpees were usually given a mental set to discuss problems that were real for them and to allow the interaction to flow according to how helpful the helper was, the affects and problem areas presented served to decrease the variability between standard helpees and thus yielded a more reliable means of assessment. All prospective helpers saw similar types of helpees, both before and after training. Accordingly, prepost-testing involving casting the helper in the helping role was employed in the assessments of the effects of training and treatment in a large number of studies (Berenson, Carkhuff, & Myrus, 1966; Carkhuff, Kratochvil, & Friel, 1968; Kratochvil, 1969; Martin & Carkhuff, 1968; Pagell, Carkhuff, & Berenson, 1968; Pierce, Carkhuff, & Berenson, 1967). This process, while time consuming, is extremely effective. Indeed, *if the conditions are available, casting prospective helpers in the helping role appears to be the preferred method of assessing communication.* In addition to the objective ratings of trained raters, this method affords us an opportunity to assess the standard helpee's experience with some degree of accuracy. That is, highly trained standard helpees give accurate estimates of the level of facilitative and action-oriented conditions that they experienced the helper as offering. On the other hand, real patients, for whom interpersonal distortion is often an integral part of their problems, do not provide estimates that are nearly so reliable or valid (Burstein & Carkhuff, 1969; Hansen, Moore, and Carkhuff, 1968; Truax, 1966). Nevertheless, under certain conditions real patients might be preferred. Pierce and Drasgow (1969) preferred to employ patients as helpees in the posttesting of their program to train patients to become helpers because the program was preparing the patient-helpers for service to their fellow-patients. In a variation of this approach Anthony and Carkhuff (1969) effectively employed both standard disability cases and student helpees in order to assess a rehabilitation-counselor training program.

The first research project to employ the standard communication index directly as a predictor was a summer workshop in counseling involving experienced teachers in their first counselor training experience (Carkhuff, 1969b). The training program incorporated both the didactic and experiential aspects of training built systematically around training on the rating scales of the core conditions. Both the communication and discrimination indexes were employed in a pretraining battery, and the ratings of actual counseling interviews with school-age children as well as with adults were employed as outcome measures. It was found that within the restrictive levels on which the trainees were functioning (below level 2), the trainees who entered training above level 1.7 gained significantly more and functioned at significantly higher absolute levels of functioning following training with a high-level trainer. The trainees who were functioning at lower levels also gained, but with the exception of one trainee these changes were minimal. Any generalizations, however, are qualified by the highly complex interaction between initial trainee and trainer levels of functioning.

Thus, for example, in other studies in which the trainers were not functioning at quite so high a level and the trainees were functioning at relatively high initial levels (around level 2 over-all) the gains were neither as substantial nor the effectiveness of the predictors as fine. In a study of an integrated training program for beginning graduate students (Carkhuff, Friel and Kratochvil, 1969) the discrimination and communication indexes were employed prior to training, and actual interviews with standard helpees were used following training. While the trends toward growth or change over time were not quite so clear, in part due perhaps to the lack of a significant differential between initial levels of trainer and trainee functioning, in general those trainees who were communicating or functioning at the highest absolute levels at the beginning of training were communicating at the highest absolute levels following training.

In another study (Carkhuff, Collingwood, & Renz, 1969) senior seminar psychology undergraduates went through an exclusively didactic experience in discrimination training. All experience or practice in the helping role was omitted or excluded. Again both standard discrimination and communication indexes were administered prior to training. Following training the same instruments were again administered in conjunction with an interview of a standard interviewee. The findings indicated that a group functioning at initially low levels of discrimination and communication (below level 2) gained significantly in discrimination, with only minimal changes in communication. The communication index did not predict any changes in discriminaton. The conclusion was that even in interaction with a high-level trainer, if the focus is exclusively upon didactic discrimination training there will be little or no generalization to communication among low-level–functioning trainees. The results are consistent with those of the training control groups of other studies (Berenson, Carkhuff, & Myrus, 1967; Martin & Carkhuff, 1967) as well as with those of graduate training (Carkhuff, Kratochvil, & Friel, 1968) where the traditional focus is upon discrimination training.

On the other hand, in a demonstration study of the effects of practice in written communication (Berenson, Carkhuff, Friel, & Leitner, 1968) with a large group of low-functioning undergraduate students pre- and posttraining administrations of alternate forms of the discrimination and communication indexes yielded substantial gains in written communication and discrimination. Again while the trends toward change were complex, in general those trainees communicating at the highest absolute levels initially were also functioning at the highest absolute levels following training.

Findings of a program to train parents to communicate effectively with each other in order to work effectively with their children (Carkhuff & Bierman, 1969) are similar. In a program that emphasized practice in communication, and discrimination only insofar as it followed communication, the discrimination and communication indexes were administered before and after training. In addition, the parents were also cast in the helping role with each other and with their children in order to assess the effects of training. The results indicated that the communication index is the best predictor of both degree of change and absolute level of functioning following training. Those parents functioning at the higher levels within a restrictive range (below level 2) made the greatest gains and functioned at the highest final levels following training with a high-level trainer.

These findings are replicated in human relations workshops and lay counselor training programs focusing upon improved interpersonal skills both within and between races and generations (Carkhuff & Banks, 1969; Carkhuff & Griffin, 1969a, 1969b). Again initial level of communication as obtained by the standard index was predictive of both degree of change and final level of absolute functioning. Those parents, teachers, and counselors functioning at the highest levels initially were found, in conjunction with a high-level trainer, to be functioning at the highest levels following the training experience.

The complexities of the interactions is further underscored by a study of the effects of a volunteer companion program (Carkhuff, 1969c). In a program involving no formal selection or training experiences except for periodic supervisory sessions with low-level–functioning supervisors (below level 2 over-all) a group of companions functioning at very low levels initially (1.5 over-all) demonstrated no positive change in themselves or their patients. Indeed, the attrition rate of over 50 percent of the companions gives sober testimony to the ineffectiveness of such an unstructured program and contrasts vividly with *the absence of attrition of systematic programs run by high-level trainers.*

In summary, the functional utility of the communication indexes involves a number of highly complex contingencies. The effectiveness of

these indexes depends upon the level of trainer and trainee functioning and upon the type of program being conducted, each as a significant
source of effect alone and in their various interactions. In general, however, there are direct indications that these devices can provide an
accurate estimate of future level of functioning in the helping role if
the relevant variables are known. The relevant variables will be discussed
more fully in the training section of this book.

EXTENSIONS AND LIMITATIONS

In naturalistic extensions of these studies an intensive exploration of
the demographic and biographic characteristics, including measures of
physical, emotional, and intellectual functioning, of the top and bottom
10 percent of communicators in a personality development course of
over 150 students was conducted (Frankel, 1968). Since the communication levels of the highest-rated students ranged from 2.03 to 2.62,
these individuals must be considered moderate- rather than high-level
communicators, while the lows were very low indeed (1.06 to 1.26).
In this context, among other things, the higher communicators were
found to be higher discriminators, to have a higher high school grade-
point average and tended to have listed some helping profession as their
vocational choice, and to list more achievements reflecting creativity and
productivity. In general, they appeared more competent than their
lower-functioning counterparts.

Devoid of either training or treatment orientation, Greenberg (1968)
in a counterbalanced design established the close relation among the
following three conditions: (1) responding in a written form to helpee
stimulus expressions; (2) responding verbally to helpee stimulus expressions; (3) responding in the helping role. This research established that
both written and verbal responses to helpee stimulus expressions are
valid indexes of assessments of the counselor in the actual helping role.
Antonuzzo and Kratochvil (1968), in turn, established a close relation
between (1) the verbal or recorded presentation of the helpee stimulus
expressions and the written responses of subjects and (2) the written
presentation of the helpee stimulus expressions and the written responses
of subjects. In each of these projects, however, certain discrepancies
between the functioning of the high- and low-level communicators were
evident. The results of the low-level communicators were variable; that
is, they were relatively high on one index and low on another, almost
as if they had specialties in functioning. On the other hand, the high-
level communicators tended to be consistent across all indexes. Thus,

it was only when the results of high- and low-functioning persons were combined that these relationships were obtained. These results are consistent with others to be discussed more fully in later chapters concerning training and treatment.

A related topic is that of item analysis of the standard communication index, both internal (the relation of each item to the over-all score or level of functioning for all items) and external (the relation of each item to the assessed level of functioning on the final outcome criteria). While there was variability within and between studies, the items relating most highly to the over-all ratings as well as to final outcome criteria are the confrontations of the counselor in different affects. Thus, we obtain an index not only of the over-all level of functioning with these items but also of how the prospective helper responds to the most difficult situations, the crises for which he is least prepared and has the fewest responses available. These findings have implications for the administration of an abbreviated version of the helpee stimulus expressions.

Together these studies suggest that the level of communication of the prospective helpers may be obtained by standardized and abbreviated indexes of communication. The question of written helper responses in response to helpee expressions raises the question concerning the amount of material that might be lost. In particular, for example, written statements may lose the quality of affective expression of the audio recording. In the same vein many other behavioral expressions are lost when audiovisual means of recording are not available. In addition, there is in general some tendency for the written responses of high-level–functioning helpers to receive lower ratings than the verbal responses of these helpers in interaction with a helpee in the helping role. The high-level helpers are much more spontaneous and accurate in their responses when they have the feedback of the helpee's behavior in person. However, the prospective helpers who have received high ratings on the written form invariably receive high ratings in the helping interaction. The basic question is not whether the response may be modified in writing but whether or not the helper has an effective response in his repertoire of responses. In general, the written format for prospective helper responses offers a satisfactory level of discrimination and an economic and efficient means of collecting data.

In regard to whether the helpee expressions should be administered by audio tape or in written form, suffice it to say that research may be conducted in large groups just as easily with an audio recording as with the written form. The written form would seem to be most appropriate when the taped procedure is not possible—for example, when groups cannot be brought together or when assessments are sought through the mail or at some distance. In general, then, under ordinary circumstances the presentation of the recorded helpee stimulus expressions and the written recording of the prospective helpers is recommended as offering maximum efficiency.

In summary, the vast amount of evidence relating counselor-communicated facilitative and action-oriented dimensions to indexes of constructive helpee change or gain has been employed as the base for the development of valid selection procedures. Indexes of communication have been devised, standardized, and validated in the most direct, straightforward, and economical ways, and the empirical research testifying to such has been presented. While the best index of future functioning in the helping role remains present functioning in the helping role, written helper responses to standard, audio helpee stimulus expressions yield fairly accurate and efficient estimates of the helper's functioning in the helping role, particularly when ratings on the written form are high. With extreme time limitations even briefer versions, such as confrontation items, may be employed if necessary. However, the relatively small percentage of persons equipped to relate effectively with persons in need of help necessitates further exploration of discrimination as a selection device. Nevertheless, at present, *the communication assessments derived from responses to helpee stimulus expressions are the most valid standard indexes for selecting persons equipped to function effectively in the helping role.*

REFERENCES

For an exploration of the methodologies involved in the projects cited in this chapter see the asterisked research articles.

Anthony, W., & Carkhuff, R. R. The effects of rehabilitation counselor training upon discrimination, communication and helping attitudes. *Journal of Counseling Psychology*, in press.

Antonuzzo, R., & Kratochvil, D. The differential effects of written and audio stimulus material upon counselor responses. Unpublished research, State University of New York at Buffalo, 1968.

Berenson, B. G., Carkhuff, R. R., Friel, T., & Leitner, L. The effects of brief written communication training in large groups. Unpublished research, State University of New York at Buffalo, 1968.

Berenson, B. G., Carkhuff, R. R., & Myrus, P. The interpersonal functioning and training of college students. *Journal of Counseling Psychology*, 1966, 13, 441–446.

Burstein, J., & Carkhuff, R. R. Objective, client and therapist ratings of therapist-offered facilitative conditions of moderate and low functioning therapists. *Journal of Clinical Psychology*, in press, 1969.

Carkhuff, R. R. Toward a comprehensive model of facilitative interpersonal processes. *Journal of Counseling Psychology*, 1967, **14**, 67–72.

Carkhuff, R. R. Helper communication and discrimination as a function of helpee affect and content. *Journal of Counseling Psychology*, 1969, **16**, 126–131. (a)

*Carkhuff, R. R. The prediction of the effects of teacher-counselor training: The development of communication and discrimination selection indexes. *Counselor Education and Supervision*, in press, 1969. (b)

Carkhuff, R. R. The effects of a volunteer companion program. Unpublished research, State University of New York at Buffalo, 1969. (c)

Carkhuff, R. R. & Banks, G. The effects of a human relations workshop for Negro parents and white teachers. Unpublished research, American International College, Springfield, Mass., 1969.

*Carkhuff, R. R., & Berenson, B. G. *Beyond counseling and therapy.* New York: Holt, Rinehart and Winston, Inc., 1967.

Carkhuff, R. R., & Bierman, R. The effects of human relations training upon child psychiatric parents in treatment. *Journal of Counseling Psychology*, in press, 1969.

Carkhuff, R. R., Collingwood, T., & Renz, L. The prediction of the effects of didactic training in discrimination. *Journal of Clinical Psychology*, in press, 1969.

Carkhuff, R. R., Friel, T., and Kratochvil, D. The differential effects of training in responsive and initiative dimensions. *Counselor Education and Supervision*, in press.

Carkhuff, R. R., & Griffin, A. The effects of training in interpersonal skills in Project "Head Start." Unpublished research, American International College, Springfield, Mass., 1969. (a)

Carkhuff, R. R., & Griffin, A. The effects of training in interpersonal skills in Project "CEP." Unpublished research, American International College, Springfield, Mass., 1969. (b)

*Carkhuff, R. R., Kratochvil, D., & Friel, T. The effects of professional training: The communication and discrimination of facilitative conditions. *Journal of Counseling Psychology*, 1968, **15**, 68–74.

Carkhuff, R. R., & Truax, C. B. Lay mental health counseling: The effectiveness of lay group counseling. *Journal of Consulting Psychology*, 1965, **29**, 426–431. (a)

Carkhuff, R. R., & Truax, C. B. Training in counseling and psychotherapy: An evaluation of an integrated didactic and experiential approach. *Journal of Consulting Psychology*, 1965, **29**, 333–336. (b)

Frankel, S. The biographic and demographic characteristics of high and low discriminators and communicators. Unpublished research, State University of New York at Buffalo, 1968.

Greenberg, B. The differential ratings of counselor responses to client expressions in a written, audio and real life form. Unpublished research, State University of New York at Buffalo, 1968.

Hansen, J., Moore, G. D., & Carkhuff, R. R. The differential relationships of objective and client perceptions of counseling. *Journal of Clinical Psychology*, 1968, **24**, 244–246.

Kratochvil, D. Changes in values and interpersonal functioning of nurses in training. *Counselor Education and Supervision*, 1969, **8**, 104–107.

Pagell, W., Carkhuff, R. R., & Berenson, B. G. The predicted differential effects of the level of counselor functioning upon the level of functioning of out-patients. *Journal of Clinical Psychology*, 1967, **23**, 510–512.

Pierce, R., Carkhuff, R. R., & Berenson, B. G. The differential effects of high and low functioning counselors upon counselors-in-training. *Journal of Clinical Psychology*, 1967, **23**, 212–215.

Pierce, R., & Drasgow, J. The effects of human relations training upon VA neuropsychiatric patients. *Journal of Counseling Psychology*, in press, 1969.

Martin, J., & Carkhuff, R. R. The effects of training upon changes in trainee personality and behavior. *Journal of Clinical Psychology*, 1968, **24**, 109–110.

Truax, C. B. Therapist empathy, warmth and genuineness and patient personality change in group psychotherapy: A comparison between interaction unit measures, time sample measures, patient perception measures. *Journal of Clinical Psychology*, 1966, **22**, 225–229. (a)

Truax, C. B. Therapist empathy, warmth and genuineness and patient personality change in group psychotherapy: A comparison between interaction unit measures, time sample measures, patient perception measures. *Journal of Clinical Psychology*, 1966, **22**, 225–229. (b)

8

ASSESSING DISCRIMINATION

Indexes of communication that have been derived from a great body of empirical research indicate those helpers who can relate effectively with persons seeking help. Unfortunately, depending upon a number of variables, the number of effective helpers is very limited—indeed, there are far too few to meet the ever-growing needs of our society. It was in this context that we explored the various correlates of discrimination. Our hope was that discrimination, as a necessary but not sufficient condition of communication, would offer the highest probability of direct translation to communication. Our expectation was that persons discriminating at high levels would be able to interpret their training experiences and translate their discriminations into communicative skills. Our most efficient and economical training efforts, then, would involve those persons best equipped to utilize their training experiences. With the hope of developing the largest possible reservoir of potential helpers— those persons who with communication training could discharge their full treatment responsibilities—we turned to those individuals who could discriminate but did not communicate, those who could see but did not articulate nor act but who, at least apparently, had immediately available the necessary resources to be trained in these skills. So went the reasoning behind our original explorations of discrimination. Unfortunately, the results of our studies do not support the efficacy of this dimension in the manner we had hoped.

Nevertheless, the dimension of discrimination remains one of potentially critical significance. At a very minimum we must select raters to discriminate effective from ineffective helping processes. Indeed, whether assessing an interaction in the helping role or a response to a standard tape, accurate discriminations constitute the basis for selecting prospective helpers on the basis of communication. At a maximum the dimension of discrimination, in various combinations, constitutes a rich source of inquiry and research. If, for example, we can find some direction in answer to the problem of why discrimination does not translate easily and readily to communication, then we will be one step closer toward understanding the problem of the differential between insight and action with helpee populations. Perhaps most important, the effective helper employs his accurate discriminations most fully in enabling the helpee to attain higher and more effective levels of both discrimination and communication.

With these thoughts in mind we examine this index of discrimination. Following the elicitation of spontaneous responses from the prospective helpers to the helpee stimulus expressions, then, we can attend to obtaining an index of discrimination.

II. *Counselor responses to helpee stimulus expressions: The best index of discriminative functioning involves an assessment of the ratings of standardized and representative helper responses to standardized and representative helpee stimulus expressions.*

Brief helper responses have been developed to cover a representative sampling of potential helper responses to the wide range of helpee stimulus expressions. The prospective helper is usually simply asked to employ a form yielding gross ratings of facilitative interpersonal functioning (see Fig. 8-1) in rating the level of helper communication to helpee expressions, although he may be given no mental set at all and may simply be asked to rate the responses from 1 (poor) to 5 (good) solely on the basis of his own experience.

Again the helper responses as well as the helpee expressions may be administered in audio or written form. The prospective helper's discrimination scores are obtained from his deviation from the ratings of experts with demonstrated predictive validity. Thus, the following set of instructions and helper responses to helpee stimulus expressions are presented to the prospective helper trainee.

A DESCRIPTION OF HELPER RESPONSES TO HELPEE STIMULUS EXPRESSIONS: AN INDEX OF DISCRIMINATION

Introduction and Instructions

The following excerpts involve a number of helpee stimulus expressions and in turn a number of helper responses. There are 16 expressions

1.0	1.5	2.0	2.5	3.0	3.5	4.0	4.5	5.0

None of these conditions are communicated to any noticeable degree in the person.	Some of the conditions are communicated and some are not.	All of the conditions are communicated at a minimally facilitative level.	All of the conditions are communicated, and some are communicated fully.	All of the conditions are fully communicated simultaneously and continually.

Figure 8-1. Gross ratings of facilitative interpersonal functioning.

The facilitator is a person who is living effectively himself and who discloses himself in a genuine and constructive fashion in response to others. He communicates an accurate empathic understanding and a respect for all of the feelings of other persons and guides discussions with those persons into specific feelings and experiences. He communicates confidence in what he is doing and is spontaneous and intense. In addition, while he is open and flexible in his relations with others, in his commitment to the welfare of the other person he is quite capable of active, assertive, and even confronting behavior when it is appropriate.

You will hear a number of excerpts taken from therapy sessions. Rate each excerpt 1.0, 1.5, 2.0, 2.5, 3.0, 3.5, 4.0, 4.5, *or* 5.0, using the above continuum.

by helpees of problems, and in response to each expression there are four possible helper responses.

These helpees can be considered to be helpees in very early contacts. They may not be formal helpees. They may simply be people who sought the help of another person in a time of need. In this example the same helpee and the same helper are involved.

You may rate these tapes, keeping in mind that those helper responses which the helpee can employ most effectively are rated the highest.

Excerpt 1

HELPEE: I don't know if I am right or wrong feeling the way I do. But I find myself withdrawing from people. I don't seem to socialize and play their stupid little games any more. I get upset and come home depressed and have headaches. It all seems so superficial. There was a time when I used to get along with everybody. Everybody said, "Isn't she wonderful. She gets along with everybody. Everybody likes her." I used to think that was something to be really proud of, but that was who I was at that time. I had no depth. I was what the crowd wanted me to be—the particular group I was with.

HELPER RESPONSES:

(1) You know you have changed a lot. There are a lot of things you want to do but no longer can.

(2) You are damned sure who you can't be any longer but you are not sure who you are. Still hesitant as to who you are yet.

(3) Who are these people that make you so angry? Why don't you tell them where to get off! They can't control your existence. You have to be your own person.

(4) So you have a social problem involving interpersonal difficulties with others.

Excerpt 2

HELPEE: I love my children and my husband and I like doing most household things. They get boring at times but on the whole I think it can be a very rewarding thing at times. I don't miss working, going to the office every day. Most women complain of being just a housewife and just a mother. But, then, again, I wonder if there is more for me. Others say there has to be. I really don't know.

HELPER RESPONSES:

(1) Hmm. Who are these other people?

(2) So you find yourself raising a lot of questions about yourself—educationally, vocationally.

(3) Why are you dominated by what others see for you? If you are comfortable and enjoy being a housewife, then continue in this job. The role of mother, homemaker can be a full-time, self-satisfying job.

(4) While others raise these questions, these questions are real for you. You don't know if there is more out there for you. You don't know if you can find more fulfillment than you have.

Excerpt 3

HELPEE: Sometimes I question my adequacy of raising three boys, especially the baby. I call him the baby—well, he is the last. I can't have any more. So I know I kept him a baby longer than the others. He won't let anyone else do things for him. If someone else opens the door, he says he wants Mommy to do it. If he closes the door, I have to open it. I encourage this. I do it. I don't know if this is right or wrong. He insists on sleeping with me every night and I allow it. And he says when he grows up he won't do it any more. Right now he is my baby and I don't discourage this much. I don't know if this comes out of my needs or if I'm making too much out of the situation or if this will handicap him when he goes to school— breaking away from Mamma. Is it going to be a traumatic experience for him? Is it something I'm creating for him? I do worry more about my children than I think most mothers do.

HELPER RESPONSES:
(1)   So you find yourself raising a lot of questions as to if what you are doing is right for your child.
(2)   Is it perhaps possible for you to have the child become involved in a situation such as some experiences in a public park where the child could play and perhaps at a distance you could supervise—where the child can gain some independence?
(3)   Could you tell me—have you talked to your husband about this?
(4)   While you are raising a lot of questions for yourself about yourself in relation to your youngest child, you are raising some more basic questions about yourself in relation to you. In lots of ways you're not certain where you are going—not sure who you are.

Excerpt 4

HELPEE: It's not an easy thing to talk about. I guess the heart of the problem is sort of a sexual problem. I never thought I would have this sort of problem. But I find myself not getting the fulfillment I used to. It's not as enjoyable—for my husband either, although we don't discuss it. I used to enjoy and look forward to making love. I used to have an orgasm but I don't anymore. I can't remember the last time I was satisfied. I find myself being attracted to other men and wondering what it would be like to go to bed with them. I don't know what this means. Is this symptomatic of our whole relationship as a marriage? Is something wrong with me or us?

HELPER RESPONSES:
(1)   Perhaps you feel your marriage and role of mother is holding you back and preventing you from being something else you want to be. Your resentment here against your husband is manifested in your frigidity. Perhaps it is your way of paying him back for keeping you down in this role, for confining you, for restricting you.
(2)   What about your relationship with your husband, his role as father and companion?
(3)   You don't quite know what to make of all this but you know something is dreadfully wrong and you are determined to find out for yourself, for your marriage.
(4)   What's happened between you and your husband has raised a lot of questions about you, about him, about your marriage.

Excerpt 5

HELPEE: Gee, those people! Who do they think they are? I just can't stand interacting with them anymore. Just a bunch of phonies. They leave me so frustrated. They make me so anxious. I get angry at myself. I don't even want to be bothered with them anymore. I just wish I could be honest with them and tell them all to go to hell! But I guess I just can't do it.

HELPER RESPONSES:

(1) They really make you very angry. You wish you could handle them more effectively than you do.
(2) Damn, they make you furious! But it's just not them. It's with yourself, too, because you don't act on how you feel.
(3) Why do you feel these people are phony? What do they say to you?
(4) Maybe society itself is at fault here—making you feel inadequate, giving you this negative view of yourself, leading you to be unable to successfully interact with others.

Excerpt 6

HELPEE: They wave that degree up like it's a pot of gold at the end of the rainbow. I used to think that, too, until I tried it. I'm happy being a housewife; I don't care to get a degree. But the people I associate with, the first thing they ask is, "Where did you get your degree?" I answer, "I don't have a degree." Christ, they look at you like you are some sort of a freak, some backwoodsman your husband picked up along the way. They actually believe that people with degrees are better. In fact, I think they are worse. I've found a lot of people without degrees that are a hell of a lot smarter than these people. They think that just because they have degrees they are something special. These poor kids that think they have to go to college or they are ruined. It seems that we are trying to perpetrate a fraud on these kids. If no degree, they think they will end up digging ditches the rest of their lives. They are looked down upon. That makes me sick.

HELPER RESPONSES:

(1) You really resent having to meet the goals other people set for you.
(2) What do you mean by "it makes me sick?"
(3) Do you honestly feel a degree makes a person worse or better? And not having a degree makes you better? Do you realize society perpetrates many frauds and sets many prerequisites such as a degree. You must realize how doors are closed unless you have a degree, while the ditches are certainly open.
(4) A lot of these expectations make you furious. Yet, they do tap in on something in yourself you are not sure of—something about yourself in relation to these other people.

Excerpt 7

HELPEE: I get so frustrated and furious with my daughter. I just don't know what to do with her. She is bright and sensitive, but damn, she has some characteristics that make me so on edge. I can't handle it sometimes. She just—I feel myself getting more and more angry! She won't do what you tell her to. She tests limits like mad. I scream and yell and lose control and think there is something wrong with me—I'm not an understanding mother or something. Damn! What potential! What she could do with what she has. There are times she doesn't use what she's got. She gets by too cheaply. I just don't know what to do with her. Then she can be so nice and then, boy, she can be as onery as she can be. And then I scream and yell and I'm about ready to slam her across the room. I don't like to feel this way. I don't know what to do with it.

HELPER RESPONSES:

(1) So you find yourself screaming and yelling at your daughter more frequently during the past three months.

(2) Why don't you try giving your daughter some very precise limitations. Tell her what you expect from her and what you don't expect from her. No excuses.

(3) While she frustrates the hell out of you, what you are really asking is, "How can I help her? How can I help myself, particularly in relation to this kid?"

(4) While she makes you very angry, you really care what happens to her.

Excerpt 8

HELPEE: He is ridiculous! Everything has to be done when he wants to do it, the way he wants it done. It's as if nobody else exists. It's everything he wants to do. There is a range of things I have to do—not just be a housewife and take care of the kids. Oh no, I have to do his typing for him, errands for him. If I don't do it right away, I'm stupid—I'm not a good wife or something stupid like that. I have an identity of my own, and I'm not going to have it wrapped up in him. It makes me—it infuriates me! I want to punch him right in the mouth. What am I going to do? Who does he think he is anyway?

HELPER RESPONSES:

(1) It really angers you when you realize in how many ways he has taken advantage of you.

(2) Tell me, what is your concept of a good marriage?

(3) Your husband makes you feel inferior in your own eyes. You feel incompetent. In many ways you make him sound like a very cruel and destructive man.

(4) It makes you furious when you think of the one-sidedness of this relationship. He imposes upon you everywhere, particularly in your own struggle for your own identity. And you don't know where this relationship is going.

Excerpt 9

HELPEE: I finally found somebody I can really get along with. There is no pretentiousness about them at all. They are real and they understand me. I can be myself with them. I don't have to worry about what I say and that they might take me wrong, because I do sometimes say things that don't come out the way I want them to. I don't have to worry that they are going to criticize me. They are just marvelous people! I just can't wait to be with them! For once I actually enjoy going out and interacting. I didn't think I could ever find people like this again. I can really be myself. It's such a wonderful feeling not to have people criticizing you for everything you say that doesn't agree with them. They are warm and understanding, and I just love them! It's just marvelous!

HELPER RESPONSES:
(1)   Sounds like you found someone who really matters to you.
(2)   Why do these kind of people accept you?
(3)   That's a real good feeling to have someone to trust and share with. "Finally, I can be myself."
(4)   Now that you have found these people who enjoy you and whom you enjoy, spend your time with these people. Forget about the other types who make you anxious. Spend your time with the people who can understand and be warm with you.

Excerpt 10

HELPEE: I'm really excited! We are going to California. I'm going to have a second lease on life. I found a marvelous job! Its great! It's so great I can't believe it's true—it's so great! I have a secretarial job. I can be a mother and can have a part-time job which I think I will enjoy very much. I can be home when the kids get home from school. It's too good to be true. It's so exciting. New horizons are unfolding. I just can't wait to get started. It's great!

HELPER RESPONSES:
(1)   Don't you think you are biting off a little bit more than you can chew? Don't you think that working and taking care of the children will be a little bit too much? How does your husband feel about this?
(2)   Hey, that's a mighty good feeling. You are on your way now. Even though there are some things you don't know along the way, it's just exciting to be gone.
(3)   Let me caution you to be cautious in your judgment. Don't be too hasty. Try to get settled first.
(4)   It's a good feeling to contemplate doing these things.

Excerpt 11

HELPEE: I'm so pleased with the kids. They are doing just marvelously. They have done so well at school and at home; they get along together. It's amazing. I never thought they would. They seem a little older.

They play together better and they enjoy each other, and I enjoy them. Life has become so much easier. It's really a joy to raise three boys. I didn't think it would be. I'm just so pleased and hopeful for the future. For them and for us. It's just great! I can't believe it. It's marvelous!

HELPER RESPONSES:
(1) It's a good feeling to have your kids settled once again.
(2) Is it possible your kids were happy before but you never noticed it before? You mentioned your boys. How about your husband? Is he happy?
(3) Do you feel this is a permanent change?
(4) Hey, that's great! Whatever the problem, and you know there will be problems, it's great to have experienced the positive side of it.

Excerpt 12

HELPEE: I'm really excited the way things are going at home with my husband. It's just amazing! We get along great together now. Sexually, I didn't know we could be that happy. I didn't know anyone could be that happy. It's just marvelous! I'm just so pleased, I don't know what else to say.

HELPER RESPONSES:
(1) It's a wonderful feeling when things are going well maritally.
(2) It's really exciting to be alive again, to feel your body again, to be in love again.
(3) Is your husband aware of these changes?
(4) Now don't go overboard on this right now. There will be problems that lie ahead and during these periods that you have these problems I want you to remember well the bliss you experienced in this moment in time.

Excerpt 13

HELPEE: I'm so thrilled to have found a counselor like you. I didn't know any existed. You seem to understand me so well. It's just great! I feel like I'm coming alive again. I have not felt like this in so long.

HELPER RESPONSES:
(1) Gratitude is a natural emotion.
(2) This is quite nice but remember, unless extreme caution is exercised, you may find yourself moving in the other direction.
(3) That's a good feeling.
(4) Hey, I'm as thrilled to hear you talk this way as you are! I'm pleased that I have been helpful. I do think we still have some work to do yet, though.

Excerpt 14

HELPEE: No response. (*Moving about in chair.*)

HELPER RESPONSES:
(1) You can't really say all that you feel at this moment.
(2) A penny for your thoughts.
(3) Are you nervous? Maybe you haven't made the progress here we hoped for.
(4) You just don't know what to say at this moment.

Excerpt 15

HELPEE: Gee, I'm so disappointed. I thought we could get along together and you could help me. We don't seem to be getting anywhere. You don't understand me. You don't know I'm here. I don't even think you care for me. You don't hear me when I talk. You seem to be somewhere else. Your responses are independent of anything I have to say. I don't know where to turn. I'm just so—doggone it —I don't know what I'm going to do, but I know you can't help me. There just is no hope.

HELPER RESPONSES:
(1) I have no reason to try and not to help you. I have every reason to want to help you.
(2) Only when we establish mutual understanding and trust and only then can we proceed to work on your problem effectively.
(3) It's disappointing and disillusioning to think you have made so little progress.
(4) I feel badly that you feel that way. I do want to help. I'm wondering, "Is it me? Is it you, both of us?" Can we work something out?

Excerpt 16

HELPEE: Who do you think you are? You call yourself a therapist! Damn, here I am spilling my guts out and all you do is look at the clock. You don't hear what I say. Your responses are not attuned to what I'm saying. I never heard of such therapy. You are supposed to be helping me. You are so wrapped up in your world you don't hear a thing I'm saying. You don't give me the time. The minute the hour is up you push me out the door whether I have something important to say or not. I—uh—it makes me so goddamn mad!

HELPER RESPONSES:
(1) You are suggesting I'm wrapped up in myself. Do you think that perhaps, in fact, this is your problem?
(2) I'm only trying to listen to you. Really, I think we are making a whole lot of progress here.

(3)   You are pretty displeased with what has been going on here.
(4)   All right, you are furious, but I wonder if it's all mine or is there something else eating you.

Ans p 124 (circled)

> **Stop! If the reader is administering or being administered the standardized counselor responses to helpee stimulus expressions in order to assess level of discrimination, he should proceed no further until all relevant persons have responded in accordance with instructions.**

DISCRIMINATION ASSESSMENTS: EVIDENCE

The standard discrimination assessment procedure, then, is designed to assess the level of discrimination in prospective helpers. The design of the helper responses to the helpee stimulus expressions is caculated to represent different stereotyped modes of helper responses (see Table 8-1).

The two variables that were manipulated in formulating helper responses were (1) the level of facilitative conditions offered by the helper and (2) the helper's action orientation. Although the process of implementing high levels of facilitative conditions will be quite clear, that of implementing high levels of action orientation deserves further elucidation, given the relative brevity of the helper responses. The intent was not to establish a high verbal activity level, although the responses did involve more verbal activity than all but the high action-oriented, low-level facilitative responses; nor was it to effect and sustain a high level of intense, optimistic affect, although relative to the other responses, this approach offered direction. Rather, while in keeping with the affect and content expressed by the helpee, the objective of the higher-level action responses was to represent a response of a helper who in his brief response searches and develops directions of inquiry that ultimately offer the helper the promise of direction.

Thus, in response to each helpee stimulus expression four possible combinations of helper responses occurred in random order: high facilitative (HF)-high active (HA); high facilitative (HF)-low active (LA); low facilitative (LF)-high active (HA); low facilitative (LF)-low active (LA). As can be seen, the over-all ratings assigned the responses are closely related to the variations in levels of facilitative conditions and action orientation, with the responses ranking in the following order: (1) HF-HA; (2) HF-LA; (3) LF-HA; (4) LF-LA. Two experienced and expert raters who had demonstrated a great deal of predictive validity in previous studies agreed upon the ratings assigned in each instance.

Table 8-1. Key to Design and Expert Ratings of Counselor Responses to Helpee Stimulus Expressions

| Helpee Stimulus Expressions | Counselor Responses | Design Level of: | | Over-all Ratings |
		Facilitation	Action Orientation	
I	1	High	Low	3.0
	2	H	H	4.0
	3	L	H	1.5
	4	L	L	1.5
II	1	L	L	1.0
	2	H	L	3.0
	3	L	H	1.5
	4	H	H	3.5
III	1	H	L	3.0
	2	L	H	1.5
	3	L	L	1.0
	4	H	H	4.0
IV	1	L	H	1.5
	2	L	L	1.5
	3	H	H	3.5
	4	H	L	3.0
V	1	H	L	3.0
	2	H	H	4.0
	3	L	L	1.0
	4	L	H	1.5
VI	1	H	L	3.0
	2	L	L	1.0
	3	L	H	1.5
	4	H	H	3.5
VII	1	L	L	1.0
	2	L	H	1.5
	3	H	H	4.0
	4	H	L	3.0
VIII	1	H	L	3.0
	2	L	L	1.0
	3	L	H	1.0
	4	H	H	4.0
IX	1	H	L	3.0
	2	L	L	1.0
	3	H	H	4.0
	4	L	H	1.5
X	1	L	H	1.5

	2	H	H	3.5
	3	L	L	1.0
	4	H	L	3.0
XI	1	H	L	3.0
	2	L	H	1.5
	3	L	L	1.0
	4	H	H	4.0
XII	1	H	L	2.5
	2	H	H	4.0
	3	L	L	1.0
	4	L	H	1.0
XIII	1	L	L	1.0
	2	L	H	1.0
	3	H	L	3.0
	4	H	H	4.0
XIV	1	H	H	3.5
	2	L	L	1.5
	3	L	H	1.5
	4	H	L	3.0
XV	1	L	L	1.0
	2	L	H	1.0
	3	H	L	3.0
	4	H	H	3.5
XVI	1	L	H	1.5
	2	L	L	1.0
	3	H	L	3.0
	4	H	H	3.5

As Table 8-1 also indicates, the over-all ratings are biased in favor of the level of facilitative conditions. Thus, on the average the HF-LA response receives a rating of 3.0 while the LF-HA receives a rating of 1.5. The direct implication is that the facilitative dimensions are the necessary but not sufficient conditions of constructive helpee change or gain. Nothing can happen without empathic understanding and the other facilitative dimensions and something can happen when these dimensions are present. On the other hand, in the context of understanding and the other facilitative dimensions the introduction of the action-oriented dimensions adds appreciably to the ratings, as is reflected in ratings between 3.5 and 4.0. *Without high levels of understanding, then, directionality is meaningless.* On the other hand, high levels of action-oriented dimensions make high levels of understanding meaningful. The evidence to support these propositions will be explored more fully in the sections on training and treatment. We might briefly note that the same biases hold in the ratings of prospective helpers' responses to the standard helpee stimulus expressions on the communication index.

In terms of discrimination the evidence indicates that the general population and undergraduate college students tend to deviate a level or more from the assessments of experts, with, interestingly enough, companion volunteers and campus leaders deviating more from the ratings of experts than unselected undergraduates. The over-all base rate data appear in Table 8.2. Similarly, professional teachers tend to deviate a level from the expert ratings. In general, then, a response rated at level 2 by the experts might be rated somewhere around 1 or 3, or one rated at level 4 might be rated somewhere around 3 or 5. Again the relatively inexperienced but somewhat more sophisticated graduate students demonstrated an average deviation ranging from above one level to slightly above three fourths of a level, depending upon the programs in which they were enrolled, while unselected and untrained but experienced counselors and therapists demonstrated an average deviation of slightly over one half of a level. Finally, persons who were both trained and experienced demonstrated the lowest mean deviation, nearly one third of a level.

As in communication, there were no functionally meaningful differences in the discriminations according to affect and content. However, the deviations by helpee stimulus expression items indicated that the greatest discrepancies between the ratings of experts and subjects occurred for those helper responses incorporating the low-level facilitative conditions and the high-level action response tendencies generally and for the LF-HA response specifically. In general, all groups deviated most sharply from the experts on the LF-HA item, with those groups that deviated the most over-all deviating significantly more than others on this item. Since the item was low rated (about 1.5) by experts, this means that the groups tended to rate this response high, with the most deviant groups rating it two or more levels above the experts on the average. The direct implication, and a somewhat ironical one for the more experienced groups, is that people prefer the highly action-oriented response independent of whether or not it is based in understanding. This finding is understandable for the inexperienced groups, who perhaps maintain a stereotype of the helper as sizing things up quickly and giving a prescription. Thus, in the role of helpee as well as helper inexperienced persons tend to prefer the action-oriented responses. Indeed, it will be recalled that even among high-functioning inexperienced persons there is a distinct tendency toward being very directive in order to do something about a given problem area. However, with the stress on empathic understanding and the like, at least verbally, in many graduate training

Table 8-2. Discrimination: Deviations in Levels of Counselor Responses to Helpee Stimulus Expressions

Populations (Levels)	N (No. of subjects)	Level of Discrimination (Absolute deviations of helper ratings from experts)	
		Mean	Standard Deviation
1. *General population*			
Outpatients	10	1.5	0.3
Parents	20	1.4	0.4
2. *Undergraduates*			
Freshman	330	1.1	0.3
Upperclass philosophy	30	1.1	0.3
Student leaders	30	1.3	0.4
Volunteer helpers	30	1.2	0.3
Senior psychology	30	1.1	0.2
3. *Lay personnel*			
Lay teachers	50	1.2	0.3
Lay counselors	50	1.2	0.4
4. *Professionals*			
Teachers	10	1.0	0.3
Beginning psychology graduate students	10	0.8	0.2
Experienced counselors (not systematically trained)	20	0.6	0.2
Experienced counselors (systematically trained)	10	0.4	0.1

programs it is interesting to note that relative to their discriminations of other responses the experienced practitioners also deviated the most on the LF-HA. Of course, these differences are relative to their own norm groups, and over-all the experienced practitioners deviated less on the LF-HA items than the inexperienced groups on any single category. Nevertheless, questions concerning the preference for the directive, often authoritarian, responses must be asked.

In general, then, along with increasingly higher levels of communication and response frequency with experience or training or both, increasingly finer discriminations may be discerned. Indeed, in contrast to the large jump in communication and response frequency level from experienced but not systematically trained practitioners to experienced and systematically trained practitioners the discrimination data present an essentially linear function from inexperienced to experienced and systematically trained helpers. Relative to inexperienced helpers, however, the experienced but not systematically trained helpers do not communicate nearly as well as they discriminate. Although high-level communicators are also high-level discriminators, the frequency of high-level communicators is small, perhaps less than 10 in 100. Thus, in spite of the consistency of the trends, which lend construct validity to the dimensions involved, high levels of discrimination are not necessarily related to high levels of communication.

Perhaps one major clinical problem confronting the helping profession involves the communication-discrimination differential. We can only conjecture concerning the underlying dynamics of why people cannot translate discrimination into communication. There may be a socially conditioned base of experience that precludes acting upon insights out of fear of negative reinforcements or punishment. This is not to say that training or treatment or both cannot overcome this handicap. The evidence from systematically trained practitioners suggests that it can. There are, however, no indications that high-level discriminators have any advantage over low-level discriminators in any learning tasks except those that emphasize discrimination exclusively.

STUDIES OF OUTCOME

Studies relating the discrimination assessments to meaningful indexes of training outcome have not been as fruitful as they were with communication. In the first of the series, during early phases of the development of discrimination assessment devices (Carkhuff, Kratochvil, & Friel, 1968), a cross-sectional study of the effects of graduate training in clinical psychology was conducted. As relates to discrimination, both clinical and nonclinical students demonstrated identical levels and trends toward improvement in discrimination over four years of graduate training, the implication being that while there is improvement, the effect appears to derive from the over-all graduate training experience rather than from the clinical training experience per se. However, there was a negative relationship with functioning in the helping role, since the trainees demonstrated lower levels of functioning following four years of training.

Anthony and Carkhuff (1969), in an extension of the earlier work, employed the discrimination index as one of the indexes in assessing the effects of graduate training in a two-year rehabilitation-counseling program. In terms of the hypotheses (Carkhuff, 1967) they found that over the course of training the trainees demonstrated improvement in their discriminations in the direction of the staff that was training them. The average deviation of more than one level suggests that the first-year students are essentially unselected when compared with other undergraduates. However, after two years with a staff that makes relatively accurate discriminations (a level of deviation of approximately one half) their deviations averaged less than three quarters of a level. In this instance the gains were related to similar positive changes in communication level. However, the results were not inconsistent with those of the previous study, since the direction of change was based in large part upon the differential between the levels of functioning of trainer and trainee, a subject to be discussed more fully in the section on training.

Studies employing the discrimination index as a predictor began with that of experienced teachers in their first counseling training experience, an integrated didactic and experiential program (Carkhuff, 1969). Employing the ratings of actual counseling interviews with both adults and school-age children as criteria, the results indicated that while initial communication level was related to the outcome criteria, discrimination level was not. Thus, those who discriminate at relatively high initial levels have no observable advantage over those who do not in systematic programs conducted by high-level trainers. Again discrimination remains unrelated to communication among low-level communicators.

A second study assessed senior seminar psychology undergraduates involved in an exclusively didactic experience in discrimination training (Carkhuff, Collingwood, & Renz, 1969). Interviews of standard interviewees as well as a second administration of the communication and discrimination assessment devices were employed as criteria. While there was little generalization to communication, the trainees demonstrated significant improvement in discrimination, and these changes were related to initial discrimination scores. Thus, although there is other evidence to indicate that high-level communicators will generalize from improved discrimination to other areas of functioning, the results demonstrate that an exclusive and didactic focus upon discrimination to the exclusion of practice in communication yields changes only in discrimination among low-level–functioning communicators. The direct implication is that there is very little generalization of learning among low-level communicators: they appear to learn what they are taught and no more. In relation to prediction, the results indicate that the best index of future discrimination is a previous index of discrimination.

Another study assessed the predictive capacity of the discrimination index in a systematic and integrated didactic and experiential program for beginning graduate students (Carkhuff, Friel, & Kratochvil, 1969).

Posttraining standard interviews and a posttraining administration of the communication and discrimination assessment devices were employed as outcome measures. Significant improvement in *both* discrimination and communication was established. Again while initial communication level was related to final communication level, initial discrimination level was related only to final discrimination level.

A demonstration project researched the effects of large-group didactic training experiences upon indexes of both communication and discrimination and found that in addition to changes in written communication on alternate forms of the index there also were significant changes on the discrimination scores on the alternate form (Berenson, Carkhuff, Friel, & Leitner, 1968). Here too discrimination predicted discrimination and not communication. The conclusion drawn was that some changes in discrimination could be effected in large groups of people in relatively brief periods of time, say from 10 to 12 hours.

Finally, still another study employed the discrimination and communication indexes as well as a variety of other assessment devices to predict and then to assess communication and discrimination (Carkhuff, 1969c). A loosely conceived and loosely structured volunteer companion program involving aperiodic and poor supervision and no systematic selection or training experiences provided an opportunity for assessing the results of programs conducted by low-level trainers and involving low-level trainees. Neither the companions nor their patients gave evidence of any demonstrable changes over the course of a year. More than half of the companions dropped out, often leaving their patients without information as to why they left and sometimes leaving the patients worse off than they found them. Needless to say, no significant relationships obtained between discrimination and any other criteria other than discrimination, which did not change significantly. *No experiences are better than some experiences!*

Only the program training parents to communicate effectively with each other (Carkhuff & Bierman, 1969) yielded a positive relationship between initial level of discrimination and final level of communication. However, in general, performance on one index does not relate to performance on another among low-functioning communicators. Only high-functioning communicators appear able to generalize their performance from one area to another.

EXTENSIONS AND LIMITATIONS

An intensive investigation of the demographic and biographic characteristics of moderately high- and low-level discriminators (the top and bottom 10 percent of a group of over 150 students) yielded similar results (Frankel, 1968). While level of communication was found to be related to a variety of indexes of productivity and creativity, there were no significant relationships for discrimination. It almost appears as if discrimination is one of the specialization areas that is unrelated to anything else.

In regard to the methodology of discrimination, Carkhuff, Kratochvil, and Friel (1968) addressed themselves to the question of whether the set given by the rating scales would elicit ratings different from five-point scales rated from good to poor without descriptions of facilitative functioning. The authors found that while the mean discriminations among the two groups of senior psychology students were not significantly different, the group employing the descriptions demonstrated significantly less variability in the ratings. It is noteworthy that the deviation scores are represented by a linear relationship from senior psychology students (most deviant) to first-year graduate students in psychology to fourth-year psychology graduate students (least deviant).

Again, Antonuzzo and Kratochvil (1968) established a fairly close relation between discrimination scores of (1) the verbal or recorded presentation and (2) the written presentation of both helpee expressions and helper responses. Such results support the employment of written forms as providing a method for obtaining a quick and reasonable indication of the level of discrimination of a large number of individuals. Although the results were positive and provided the basis for investigations that might otherwise not have been conducted, our bias in favor of functional indexes approximating real-life experiences as closely as possible leads us to favor the audio form where possible.

The question of presenting discrimination material in abbreviated form is further attended by the item analyses, which suggested that, similar to communication, the discrimination of the confrontation items gives the best over-all index of discrimination. Again, and this is particularly true in regard to the selection of raters, that affect (in general, the depressive affect is dominant in most but not necessarily all helping situations) and that problem area which the rater is likely to be rating will constitute the best abbreviated form.

In an effort to get at the predisposition of raters to prefer one kind of response to another, Greenbaum (1968) implemented a design under three conditions, the latter two in a counterbalanced order: (1) the subjects, who were perceived as undergraduate campus leaders with expressed interests in the helping area, were presented with the helpee stimulus expressions in order to obtain an index of their communicative functioning; (2) half of the subjects were then presented with (a) the helper responses in the absence of the helpee expressions and (b) the helper responses in conjunction with the helpee expressions; (3) the remaining half of the subjects were presented with the same conditions in reverse order. The results of this study with this extremely low-functioning group indicated that the conditions with or without hearing the helpee expressions did not make a difference. The subjects rated the helper responses as if the helpee did not exist. Obviously their deviations from the expert ratings were very high (deviant), indicating that they made very poor discriminations. Thus, we are provided with some critical insights into the poorest discriminators. Such individuals prefer certain helper responses independent of hearing helpee affect and problems, and indeed, independent of helpee benefits.

In summary, accurate discriminations are essential to the rating that constitutes the basis for the entire selection process. We understand something about the nature of this dimension. We need to know much more. While the results of the explorations of discrimination did not lead us to the conclusion we originally anticipated, the dimension remains a rich source of investigation. For one thing we know that high-level–functioning persons know how to employ their discriminations while low-level–functioning persons do not. Indeed, while discrimination remains unrelated to communication among low-level communicators, the very highest levels of discrimination are predictive of high levels of communication. Further, we might even hypothesize that didactic programs focusing upon discrimination to the exclusion of practice in communication could yield results on communication simply because of the flexibility of the high-level person in making the necessary generalizations from understanding to action. We know that this is not so for the low-functioning trainee, and in all probability the most effective mode of training the low-level person would be to practice communication before teaching discrimination. A related area deserving further investigation involves the differential between discrimination and communication. We might attempt different training and treatment programs with persons selected according to various combinations of high and low levels of functioning on both discrimination and communication. Finally, the finding that written responses, verbal responses to tapes, verbal responses in the helping role, and discrimination do not relate to each other or to anything else among low-level communicators (functioning on one index does not relate to functioning on other apparently related indexes) while the fact that high levels of consistency have been demonstrated among and between performance indexes of high-level communicators suggests that we may, in fact, be talking about persons who are functioning in structurally rather than quantitatively different ways.

REFERENCES

For an exploration of the methodologies involved in the projects cited in this chapter see the asterisked research articles.

Anthony, W., & Carkhuff, R. R. The effects of rehabilitation counselor training upon discrimination, communication and helping attitudes. *Journal of Counseling Psychology*, in press, 1969.

Antonuzzo, R. & Kratochvil, D. The differential effects of written and audio stimulus material. Unpublished research, State University of New York at Buffalo, 1968.

Berenson, B. G., Carkhuff, R. R., Friel, T., & Leitner, L. The effects of brief written communication training in large groups. Unpublished research, State University of New York at Buffalo, 1968.

Carkhuff, R. R. Toward a comprehensive model of facilitative interpersonal processes. *Journal of Counseling Psychology*, 1967, 14, 67–72.

Carkhuff, R. R. Helper communication and discrimination as a function of helpee affect and content. *Journal of Counseling Psychology*, in press, 1969. (a)

*Carkhuff, R. R. The prediction of the effects of teacher-counselor training: The development of communication and discrimination selection indexes. *Counselor Education and Supervision*, in press, 1969. (b)

Carkhuff, R. R. The effects of a volunteer companion program. Unpublished research, State University of New York at Buffalo, 1969. (c)

*Carkhuff, R. R., & Berenson, B. G. *Beyond counseling and therapy*. New York: Holt, Rinehart and Winston, Inc., 1967.

Carkhuff, R. R., & Bierman, R. The effects of human relations training upon child psychiatric parents in treatment. *Journal of Counseling Psychology*, in press, 1969.

Carkhuff, R. R., Collingwood, T., & Renz, L. The prediction of didactic training in discrimination. *Journal of Clinical Psychology*, in press, 1969. (a)

*Carkhuff, R. R., Kratochvil, D., & Friel, T. The effects of professional training: The communication and discrimination of facilitative conditions. *Journal of Counseling Psychology*, 1968, 15, 68–74.

Frankel, S. The biographic and demographic characteristics of high and low discriminators and communicators. Unpublished research, State University of New York at Buffalo, 1968.

Friel, T., Kratochvil, D., & Carkhuff, R. R. The prediction of counselor functioning in the helping role from a variety of selection indexes. Unpublished research, State University of New York at Buffalo, 1968.

Greenbaum, S. The discrimination of counselor responses with and without client expressions. Unpublished research, State University of New York at Buffalo, 1968.

Kratochvil, D., Carkhuff, R. R., & Berenson, B. G. The effects of parent and teacher offered levels of facilitative conditions upon indexes of student physical, emotional and intellectual functioning. *Journal of Educational Research*, in press, 1969.

9

APPLICATIONS IN SELECTION

The problems associated with the application of selection procedures are numerous, depending upon a variety of variables only a few of which are explicitly considered in most training centers. In considering selection procedures we must first define our training goals and then determine the relevancy of our selection indexes to our goals. We must in addition answer questions concerning the relevancy of the type and orientation of the training program to the training goals we have cited and, in turn, the relevancy of the selection procedures to the kind of program being implemented.

Once these issues are resolved a question frequently raised is, "How do we get the best possible trainees?" A more basic question is, "How do we get the best possible trainers?" Without knowledge of our training personnel we cannot determine the individuals who should be selected as trainees. If we know the level of functioning of our training personnel, however, we are in a better position to make sound decisions concerning the selection of trainees. We can best understand the selection process when we place it in the context of ongoing training and treatment programs. In this chapter we explore these issues and determine pragmatic recommendations and applications for effective selection procedures.

TRAINING GOALS AND PROGRAMS

The goals of professional and subprofessional training are, to be sure, different in critical respects. However, while some graduate training programs claim specifically that they are not training students to help people and that they leave this consideration instead to the internship programs, it is our belief that the professional programs should be most broadly based in all aspects of training people to help people. It is our firm conviction that *the core of training in the helping professions should involve training in helping.*

Professional programs, of course, emphasize many other goals in training. It is traditional, for example, to give at least verbal emphasis to the research orientation in doctoral study. However, even in this area there are a number of relevant considerations. First, it is clear from the available follow-up data that graduate programs in the helping profession have failed in this regard. It has been found, for example, that 95 to 99 percent of the graduates of many professional programs never go on to conduct another research project beyond their doctoral thesis. Second, if the academic emphasis is upon research to the exclusion of training in helping, at a minimum the trainees should be researching the efficacy of both helping and internship training, which they do not do at present. Finally, in order to accomplish the research goal of training, the researcher of the helping process must be able to (1) discern the dimensions of the helping process that need research and (2) understand the clinical implications of his research problems. The interaction of empirical and experiential data implies the necessity for the trainee's demonstrated effectiveness in the helping process.

Hopefully, effective graduate training will prepare individuals for a number of professionally meaningful roles that might best be summarized in the role of mental health consultant. Hopefully, the trainee will be prepared to assess ongoing helping programs. Hopefully, he will be prepared to institute, administer, and teach training programs for both professional and nonprofessional helpers. Hopefully, he will be able to assess the effects of these programs not only in the course of training but in the treatment programs that follow. Hopefully, all aspects of helping, training, teaching, and administering can be assessed. Unfortunately, our traditional indexes do not provide us with the degree of predictive discrimination we need in this area.

The indexes that are usually employed as predictors have been (1) undergraduate grade-point average (UGPA), which is sometimes subclassified as (a) UGPA: psychology and (b) UGPA: mathematics and science; (2) the Miller Analogies Test; and (3) the Graduate Record Examination. These predictors have been related to five measures of graduate school success, some of which may be more irrelevant than relevant. In general, these predictors have yielded highly variable results, with relationships ranging from negative to positive correlations in the neighborhood of .60 with the following indexes: (1) academic criteria such as graduate grade-point average (GGPA), rated academic performance, marks on doctoral preliminary examinations, and advanced degree attainment; (2) research criteria such as rated research competence and assessments of potential scientific contribution; (3) clinical criteria such as rated clinical competence. In summary, the predictability is quite variable and low. In addition, such criteria as GGPA are often of questionable validity. Indeed, there are strong indications that UGPA is related to GGPA and nothing else. The real question is whether GGPA is related to any meaningful activity. Further, staff knowledge of trainee performance often leads to self-fulfilling prophesies where the trainee fulfills the expectations of the staff according to trainee performance on the selection indexes. Finally, all too few investigations have involved long-term follow-up studies of effectiveness in research, teaching and training, and helping and administration. That is, the measures of these criteria most frequently employed are immediate to the graduate training setting and thus, in a very real sense, constitute measures of process and not of final outcome. All of these factors lead to a consideration of the nature of graduate training, which is, at present, often independent of the goals described.

While the professional training programs allegedly emphasize a research orientation, there is substantial evidence, both experiential and empirical, to indicate that they are preparing incorporators rather than promulgators of research, passive recipients rather than active participants in the process of making enlightened and systematic inquiries into what they are professing to do. The few thrusts into clinical effectiveness, in turn, in the area of personality and behavior prediction have yielded negative results. In conjunction with these other results the main inference that can be drawn from the positive findings concerning the increased ability to discriminate effectiveness in the helping role is that the *graduate programs are training critics rather than active and effective participants in a world that is in need of the latter.*

In summary, then, not only are the training programs unrelated to the goals described but also none of the predictors or criteria give us adequate and reliable measures of helping effectiveness, the core of professional as well as nonprofessional training programs. If we accept that our principal goal of training is helping, and if we accept that the best index of a future criteria is a previous index of that criteria, then our need is for functional predictors and criteria by which to judge what we are attempting to accomplish, namely, effectiveness in the helping role. In this regard the best recommendation is that each program conduct its own long-term assessment of itself in terms of its own purposes.

If its purposes involve, in addition to training in helping, the selection of highly research-oriented persons to train for broadly professional purposes, then it would do well to develop selection indexes of similar functional utility. That is, the best indexes of future research competency are previous indexes of research competency. If the purposes of the program are focused exclusively upon helping, it would do well to employ those indexes of helping effectiveness presently available and to attempt to intensify these levels over the course of training. If the purposes of the program are even more narrowly defined, such as rater selection, it might simply employ indexes of the discrimination of helping effectiveness and attempt to intensify these levels over training.

TRAINER AND TRAINEE PERSONNEL

Before selecting trainees we must assure ourselves that we have made wise decisions in choosing trainer personnel. We must assure ourselves of the trainer's level of functioning in order to have confidence in the positive results of our program. Any equation employed to predict either change over the course of training or final level of trainee functioning necessitates a thorough knowledge of the initial level of both trainer and trainee functioning. This subject will be discussed more extensively in the section on training, but suffice it to say for the present that trainees, and for that matter trainers, may demonstrate both positive and negative changes. At the extremes trainees coming in at relatively low (but not too low) levels may gain a great deal in interaction with trainers functioning at relatively high levels, while trainees entering at relatively high levels may lose significantly over time in interaction with trainers functioning at relatively low levels. The problem of trainer level of functioning is not to be avoided by placing the burden upon the internship. The same principles hold for the directors of internship training that hold for the directors of graduate training. In addition, the same conditions of functioning dominate a graduate training program that dominate any interpersonal process.

Knowing the trainer level of functioning, then, we can explore the possibilities of trainee selection. If the trainers are functioning at very high levels, we may select the highest-level–functioning trainees available so that we might achieve the maximum absolute levels of helping effectiveness in a minimum period of time. If we wish to demonstrate maximum change over a given time, we may select those trainees functioning at the lowest levels, providing the greatest differential between trainer and trainee level of functioning and thus the prospects for maximum relative change. On the other hand, if our trainers are functioning at low to moderate levels, we may wish to conduct inservice training programs in order to enable them to function at effective levels. At the lowest levels we may wish to involve our trainers in both longer-term treatment and training or—and this is the last alternative—eliminate them from responsible positions within the program. If our trainers are functioning at low levels, we can generate predictions only of deteriorative change for relatively high-functioning entering trainees. Indeed, if we must maintain staffs of low-functioning trainers, we would minimize our losses by selecting even lower-functioning trainees, all of which, of course, neglects the purpose of training—to aid the helpee.

The same principles hold for a program geared to the production of enlightened investigators. Just as those persons demonstrating the most experience and expertise in helping are most effective in discriminating and/or training effective helpers, so also will those persons with the greatest experience and expertise in research be the most effective in discriminating and/or training effective researchers. The demands are high indeed for the person who would both train helpers and research the effectiveness of helping. The program developed must be coordinated and systematically geared toward the development of a similarly fully functioning professional.

THE SELECTION PROCESS

Under optimum conditions the most desirable approach to selecting a helper, whether professional or subprofessional, would be to cast him in the helping role. In addition, depending upon the specific purposes of the program involved, we would do best to employ standard helpees or helpees representative of the population or populations for which the trainee is being prepared. At a minimum in the event that training is not effective we will have a good index of the future levels of functioning of such individuals. Even if the training program is effective and there is some loss in functioning over time perhaps following training in a setting that does not support a high level of functioning, trainee movement will be in the direction of original functioning and we will have a good index of that. In other words, while we may maximize our chances for gain with trainees functioning in lower ranges, we maximize our chances of having our helper product function at effective levels following training by selecting those trainees who function initially at the highest levels, assuming, of course, a high level of trainer functioning.

While casting the prospective helper in the helping role with a representative of a relevant population is the single most effective selection procedure we could employ, there are a variety of other approaches that would be meaningful given sufficient time, if for no other reason than to assess their effectiveness in building up local or institutional norms. Just as we cast the prospective helper in the helping role, we might also cast him in the helpee role in order to obtain an index of his ability to utilize such an experience. While there is some relation between functioning in both roles, we might take an index of the helper's level of self-exploration. Obviously, we have to have an index of the helper's level of functioning with regard to the helpee in this instance. Again, obviously, this procedure will be most effective and meaningful for the helpee when the helper is functioning at high levels.

Similarly, we might obtain a brief index of suitability for training by casting the prospective helper in the trainee's role for a brief period. For example, we might expose the prospective trainee to brief empathy training and obtain indexes of change both before and after training. Again this procedure will be most effective if (1) it involves the training personnel who will be involved in later training and (2) these personnel are functioning at high levels of facilitative and action-oriented dimensions.

Finally, if the options for such intensive and personalized selection procedures are not available or possible, the standardized indexes of communication and discrimination offer a reliable and valid means of estimating a prospective helper's level of functioning. In addition to being economical and efficient means which may be employed in groups or through the mail, both the audio and written versions provide estimates of responsiveness to a cross-section of different experiences in helping. Under optimum circumstances it would be advantageous to exhaust the prospective helper's response repertoire by repeated administration. This will give us another index of the reliability of our measure in addition to an estimate of the depth of the helper's sensitivity and perseverance or ability to continue to respond as it is appropriate. Under the most limited circumstances abbreviated versions of the indexes may be employed. In its most abbreviated form the three confrontation expressions in different affects may be employed. The item analyses indicate that these are the most efficient estimates of over-all functioning. In addition, these items provide an index of the prospective helper's ability to employ his understanding of himself and another in functioning in a crisislike situation. Finally, the three confrontation items might be combined best with the four depression expressions in different problem areas, since these items are representative of the dominant affect dealt with in the helping process. Thus, such a seven-item test might present a valid estimate of over-all functioning. Depending upon the ultimate purpose of the training, that is, the populations to be dealt with, a given setting might select those items that are most relevant for their purposes or create their own. Again it must be remembered that in general responses, whether written or otherwise, to taped stimulus expressions will tend to yield somewhat depressed ratings at the higher levels. In other words, individuals who receive the highest ratings for their responses to standard stimuli will probably receive even higher ratings when cast in the helping role.

Of course, the different indexes of functioning in the helping role need not be employed to the exclusion of each other. One effective mode of operation is to employ the standard helpee and helper expressions as a preliminary screening device, following which those prospective helpers functioning above a given level may be cast in the helping role. In addition, when dealing with experienced helpers we may wish to ask for tapes that such persons feel are representative of their counseling activities. While the evidence suggests a high degree of relationship between ratings of such tapes and standard interviews, in a given setting we may wish to ascertain this relationship with the thought of employing such tapes in the selection process.

In addition to providing an estimate of over-all functioning of prospective helpers, the helpee expressions and helper responses provide us with comparative norms and a standardized basis for research of the complex interactions involved in human relations training. In this regard a given setting may wish to establish its own validity. Rather than to select people on the basis of functioning, then, it may wish to accept all candidates, high-, moderate-, and low-functioning, in order to determine the effects of training in this particular setting upon the candidates. The key to these studies is again the degree of change over the course of training as opposed to final level of functioning. To be sure, under specifiable conditions the degree of change and the absolute level of functioning are not mutually exclusive. Although under ordinary circumstances we must be most concerned with the final level of functioning of those who will affect the lives of others, a case can be made for individuals who demonstrate a positive growth trend. A quick analogy might be drawn in almost any area concerned with delivery or productivity. We are most sure of our results with persons who demonstrate the highest absolute level of functioning, especially if they have demonstrated recent positive change, although in given instances we may wish to invest responsibilities in those with the most positively accelerating growth curves.

We must remember that the selection process is a highly interactive and ongoing one in which both trainer and trainee are continuously selecting and reselecting themselves as well as others. The trainer does not merely choose trainees—he himself is chosen or not chosen by the trainees. This point is illustrated by the high-level trainees who terminate training conducted by low-level trainers. The evidence in treatment is analogous. Similarly, the conditions of training should be such as to allow both trainees and trainers to, so to speak, select themselves out or counsel themselves out of training when appropriate.

In addition, the need to follow up on the selection process is apparent. This should occur at two principal points, namely, after training and after treatment. The posttraining evaluation allows us to assess the degree to which we have achieved the goals of training. Hopefully, it will not be unrelated to the goals of treatment. However related the indexes are to treatment though, the training indexes do not constitute final outcome indexes of treatment effectiveness. Here we wish to know how the helper product functions in his helping role, and more important, what the effects are upon his helpees' functioning in their lives outside of treatment and over a period of time. This information can be obtained only through long-term follow-up studies of a variety of indexes that will be discussed more fully in Volume II.

While our emphasis has been upon communication as an index of functioning in the helping role, the index of discrimination serves several necessary functions. Although it does not necessarily relate to communication among low-level communicators, high-level discrimination scores add weight to evidence of high-level communication. Those trainees communicating and discriminating at the highest relative levels are the best prospects for selection. In addition, assessments of discrimination allow us to develop research projects assessing the effects of, or upon, persons functioning differentially at high and low levels of communication and discrimination. Perhaps most important, the discrimination index provides us with the basis for selecting the persons best equipped to make the accurate discriminations necessary for rating or those whose scores indicate that we can intensify the accuracy of their discriminations with training. If for no other purpose, *in order to carry on a selection process we need accurate discriminators to assess the level of responses of our prospective helpers to helpee expressions.*

Finally, in regard to both discrimination and communication, persons in a given setting may wish to develop their own excerpts and norms relevant to that particular setting. This is a desirable tendency. It may also be necessary, for example, in the event that these standard materials become known to the persons we are attempting to select. In addition, the sex of the helpee in the standard indexes is female. A given setting may work predominantly or exclusively with males and may, accordingly, wish to represent them in their indexes. It would be valuable indeed to have representation of all potentially relevant demographic characteristics in such assessment procedures. In any event an alternate form of the discrimination and communication indexes is valuable for follow-up assessment studies.

SOME CASES IN POINT

Although our efforts in the study of selection have largely involved the inclusion and random assignment of all prospective helpers in order to determine the validity of our selection instruments, and indeed the trainers in a given setting may wish to do likewise, we have learned a number of lessons from our selection and training studies. First and foremost we have come to understand the dangers associated with such work. Initial phases in the development of new programs and new instruments dictate certain research strategies that involve responsibilities for the psychological welfare of the individuals involved. Thus, for an example in the extreme, in the development of lay training programs we have accepted essentially all volunteers. In some instances these volunteers have been low-functioning persons whose own adjustments have been somewhat tenuous. In allowing these persons into the program we have taken responsibility for them and for the people they might ultimately affect. In most cases we have assumed this responsibility by employing the highest-level trainer available. Accordingly, we have had little difficulty because the trainers have brought their full energies and responsibilities to the task. In this regard evidence from the large number of systematic training programs we have conducted indicates that, in addition to the consistent demonstration of positive change, *we have never had a drop-out*, an unusual record for an innovating project. However, in those few instances in which we have studied the differential effects of moderate- (never low-) functioning trainers we have had a number of trainee terminations in addition to other difficulties. In one case, the moderate-level trainer obviously fed into the dynamics of the pathology of a very low-level–functioning trainee, and while the immediate consequences were not serious, the long-term dangers could have been great. *While such incidents are no more serious than much of the teaching, counseling, and psychotherapy that goes on daily, the potential jeopardy of the lives of others, psychologically or physically, places a burden of responsibility on the administrator and trainers of all programs, professional and subprofessional.*

In another case we accepted an extremely low-functioning trainee who might easily have been a neuropsychiatric patient in another setting as a challenge to the effectiveness of our training program. If we cannot, we reasoned, effect significant constructive change in several thousand hours of graduate training, then how can we expect to effect significant constructive change in 1 or 30 or 100 hours of counseling or psychotherapy? Although the candidate improved greatly, as reflected in his level of functioning as well as in other productive and creative activities, his improvement was possible only through an extraordinary amount of personal attention and guidance, including long-term individual and group psychotherapy. Again while the candidate improved, his final absolute level of functioning, while better than many of his colleagues in the helping profession, was not what we would consider minimally facilitative. Having continued his training, ultimately we had to decide whether to graduate him or not. In such situations we usually decide positively because of our commitment to the trainee. However, in doing so we must assume the responsibility for the future helping activities of such individuals with other distressed persons.

Other individual cases illustrate the problems involved in the selection process. There is, for example, the experienced and knowledgeable helper who may know what the assessment is all about or who may have studied many techniques in order to receive evaluations at relatively high levels. The ratings of such a person may obviously be inflated, and control of this possibility may be established by a few simple standard questions or an interview. In any event the ratings of such a candidate should not be compared to those of naïve candidates.

Another case involves the prospective helper with the appropriate resources and feelings but without the language to communicate them. In particular, we must be on guard for individuals with writing or verbal communication problems. Cast in the helping role or even in an interview situation, the individual's struggle to put into words a large capacity to understand may become apparent. In some few cases the reservoir of energy, sensitivity, and talent may be so great that there has been no appropriate outlet for all the individual has to offer. In addition to a few basic communicative skills, these persons usually need little more than the confidence or permission to become effective helpers. If in doubt, then, where questions such as these appear from the standard indexes, interviews should be conducted.

There is, furthermore, the very difficult instance of the entering high-level–functioning person for whom the program does not move along rapidly enough. Every trainer must make decisions concerning whether to begin and continue to attend to everyone in the group, to the modal level of the group, or to the highest level in the group. Usually, the trainer who is functioning at a high level is able to involve all trainees in a constructive change process, which is reflected on the training outcome indexes. The high-level trainee, however, may not feel that he has moved as significantly as he feels he is capable, for each person in his own way seeks out his own modal level of functioning, both relative to himself as well as to others. Accordingly, such an individual may test the limits of both trainer and group. Often these persons can be used effectively in a co-trainer capacity, which gives them the level of recognition and responsibility that will spur them on to greater efforts.

In general, then, selection procedures are most effective when the groups of candidates are equated on experience. On the one hand, with groups of knowledgeable candidates we can be confident that those with low ratings are not likely to become effective helpers. In this instance we must make further and finer discriminations among those receiving relatively high ratings in order to discern those best equipped to utilize the training experience and to deliver constructive change in their later helping efforts. On the other hand, with groups of naïve candidates we can be confident that those with high ratings will become effective helpers. Here we must make further and finer discriminations among those receiving low ratings in order to discern those most likely to be successful trainees and practitioners. In each instance the ratings will reflect the individual's ability or inability to incorporate significant learnings concerning the helping process, whether these were derived from systematic teaching or intuitive living.

In addition to discriminating potential helpers from nonhelpers, the selection procedures serve other purposes vital to effective helping processes. First, they serve to initiate a process of search and research. They discharge the first stage of a commitment to make systematic inquiries into our efforts. Second, and perhaps most important, if meaningfully employed by a high-level–functioning helpee, the selection process initiates the learning experience concerning helping. The prospective trainees are introduced to what they know and do not know about the critical ingredients of effective helping, and the best of them will be motivated for the training process that follows. Indeed, some will demonstrate positively accelerating learning curves on the selection indexes themselves, as reflected in their steadily improving communication and discrimination scores. This factor in itself can constitute a meaningful basis for selection.

In summary, both trainees and trainers come in many shapes and sizes, some good, some bad. We must learn to discriminate among those who can learn to utilize effectively their resources for constructive purposes and those who cannot. The former constitute the hope for a healthy society. The latter are another matter. There are some individuals who simply do not have the resources necessary for the helping role, and we would do best to treat such persons as helpees rather than helpers. Others can see but cannot or will not translate what they see into constructive action. More rare are those who can both see and do but who do not consistently employ their resources for constructive purposes. *Whatever the degree of investment, it is as important to exclude those who cannot utilize their resources from assuming helping positions as it is to populate the world with those who can. Those who can help, seek to populate the world with helpers, while those who cannot populate the world with helpees.*

PART FOUR

Toward Effective Training

PART FOUR EXAMINES the present state of affairs in the area of training (Chapter 10) and then explores the means for implementing effective training programs. The scales of the facilitative and action-oriented dimensions and, concomitantly, procedures for discrimination training are introduced (Chapter 11). In turn, communication training is discussed, with particular emphasis upon those guidelines that will enable the helper to function most effectively (Chapter 12). In addition, the processes involved in the initial interactions with another human being during and following training are considered and examples are given of high- and low-level facilitative and action-oriented responses (Chapter 13). Finally, applications of training in the core conditions (Chapter 14) as well as in effective ancillary modes of treatment (Chapter 15) are reviewed.

10

THE DEVELOPMENT OF EFFECTIVE
TRAINING PROCEDURES

Just as the traditional literature on selection fails to demonstrate the effectiveness of existing procedures, so also does that concerned with training, an area that is perhaps the last haven of dominance for those who choose not to inquire into the consequences of their efforts. Indeed, the maxim that those who cannot treat may teach perhaps holds a great deal more truth than mirth. In any event, in spite of the long-standing, functionally autonomous rituals of many of our traditional training orientations, *none have demonstrated their translation to tangible human benefits or the potential for such.* In fact, the empirical evidence of the few traditional programs that have been researched yield essentially "negative results." This situation, particularly as it contrasts with the positive achievements of lay and other lower-level programs, suggests our first proposition.

Proposition I. Training in the helping professions may have constructive or destructive consequences on trainee level of functioning on dimensions related to constructive change.

If we accept the assumption that training, like counseling and psychotherapy, is an additional instance of all learning or relearning processes, then training as all other interpersonal processes may be for better or for worse for trainees on indexes relevant to helpee functioning. Several corollaries flow from this basic proposition.

Corollary I. Trainees in the traditional, professional training programs demonstrate no change or negative change.

On those indexes related to constructive helpee change or gain in the few traditional, professional training programs that have been investigated, the trainees involved have demonstrated no change or deteriorative change on the communication of facilitative and action-oriented dimensions (Bergin & Soloman, 1963; Carkhuff, Kratochvil, & Friel, 1968). In the one instance in which an intermediate-level professional program demonstrated positive results, trainees functioning at very low levels initially progressed over the course of training to far less than minimally facilitative levels (Anthony & Carkhuff, 1968).

Corollary II.   Trainees in lay and lower-level training programs demonstrate largely positive results.

On indexes related to client change lay and lower-level training programs such as NDEA and other short-term guidance institutes, and including in particular patient training programs, demonstrate largely positive results (Berenson, Carkhuff, & Myrus, 1966; Carkhuff, 1969a; Carkhuff & Banks, 1969; Carkhuff & Bierman, 1969; Carkhuff & Truax, 1965a, 1965b; Kratochvil, 1969; Martin & Carkhuff, 1968; Pierce, Carkhuff, & Berenson, 1967; Pierce & Drasgow, 1969; Vitalo, 1969; and a number of others summarized in Carkhuff, 1966, and Carkhuff, 1968).

However, these demonstrated differences may be not so much the consequence of the professional status of the program as they are of the level of competency of the persons promulgating the different programs. Thus, we come to a second proposition.

Proposition II.   Constructive or destructive consequences in training may be accounted for in large part by the initial level of functioning of both trainer and trainee on dimensions related to constructive change.

Again if we accept the assumption that training is an instance of all interpersonal learning processes, then the respective level of functioning of both trainer and trainee on those facilitative and action-oriented dimensions that account in large part for constructive gain in learning and relearning should account in large part for constructive gains in training (Carkhuff, 1967). Two corollaries illuminate this proposition further.

Corollary I.   In traditional, professional programs the trainers are generally functioning at low levels and have differentially negative effects upon the trainees, depending upon the trainees' level of functioning.

Where investigations have been possible of the professional trainers' level of functioning the results have been extremely disheartening, reflecting no doubt a significant selection factor, with those trainees who remain in training demonstrating no change or deterioration in the direction of their low-level–functioning trainers (Burstein & Carkhuff, 1969; Carkhuff, Kratochvil, & Friel, 1968).

Corollary II.   In lay and lower-level training programs the trainers are generally functioning at high levels and thus have differentially positive effects upon the trainees' level of functioning.

Investigations of the trainers' level of functioning in lay and lower-level programs has yielded very positive results. In general, the trainers have been functioning at relatively high levels (again a selection factor may be operative) and have had a significantly constructive effect upon all of their trainees (Berenson, Carkhuff, & Myrus, 1966; Carkhuff, 1968a; Carkhuff & Banks, 1969; Carkhuff & Bierman, 1969; Carkhuff & Truax, 1965a; Martin & Carkhuff, 1968; Kratochvil, 1969; Pierce *et al.*, 1967; Pierce & Drasgow, 1969; Vitalo, 1969).

In this regard, there is a proposition that is basic to the types of programs promulgated.

Proposition III.   The most effective programs appear to be those that (1) focus upon primary facilitative and action-oriented dimensions complemented by secondary dimensions involving potential preferred modes of treatment and (2) integrate the didactic, experiential, and modeling aspects of learning.

The integrated programs built around core conditions have demonstrated the most constructive trainee outcomes on both experiential and empirical indexes (summarized in Carkhuff & Berenson, 1967).

Corollary I.   Traditional, professional programs have been neither built around primary conditions nor have they integrated the learning experiences.

By and large traditional training programs have focused upon secondary dimensions exclusively, that is, upon one or the other potential preferred mode of treatment which they have assumed to be preeminent. Similarly, the traditional programs have tended to be exclusively didactic, as in the psychoanalytic, trait-and-factor, and behavioristic approaches, or experiential, as in the client-centered and existential approaches. The modeling source of learning has been universally neglected (Carkhuff & Berenson, 1967).

Corollary II. Lay and lower-level training programs have tended to be integrated learning experiences built around primary core conditions.

The results obtained in studies of a host of lower-level training programs have demonstrated the effectiveness of integrating the didactic, experiential, and modeling aspects of learning around primary core conditions (Berenson, Carkhuff, & Myrus, 1966; Carkhuff, 1969a; Carkhuff & Banks, 1969; Carkhuff & Bierman, 1969; Carkhuff, Kratochvil, & Friel, 1968; Carkhuff & Truax, 1965a; Kratochvil, 1969; Martin & Carkhuff, 1968; Pierce *et al.*, 1967; Pierce & Drasgow, 1969; Vitalo, 1968).

Differences are not to be accounted for solely in terms of whether the program is a professional graduate program or a subprofessional program. Obviously, for example, there may be trainers who are functioning at high levels within the professional programs and those who are functioning at low levels in the subprofessional programs. Indeed, the results may be in part an artifact of a selection factor, reflecting those individuals who are attracted to these differing programs. A number of the research projects have addressed themselves to these questions directly. A closer look at some of the details and summary data of these projects is warranted at this point.

THE EFFECT OF TRAINER LEVEL OF FUNCTIONING: A VIEW IN DEPTH

Perhaps the most critical variable in effective counselor training is the level at which the counselor-trainer is functioning on those dimensions related to constructive helpee change. In relation to helpee change research has led us to discern what we term both facilitative and action-oriented interpersonal dimensions (empathy, respect, concreteness, genuineness, self-disclosure, confrontation, immediacy) as the critical ingredients of effective interpersonal processes (Carkhuff, 1969c; Carkhuff & Berenson, 1967, 1969). Hopefully, the trainer is not only functioning at high levels on these dimensions but is also attempting to impart learnings concerning these dimensions in a systematic manner, for only then will he integrate the critical sources of learning—the didactic, the experiential, and the modeling. In this regard it simply makes sense that whatever the task, whether it is research or counseling, science or art, *the implementer of any training program should fulfill at least the following key conditions: (1) he should be experienced in the relevant areas and (2) he should have demonstrated a level of expertise or excellence in the relevant area.*

A number of research projects assessing the effects of training have addressed themselves directly to these questions. While there are many more such projects, they do not provide us with a systematic assessment we can employ for comparative purposes. Table 10-1 summarizes the levels of over-all functioning of trainers when in the helping role with adults and the level of over-all functioning of the trainees when in the helping role with adults at the beginning and at the end of training. Thus, the table establishes the over-all effect or net trainee gain or loss over training. It should be emphasized that, independent of duration of training, only those programs or those aspects of programs that have made full discharge of all relevant aspects of training as seen by their promulgators are included for consideration. In addition, while changes in trainee level of functioning are noted, only the initial level of trainer functioning is available, and similar differentials are not recorded for the trainer. Indeed, it is likely that just as in counseling (Kratochvil, Aspy, & Carkhuff, 1967) the direction of change in trainer functioning may be as critical or more critical than absolute level of functioning.

As the table indicates, in all cases in which the data are available the trainees move in the direction of their trainers. It will be noted that in one instance, program V, trainees beginning at an extraordinarily low level progressed over the course of training to a point at which they were functioning at a level slightly (although not significantly) above their relatively low-functioning trainers. It is also apparent that in general the high-functioning trainers tended to invest themselves in the more innovating, shorter-term, "lower-level" training programs while the lower-functioning trainers became involved in longer-term, professional graduate programs. Over-all, the subprofessional trainees tended to gain more in their level of functioning over the course of brief training than professional trainees over years of training. However, again the data are not unqualified. For example, while two of the professional programs assessed (I and II) demonstrated low final levels of trainee functioning,

Table 10-1.   Mean Levels of Over-all Functioning of Beginning and Advanced Trainees and Their Trainers' Levels of Professionalization of Programs

Population Levels of Functioning	Professional				Intermediate			
	I Clinical (Ph.D.)	II Clinical (Ph.D.)	III Clinical (Ph.D.)	IV Counseling (Ph.D.)	V Rehabilitation counselor (M.A.)	VI Guidance counselor	VII Teacher counselor (M.A.)	VIII Beginning psychology (M.A.)
Beginning of training	2.0 (N = 8)	2.1 (N = 14)		2.1 (N = 10)	1.4 (N = 8)	1.9 (N = 14)	1.7 (N = 8)	1.8 (N = 10)
Advanced stage (noted)	2.0 (N = 8) 4th year	1.8 (N = 8) 2d year	3.0[b] (N = 12) 100 hours	3.0 (N = 10) 3d year	1.8 (N = 8) 2d year	2.8 (N = 14) 50 hours	2.6 (N = 8) 50 hours	2.5 (N = 10) 30 hours
Trainer level	1.9 (N = 9)	1.7[a] (N = 3)	3.3[b] (N = 2)	3.6 (N = 3)	1.6 (N = 7)	3.5 (N = 1)	4.0 (N = 1)	3.0 (N = 2)
Trainees' net change	−0.1	−0.3		0.9	0.4	0.9	0.9	0.7
Sources	Carkhuff, Kratochvil, & Friel, 1968	Carkhuff, Kratochvil, & Friel, 1968	Carkhuff & Truax, 1965a	Carkhuff, 1969b	Anthony & Carkhuff, 1969	Martin & Carkhuff, 1968	Carkhuff, 1969a	Carkhuff, Friel, & Kratochvil, 1969

within the professional programs trainees of high-level trainers demonstrated highly positive results (III and IV).[1]

The findings of studies of intermediate, subprofessional, and patient programs that demonstrated significantly positive changes with counselor-

---

[1] The results of assessments of other professional programs are consistent. For example, the transformations of the data of Bergin and Soloman (1963) indicate that the trainees' final level of functioning on only one dimension, empathic understanding, was 1.7. While the necessary data are unavailable, if we could assume that the trainees began at 2.1, the modal level of beginning professional trainees, we might make two inferences: (1) that the net change of the trainees would be −0.4 and (2) that the trainers were functioning at level 1.7 or less.

Table 10-1 continued

	Subprofessional				Helpee			
IX Nursing (Nondegree)	X Dormitory counselor (Nondegree)	XI Community volunteer (Nondegree)		XII Hospital attendant (Nondegree)	XIII Parents and teachers (Racial relations workshop)	XIV Child psychiatric parents (Treatment)	XV Inpatients (Treatment)	XVI Inpatients (Treatment)
		A	B					
1.7 (N=10)	1.8 (N=12)	1.6 (N=9)	1.5 (N=8)		1.4 (N=25)	1.5 (N=10)	1.2 (N=7)	1.2 (N=12)
2.3 (N=10) 20 hours	2.7 (N=12) 20 hours	2.4 (N=9) 20 hours	1.9 (N=8) 20 hours	2.8[b] (N=5) 100 hours	2.6[b] 20 hours	2.9[b] (N=10) 25 hours	2.4 (N=7) 25 hours	2.6 30 hours
3.0 (N=1)	3.8 (N=1)	3.1 (N=1)	2.0 (N=1)	3.3[b] (N=2)	4.0 (N=2)	4.5 (N=1)	3.5 (N=2)	3.8 (N=1)
0.6	0.9	0.8	0.4		1.2	1.4	1.2	1.4
Kratochvil, 1969	Berenson, Carkhuff, & Myrus, 1966	Pierce et al., 1967		Carkhuff & Truax, 1965a	Carkhuff & Banks, 1969	Carkhuff & Bierman, 1969	Pierce & Drasgow, 1969	Vitalo, 1969

[a] Only three of six staff members were available for assessment.
[b] Communication level between adults only where level with children was also assessed.

trainers functioning at high levels contrast sharply with those obtained with some of the professional programs. Indeed, it is noteworthy that the programs demonstrating the greatest gains were patient programs, with a variety of factors no doubt contributing to these results. In general, the results of all programs may be summarized as follows: *those trainees whose trainers were functioning (1) above minimally facilitative levels (level 3) and (2) approximately one level or more above the trainees demonstrated the most positive changes.* In this regard the fact that the trainers in many of these projects were functioning well above the norms of their membership groups is also relevant. In addition to the results of the rehabilitation-counselor program (program V), the fact that the trainer in program X who was functioning above his trainees but not at minimally facilitative levels elicited some constructive change from his trainees suggests that a trainer who comes close to meeting one of these conditions may make a contribution, albeit a limited one, to the growth of his trainees. On the other hand, those trainers who are functioning neither at minimally facilitative levels nor significantly above their trainees have nothing to offer their trainees, while those who are functioning at levels lower than their trainees can promise their trainees no change or deteriorative change.

Over-all, the results can be summarized in tabular form in terms of the trainers' levels of functioning, independent of all other considerations—that is, number of trainers or trainees, level of trainees, type and duration of program, and so on. As Table 10-2 indicates, whether or not we employ the estimates for programs IV and XII derived from Table 10-1, there is a very high degree of relation (a correlation above 0.8 in any event) between the trainer's level of functioning and the

Table 10-2.   Mean Level of Trainer Functioning and Mean Level of Trainee Gain[a]

Program	Mean Level of Trainer Functioning	Mean Level of Net Trainee Gain
XIV	4.5	1.4
VII	4.0	0.9
XIII	4.0	1.2
XVI	3.8	1.4
X	3.7	0.9
IV	3.6	0.9
XV	3.5	1.2
VI	3.5	0.9
XII	3.3	1.0[b]
III	3.3	0.9[b]
XIA	3.1	0.8
VIII	3.0	0.7
IX	3.0	0.6
XIB	2.0	0.4
I	1.9	−0.1
II	1.7	−0.3
V	1.6	0.4

[a] Carkhuff, 1969d.
[b] Estimated from Table 10-1.

mean gain in the level of functioning of the trainee. Thus, *the level of the counselor-trainer's functioning appears to be the single most critical aspect of effective training.*

Some insights into the dynamics of interpersonal functioning may be obtained by viewing the data on the discrimination of counselor functioning by trainers and trainees. Whereas on entering training trainees deviate more than one level from the ratings of experts, as with communication they demonstrate movement in the direction of their trainers' levels of discrimination over the course of training. Indeed, a high level of discrimination (a deviation of approximately one half a level from experts) by the trainers in the rehabilitation-counselor training program (Anthony & Carkhuff, 1969) may account in part for the fact that the trainees were able to go beyond their trainers in level of interpersonal functioning; that is, the trainers can make accurate discriminations concerning the trainees even if they cannot establish an accurate experiential and modeling base for training. Obviously what is most puzzling is that the trainers function at fairly high levels of discrimination and at low levels of communication, a finding that is consistent with the results establishing the independence of discrimination and communication among low-level communicators (Carkhuff, Kratochvil, & Friel, 1968). It appears that many people see but do not act upon what they see, with perhaps a dynamic base of having been conditioned to fear acting upon what they see. Since the problem is not unlike the insight-action conflict of therapeutic processes, the relevant questions might be whether systematic training or psychotherapy or both are the answers for these trainers. At a minimum we must conclude that those persons functioning at the highest levels behaviorally are not conducting our professional training programs.

LEVEL OF TRAINEE FUNCTIONING

The level of trainer functioning cannot be considered independently of the level of trainee functioning. The results of Table 10-1, which are consistent with base rate data in the field (Carkhuff, 1969c, 1969d; Carkhuff & Berenson, 1967), indicate that in general those professional trainees functioning relatively at the highest levels are selected, whether inadvertently or not, either by themselves or by the professional programs to which they apply. The intermediate-level program trainees are essentially unselected from those persons in the general population with interests in helping, with at least one program (V) apparently receiving those trainees who are functioning at unusually low levels relatively, perhaps reflecting a "left-over" nature of this sample—that is, those applicants who are unable to get into the doctoral clinical and counseling programs.

Unfortunately, the results also indicate that in general those trainees functioning at the highest levels initially tend to deteriorate over the course of training. With the professional-subprofessional dimension confounded with trainer level of functioning, the lowest-level trainees are often interacting with the highest-level trainers, and the highest-level trainees are most often interacting with the lowest-level trainers. The follow-up studies of programs I and II provide us with relevant data. In the longitudinal study of program I, by the second year there were six drop-outs from among the 14 original first-year students. The two students functioning at the highest level and four of the six functioning above level 2 terminated or were terminated. Over-all, the initial level of functioning of those who ultimately dropped out was approximately 2.2 to approximately 2.0 for those who were to continue in the programs (Carkhuff, Kratochvil, & Friel, 1968). Further, a tentative hypothesis that the best and the worst trainees might be eliminated from traditional programs received no additional support from the results of a follow-up of program I. Of the eight first-year clinical and eight first-year nonclinical trainees five had dropped out voluntarily by the first semester of the second year: the five drop-outs were five of the six trainees who were functioning above level 2; over-all, their comparative mean levels of functioning were approximately 2.3 to approximately 1.9 for those who remained. Another interesting follow-up process study (Holder, 1968) revealed that in addition to level of facilitative functioning those dropping out tended to be functioning in the more action-oriented direction (traditionally masculine)—that is, these individuals were trying to *do* something about problems of their helpees in an active way, while those who remained functioned in a more passively acceptant manner (traditionally feminine), a finding consistent with interpretations of Patterson's (1968) review of selection literature. Thus, it appears that the only consistent finding is that *the trainees functioning at the highest levels of both facilitative and action-oriented dimensions will be eliminated from traditional programs.*

Needless to elaborate, the results of programs III and IV, in which relatively high-level trainees interacted with high-level trainers, provide a vivid contrast to those of the other programs. In addition, those trainees in the intermediate, subprofessional, and patient programs who were functioning at relatively low levels initially tended to demonstrate positive gains over the course of training. Again, in general, these trainees had the benefit of interacting with high-level trainers. The positive results of the one program (V) with trainers functioning at low levels can be accounted for in part by the extraordinarily low initial level of functioning of the trainees. In effect, these trainees stood to gain by getting back to the average level of functioning of the general population.

While at first glance, then, the initial level of trainee functioning bears no relation to trainee gain, when we consider it in interaction with trainer level of functioning a number of critical trends emerge. Depending, of course, upon the intensity of the discrepancies in level of functioning, *within limits* the effect of trainee level of functioning depends upon trainer level of functioning, both within and between programs. While both relatively high- and low-functioning trainees will gain from high-level–functioning trainers, it is obvious that within a limited temporal period the trainees functioning at high levels will demonstrate a higher final level of absolute functioning. However, even if the initially low-level–functioning trainees progress at a slower rate, if the program is long enough they may close the gap between themselves and those functioning at high levels. Similarly, in interaction with low-level–functioning trainers, both high- and low-level trainees will demonstrate negative change, and even if the initially high trainees deteriorate more slowly over an extended period of time, the highs will close in on the lows' absolute level of functioning. Of course, there are contingencies. Not the least of these is the intensity of the differential between trainer and trainee functioning. Where the differential is greatest between trainees functioning initially at relatively high levels and trainers functioning at very high levels, we can generate predictions for the greatest and most rapid positive trainee change. Where the differential is greatest between trainees functioning initially at relatively high levels and trainers functioning at very low levels, we can expect the greatest negative trainee change, although perhaps more slowly over longer periods of time—at least in those instances in which the trainees do not terminate. Where the differential is smaller in either a positive or negative direction, we can anticipate lesser changes in either a positive or negative direction.

These findings, of course, have implications for selection. That is, knowing the level of trainer functioning, we can generate differential predictions according to level of trainee functioning. In several predictive validity studies (Carkhuff, 1969a; Carkhuff & Banks, 1969; Carkhuff & Bierman, 1969) indexes of communication have been found to be the best predictors of future functioning in the helping role: in interaction with a high-level–functioning trainer trainees functioning initially at relatively higher levels (1) functioned at the highest final level and (2) made the greatest gains, while those functioning initially at relatively lower levels functioned at relatively lower final levels and gained the least. In regard to discrimination, while pretraining indexes of discrimination are good predictors of posttraining discrimination, there was little or no relation between discrimination indexes and functioning in the helping role. (To be sure, in the individual instance high-level communicators may be predicted by very high discriminators). Again, in general, trainees move in the direction of their trainers on discrimination. Thus, in cases in which the trainers are discriminating at relatively high levels and communicating at low levels the trainees improve in discrimination while deteriorating in communication.

TYPE OF TRAINING PROGRAM

Trainer and trainee levels of functioning, in turn, cannot be considered independently of the type of program implemented. Again, the apparent effects of type and duration of program are confounded by the level of functioning of the trainers promulgating these programs. Thus, the professional programs conducted by low-level–functioning counselors are also characterized by the curious blend of psychoanalytic and behavioristic approaches that dominate many academic training centers today. Similarly, program V, the rehabilitation-counselor training program, is dominated by another curious blend of client-centered and trait-and-factor orientations. In each instance it may be said that the programs involved focus upon what we might call secondary dimensions or potential preferred modes of treatment rather than systematically upon those core dimensions for which we have received the greatest support (Carkhuff, 1966a, 1969c; Carkhuff & Berenson, 1967). Similarly, these programs tend to focus exclusively upon the didactic source of learning, even in the case of the client-centered training where, interestingly enough, the emphasis is upon teaching rather than the experiential base of the trainee. All too often these experiences leave the trainees in a "double-bind" situation, where for example the trainer is functioning in a manner different from his teaching. Finally, concerning the duration of the program, while the negative relationship with trainee change is confounded, the best that can be said is that these programs are wasteful in the time allotted to effect trainee functioning in the helping role.

By contrast, the remaining programs for which we have positive evidence may be considered eclectic programs that (1) focus upon core conditions shared by all interview-oriented processes for which there is research support complemented by a consideration of the unique contributions of the various potential preferred modes of treatment and (2) emphasize the integration of the different critical sources of learning. From the model that we have been employing (Carkhuff, 1966a,

1966b, 1967, 1968, 1969c; Carkhuff & Berenson, 1967) this means that the counselor-trainer not only offers high levels of facilitative and action-oriented dimensions, thus providing the trainee with the same experiential base as the helpee is to be offered, but also establishes himself as a model for an individual who can sensitively share experiences with another person as well as act upon these experiences, both within and without the pertinent interpersonal process. In addition, the training process is that much more effective when the trainer is also systematically focusing in his didactic teaching and "shaping" upon the conditions he is employing in interaction with the trainees. These programs have produced changes on not only the objective measures assessing level of functioning in the helping role but also on self and expert ratings, on the ratings of clients and significant others, and on indexes of the constructive personality change of the trainee. Further, these programs have produced changes significantly greater than training control groups of traditional programs which meet for the same period of time (Berenson, Carkhuff, & Myrus, 1966; Carkhuff, Collingwood, & Renz, 1969; Martin & Carkhuff, 1967) as well as the usual control groups. In contrast, it is worth noting briefly that experience in helping alone, without adequate training and supervision, is not sufficient to effect positive change in either the helper or the helpee (Carkhuff, 1969e).

Concerning what is taught, there is evidence to indicate that if we concentrate upon didactic teaching to the exclusion of practice in communication we obtain changes in discrimination only (Carkhuff, Collingwood, & Renz, 1969; Carkhuff, Kratochvil, & Friel, 1968). The direct implication that people functioning at low levels by and large learn only what they are taught is further buttressed by the differential findings of Anthony and Carkhuff (1969) in which changes in attitudes toward the physically handicapped were found in a program emphasizing such changes and of Kratochvil (1969) in which changes in attitudes were not found in a program placing no stress upon such changes. The fact that discrimination does not translate itself readily into functioning in the helping role in conjunction with the fact that there is no evidence to relate discrimination to client or patient benefits in any way has implications for a behavioristic approach to training.

While there is empirical as well as experiential evidence to indicate that high-level–functioning people can generalize from one learning experience to another (as, for example, from discrimination to communication), the inability of low-level persons to do likewise has implications for training both high- as well as low-functioning persons to do what we want them to do. If we want trainees to function effectively in the helping role, then we must give them plenty of practice in that role.

If we want the trainees to learn to communicate effectively, we must give them practice in communication. In particular, with regard to the low-functioning trainees, if we do not give them practice, they will be functioning at levels commensurate with the helpees whom they are treating and thus will have nothing to offer (Carkhuff, 1969e; Pagell, Carkhuff, & Berenson, 1967). We must differentially reinforce those behaviors that are in fact helpful and those that are not. We must explicitly and systematically teach what we wish trainees to learn. Again, in particular in relation to the low-functioning trainee, we must leave nothing implicit and expect no indirect effects in other spheres of the trainee's life or upon other individuals in the trainee's life (Donofrio, 1968). We must work up gradations of practice in "shaping" effective behavior. Upon conclusion of training we must further support the changes we have effected.

There are, to be sure, other considerations. For example, in regard to patient groups that demonstrated so much positive change so quickly there were a variety of other factors operating, not the least of which was the built-in motivation of the trainees. In particular, the parents who were trained to work with each other and their disturbed children (XIV) were motivated to do what they could for their troubled children, perhaps even more than they might for themselves, as in inpatient programs XV and XVI. In addition, the development of the results of other programs led to a heavy behavioristic emphasis in these programs, an emphasis that might have converged very nicely with these initially low-level populations. Finally, and perhaps even most significant, these people offered a wealth of experience in living to tap in on—not all good, but nevertheless a base of experience that contrasts vividly with that of many trainees such as undergraduate or graduate students. Even here, though, in a brief demonstration program of approximately 20 hours duration a group of over 150 undergraduate students was able to demonstrate nearly three quarters of a level improvement in written communication by practicing written responses to tapes (Berenson, Carkhuff, Friel, & Leitner, 1968). However, in addition to the problems in generalization there are the problems of retention of learning.

Again, in relation to the low-level trainee we can expect no generalization to other behaviors and other situations. We must control the environment and the systems of reinforcements within the environment to which these individuals return in order to maintain lasting effects. In particular, for the low-level–functioning trainee the immediate effects of one learning experience will be neutralized by the effects of succeeding experiences (Kratochvil & Carkhuff, 1969). Simply stated, *while the hope for low-level–functioning trainees is to enable them to function at higher levels, in general they function in a given role in a manner in which they are trained to function through all of the sources of learning under the control of the trainer. They change only if they are trained to change. Obviously, it is an advantage to begin with higher-level–functioning trainees, but even they can benefit from explicit and systematic programs offered in the context of a facilitative atmosphere.*

One alternative, then, is to select relatively high-level–functioning trainees. However, the necessity for high-level–functioning trainers in these instances is imperative. Indeed, under the present professional system and with the trainers that dominate we might minimize our trainee losses by selecting low-level trainees. Concerning selection, the evidence indicates that the best index of a future criteria is a previous index of that criteria. Thus, if we want to predict future functioning in the helping role, we must obtain an index of present functioning in the helping role. In this regard, again, there is no evidence to indicate that discrimination gives us an index of anything other than discrimination, and unless we are training persons to discriminate at high levels, as for example, research raters, there is no value to such extended efforts. Even here, however, there is clear-cut evidence to indicate that those persons who are (1) functioning at the highest levels interpersonally and (2) are most experienced in the relevant interpersonal relations, as for example, counseling and psychotherapy, are the most accurate discriminators or raters (Cannon & Carkhuff, 1969).

SUMMARY AND CONCLUSIONS

In summary, it is apparent that dependent upon the level of functioning of (1) trainers and (2) trainees and (3) the types of programs implemented in training, the effects may range from severe losses in trainee functioning over years of training to significant gains within months. We must add that, in general, *people best learn that for which they are best trained.* In this regard, in addition to assessing facilitative and action-oriented dimensions, we must learn to assess the effectiveness with which helpers implement the techniques of potential preferred modes of treatment, as, for example, how effectively a helper implements a counterconditioning process or employs and interprets a Strong Vocational Interest Blank (Carkhuff & Berenson, 1967). Accordingly, programs of both high- and low-level–functioning trainers may focus explicitly upon relevant or extraneous learnings. For example, many, if not most, programs emphasize trainee "statements of positive attitudes toward patients" and indeed eliminate those candidates who do not conform to meeting this expectation, yet the dimension emphasized remains unrelated to indexes of helpee change or gain. In the same vein many of the trainees' learnings, whether from high- or low-level–functioning trainers, have been inadvertent. For example, a high-level–functioning trainer may effect constructive trainee changes on dimensions related to helpee change even while emphasizing extraneous learnings; similarly, a low-level trainer may effect deteriorative trainee change while focusing upon very relevant dimensions. The direct implication, then, is that those programs in which high-level–functioning trainers focus explicitly upon dimensions relevant to helpee gains and make systematic employment of all significant sources of learning, including in particular modeling, are most effective.

The results have implications not only for the selection of trainers and trainees and the conduct of their training programs but also for treatment. We may, for example, be able to employ the same relevant indexes for assessing the level of functioning of helpees. In addition, within treatment the same behavioristic principles that apply to low-level–functioning trainees will apply to low-level–functioning clients. (Hopefully, a greater percentage of trainees than helpees will be functioning at relatively high levels or we must ask the question, "What is it that the prospective helper believes he has to offer to a person in need of help?") In this regard explicit teaching and systematic "shaping" and programing through differential reinforcement schedules and control of the environment at least to the point where we can anticipate and similarly program otherwise difficult conditions, particularly those involving people in the environment to which the helpee returns, may constitute a preferred mode of treatment.

Finally, the training tasks set forth are very difficult indeed for the helping professions. They may not be insurmountable, though, if professionals can overcome the previous lack of training and treatment criteria, an inherent attraction which may have brought many to the profession in the first place.

REFERENCES

Anthony, W., & Carkhuff, R. R. The effects of rehabilitation counselor training upon discrimination, communication and helping attitudes. *Journal of Counseling Psychology*, in press, 1969.

Berenson, B. G., Carkhuff, R. R., Friel, T., & Leitner, L. The effects of large group training experiences upon written communication. Mimeographed research report, State University of New York at Buffalo, 1968.

Berenson, B. G., Carkhuff, R. R., & Myrus, P. The interpersonal functioning and training of college students. *Journal of Counseling Psychology*, 1966, **13**, 441–446.

Bergin, A., & Soloman, S. Personality and performance correlates of empathic understanding in psychotherapy. *American Psychologist*, 1963, **18**, 393.

Burstein, J., & Carkhuff, R. R. Objective, client and therapist ratings of therapeutic-offered facilitative conditions of moderate and low functioning therapists. *Journal of Clinical Psychology*, in press, 1969.

Cannon, J., & Carkhuff, R. R. The effects of level of functioning and experience on accuracy of discrimination. *Journal of Consulting Psychology*, in press, 1969.

Carkhuff, R. R. Training in counseling and psychotherapy: Requiem or reveille? *Journal of Counseling Psychology*, 1966, **13**, 360–367. (a)

Carkhuff, R. R. Counseling research, theory and practice. *Journal of Counseling Psychology*, 1966, **13**, 467–480. (b)

Carkhuff, R. R. Toward a comprehensive model of facilitative interpersonal processes. *Journal of Counseling Psychology*, 1967, **14**, 67–72.

Carkhuff, R. R. The differential functioning of lay and professional helpers. *Journal of Counseling Psychology*, 1968, **15**, 417–426.

Carkhuff, R. R. The prediction of the effects of teacher-counselor training: The development of communication and discrimination selection indexes. *Counselor Education and Supervision*, in press, 1969. (a)

Carkhuff, R. R. The effects of a systematic eclectic training program. Unpublished research, State University of New York at Buffalo, 1969. (b)

Carkhuff, R. R. Counselor communication and discrimination as a function of client affect and content. *Journal of Counseling Psychology*, in press, 1969. (c)

Carkhuff, R. R. Critical variables in counselor training. *Journal of Counseling Psychology*, in press, 1969. (d)

Carkhuff, R. R. The effects of a volunteer patient companion program. Unpublished research, State University of New York at Buffalo, 1969. (f)

Carkhuff, R. R., & Banks, G. The effects of a human relations workshop for Negro parents and white teachers. Unpublished research, American International College, Springfield, Mass., 1969.

Carkhuff, R. R., & Berenson, B. G. *Beyond counseling and therapy*. New York: Holt, Rinehart and Winston, Inc., 1967.

Carkhuff, R. R., & Berenson, B. G. The counselor is a man and woman. *Personnel and Guidance Journal*, in press, 1969.

Carkhuff, R. R., & Bierman, R. The effects of human relations training upon child psychiatric patients in treatment. *Journal of Counseling Psychology*, in press, 1969.

Carkhuff, R. R., Collingwood, T., & Renz, L. The prediction of the effects of didactic training in discrimination. *Journal of Clinical Psychology*, in press, 1969.

Carkhuff, R. R., Kratochvil, D., & Friel, T. The effects of professional training: The communication and discrimination of facilitative conditions. *Journal of Counseling Psychology*, 1968, **15**, 68–74.

Carkhuff, R. R., Friel, T., & Kratochvil, D. The differential effects of training in responsive and initiative conditions. *Counselor Education and Supervision*, in press, 1969.

Carkhuff, R. R., & Truax, C. B. Training in counseling and psychotherapy: An evaluation of an integrated didactic and experiential approach. *Journal of Consulting Psychology*, 1965, **29**, 333–336. (a)

Carkhuff, R. R., & Truax, C. B. Lay mental health counseling: The effects of lay group counseling. *Journal of Consulting Psychology*, 1965, **29**, 426–432.

Donofrio, D. The effects of therapist-offered conditions upon parents in group therapy and their children. Doctoral dissertation, State University of New York at Buffalo, 1968.

Holder, B. T. A follow-up study of the activity-passivity and facilitative-nonfacilitative dimensions of continuing and terminated graduate trainees. *Journal of Clinical Psychology*, in press, 1969.

Kratochvil, D. Changes in values and interpersonal functioning of nurses in training. *Counselor Education and Supervision*, 1969, **8**, 104–107.

Kratochvil, D., Aspy, D., & Carkhuff, R. R. The differential effects of absolute level and direction of growth in counselor functioning upon client functioning. *Journal of Clinical Psychology*, 1968, **23**, 216–218.

Kratochvil, D., Carkhuff, R. R., & Berenson, B. G. The cumulative effects of facilitative conditions upon the physical, emotional and intellectual functioning of grammar school students. *Journal of Educational Research*, in press, 1969.

Martin, J., & Carkhuff, R. R. The effects of training upon changes in trainee personality and behavior. *Journal of Clinical Psychology*, 1968, **24**, 109–110.

Pagell, W., Carkhuff, R. R., & Berenson, B. G. The predicted differential effects of the level of counselor functioning upon the level of functioning of outpatients. *Journal of Clinical Psychology*, 1967, **23**, 510–512.

Patterson, C. H. The selection of counselors. Paper presented at the Conference on Research Problems in Counseling, Washington University, St. Louis, Mo., 1967.

Pierce, R., Carkhuff, R. R., & Berenson, B. G. The differential effects of high and low functioning counselors upon counselors-in-training. *Journal of Clinical Psychology*, 1967, **23**, 212–215.

Pierce, R., & Drasgow, J. The effects of human relations training upon V.A. neuropsychiatric patients. *Journal of Counseling Psychology*, in press, 1969.

Vitalo, R. The effects of training in interpersonal skills upon psychiatric inpatients. Unpublished research, V.A. Hospital, Buffalo, New York, and Buffalo State Hospital, 1969.

11

DISCRIMINATION TRAINING

There is substantial evidence to support the proposition that gains or losses in the level of functioning of trainees over the course of training are dependent upon the initial levels of functioning of both the trainer and the trainee. That is, trainee gains are in large part a function of the interaction between the trainer's and the trainee's level of functioning, with initially high-level trainers and trainees in interaction with each other tending to produce the greatest trainee gains the quickest.

There is also substantial evidence to support the proposition that a high level of discrimination, insufficient in and of itself for a high level of communication, is nevertheless critical to a high level of communication. Since a high level of communication is the basic goal of training (Carkhuff & Berenson, 1967), it as meaningful to focus upon discrimination as a first stage of effective communication in the helping process.

Simply stated, however, the evidence indicates that with most populations *communication is best learned by practicing communication.* Discrimination follows communication as insight follows action for relatively low-functioning populations. Indeed, an increased understanding following action may serve to bring the new learning from the action to culmination, thus increasing the probability of retention. Nevertheless, even when the focus is upon communication in a shaping process, the briefest of introductions to the relevant dimension usually precedes such practice. In this context we examined the dimensions involved in the selection process.

The trainee's level of discrimination, then, is largely a function of the trainer's level of both discrimination and communication as well as of the trainee's initial level of discrimination. This statement and the evidence to support it may be summarized in proposition form.

167

Proposition I.   The gains or losses in the trainee's level of discrimination are dependent in part upon the trainer's initial level of communication.

A high level of trainer communication, since it assumes a high level of trainer discrimination, is obviously the strongest factor in effecting significantly high trainee discriminations. Not only does the trainer discriminate at high levels but also he is able to communicate accurately these discriminations to the trainee. Indeed, the evidence suggests that the trainees of high-level–communicating trainers improve while those of low-level–communicating trainers demonstrate little or no positive change in discrimination (Berenson, Carkhuff, Friel, & Leitner, 1968; Burstein & Carkhuff, 1969; Carkhuff & Bierman, 1969; Carkhuff, Collingwood, & Renz, 1969; Carkhuff, Friel, & Kratochvil, 1969; Carkhuff, Kratochvil, & Friel, 1968). Again, however, the trainees of one program in which the trainers were functioning at very low levels of communication were able to demonstrate significant improvement in discrimination (Anthony & Carkhuff, 1969). It is noteworthy here, however, that while the trainers were functioning at very low levels of communication they were functioning at levels higher than the trainees on communication and they were functioning at significantly high levels of discrimination.

Proposition II.   The gains or losses in the trainee's level of discrimination are dependent in part upon the trainer's initial level of discrimination.

Trainees by and large learn what they are taught. The evidence suggests that trainees of trainers who discriminate at high levels improve in discrimination while those whose trainers discriminate at low levels demonstrate little or no positive change in discrimination (Anthony & Carkhuff, 1969; Berenson *et al.*, 1968; Burstein & Carkhuff, 1969; Carkhuff & Bierman, 1969; Carkhuff, Collingwood, & Renz, 1969; Carkhuff, Friel, & Kratochvil, 1969; Carkhuff, Kratochvil, & Friel, 1968). The inference might be made that even if trainers who discriminate at high levels are low-level communicators, they nevertheless reinforce improved levels of trainee discrimination, perhaps with their fine discriminations also allowing those trainees who can to go on to work their way through to higher levels of communication.

Proposition III.   The gains or losses in the trainee's level of discrimination are dependent in part upon the trainee's initial level of discrimination.

The trainer's level of functioning does not operate in a vacuum but rather in interaction with the trainee's level of functioning. Those trainees who are functioning at the highest levels will demonstrate the highest final level of functioning in interaction with a high-level trainer while those demonstrating the greatest differential from the trainer's level of functioning will make the greatest gains with trainers functioning at high levels. In relation to discrimination specifically, those trainees discriminating at the highest levels will demonstrate the highest final level of discrimination in interaction with trainers both communicating and discriminating at high levels while those demonstrating the greatest differential from the trainer's level of both discrimination and communication will make the greatest gains. Similarly, those trainees discriminating at the highest levels and/or demonstrating the greatest differential from the trainer will lose the most in interaction with trainers functioning at low levels. Further, those trainees discriminating at the lowest levels and/or demonstrating the least differential from the trainer will demonstrate the least change with trainers functioning at high and low levels. The evidence points in general toward these effects (Anthony & Carkhuff, 1969; Carkhuff, Collingwood, & Renz, 1969; Carkhuff, Friel, & Kratochvil, 1969; Carkhuff, Kratochvil, & Friel, 1968).

GROSS DISCRIMINATIONS: PHASE 1 OF
DISCRIMINATION TRAINING

In contrast to the traditional programs, which tend to focus exclusively upon one or another mode of treatment and exclusively upon one source of learning, programs that integrate all sources of learning and that focus in a systematic way upon primary, core conditions complemented by secondary dimensions or potential preferred modes of treatment (Carkhuff & Berenson, 1967) have been found most effective. These programs, then, focus not only upon the didactic source of learning but also upon the experiential and the modeling bases. However, depending upon the amount of time available, we may wish to modify these programs. Thus, we have found that shorter-term programs tend to concentrate upon the didactic or "shaping" approach to discrimination. As with communication, with low-level or poorly discriminating populations this approach has been demonstrated to be most effective. If, for example, we wish only to train people to become raters, the didactic approach is by far the most effective. If, in addition, our time is limited to 10 or so hours of training, heavy emphasis upon the didactic approach is most effective. To be sure, the whole process can be facilitated by the selection of initially high-level discriminators (see the discussion of low deviation scores in Chapter 8) and a trainer discriminating and communicating at levels high enough to demonstrate a differential. However, if we are interested in having the trainees incorporate and retain long-term changes in perceptions and communication and, indeed, in their life styles, then an integrated approach with teaching built upon an experiential and modeling base is most effective. With these considerations in mind, then, rating scales that have been validated in previous studies of treatment are systematically employed in discrimination and communication training. In regard to discrimination training specifically, the first task involves introducing the trainees to the rating process. A number of considerations are involved.

First, it is most economical and efficient to work with small groups, say from 8 to 10 trainees, although there is nothing magical about these numbers. While trainees could be tutored individually, this method does not make maximum use of the talents of an effective trainer. Individual tutoring, if necessary, can take place at a later stage of training by pairing less skilled trainees with more skilled trainees. On the other hand, although training has been effectively implemented with groups of 20 or more, and in one instance with over 150 students (Berenson *et al.*, 1968), groups of more than 10 or 12 trainees often become cumbersome. However, these findings are contingent in part upon the level of functioning of the trainees involved, with only high-level and experienced trainees perhaps able to make maximum use of the training experience in larger groups.

Second, the trainees with the necessary time available might be exposed initially to a wide variety of taped counseling and psychotherapy sessions as well as other available materials, visual as well as audio, on interpersonal learning or relearning processes. At a minimum these might include material from all major orientations—psychoanalytic, client-centered, existential, trait-and-factor, and behavioristic. The core group experience, then, would emphasize exposure to excerpts from this widely diversified pool of material. In addition, supplementary listening experiences can be made available by individual homework assignments to listen through entire hours and in some instances the entire helping process of particular cases. With trainees sufficiently experienced in the relevant human relations area this aspect of training may be minimized.

Third, it is most helpful in the introduction to rating to move from the global or general to the specific. Before making assessments of individual dimensions by individual rating scales, it is effective to employ some means of making gross assessments. These assessments may be based solely on the trainee's own phenomenology. For example, the trainee may simply be asked to rate the tapes from poor (level 1) to good (level 5). On the other hand, we have found it effective to provide some structure such as the gross rating scales employed with selection indexes (see Chapter 8) in making initial assessments of level of functioning.

Gross Functioning: An Illustration

Facilitative interpersonal functioning may be assessed on five-point scales moving from the communication of none of the conditions (level 1) to the full and simultaneous communication of all of the following general conditions:

The facilitator is a person who is living effectively himself and who discloses himself in a genuine and constructive fashion in response to others. He communicates an accurate empathic understanding and a respect for all of the feelings of other persons and guides discussions with those persons into specific feelings and experiences. He communicates confidence in what he is doing and is spontaneous and intense. In addition, while he is open and flexible in his relations with others and committed to the welfare of the other person, he is quite capable of assertive and confronting behavior when it is appropriate.

In listening to taped excerpts of helping sessions, then, the trainees are asked to make gross estimates of the helper's level of facilitative interpersonal functioning. In turn, each trainee is requested to record and share his estimate, along with the reasons for it, with the entire group. This procedure not only provides immediate and concrete informational feedback to each and every trainee but also establishes the basis for discussion of the dimensions involved and, perhaps most important, initiates communication among trainees.

The rating feedback introduces a shaping process that incorporates evaluations of both self and others. That is, the individual trainee must compare and sometimes defend to himself as well as others his ratings against those of others. He is exposed, usually for the first time systematically, to alternate ways of viewing helping processes along with his experience of the taped alternate modes of helping. Thus, the experience is both broadening and deepening. The following material illustrates discrimination training on the individual dimensions.

INDIVIDUAL DISCRIMINATIONS: PHASE 2 OF DISCRIMINATION TRAINING

The tasks of the second phase of discrimination training are (1) to articulate the dimensions involved; (2) to clarify the functions and effects of these dimensions; (3) to put into operation the assessments of these dimensions; and (4) to shape trainee discriminations of the levels of these dimensions. In the second phase of discrimination training, then, the trainee is introduced to the individual dimensions of effective human relations, dimensions that he has already been exposed to and, hopefully, has "discovered" in formulating his gross estimates of facilitative interpersonal functioning. Thus, the gross assessments are broken down into the individual dimensions that comprise them. The trainees are introduced to the functions and the effects of the facilitative interpersonal dimensions of empathic understanding, respect, and warmth; the facilitative and action-oriented dimensions of concreteness, genuineness, and self-disclosure; and the action-oriented dimensions of immediacy and confrontation. These dimensions are considered in detail in the treatment section of Volume II.

In general, in discrimination training we have found it helpful to use the following guidelines:

1. *The trainee will find that it is most effective to concentrate initially upon minimally facilitative levels of all dimensions.*

Initially it is most effective to concentrate upon level 3 communications on the five-point scales: empathic communications that are interchangeable in affect and meaning with those of the helpee; the absence of negative regard and an openness to communicating respect for the helpee; the absence of vague abstractions and an openness to discussion of personally relevant and concrete instances; the absence of negative cues of a discrepancy between what the helper says and what he appears otherwise to be experiencing; the openness to confrontation of discrepancies in the helpee's behavior; and the openness to interpretations of immediacy in the relationship.

2. *The trainee will find that it is most effective to then move to the higher and lower levels of the dimensions involved.*

In the context of an introduction to the minimally facilitative levels of each dimension it is useful to view the levels above and below level 3. Thus, below level 3 the helper's empathic responses are subtractive while above level 3 they are additive in affect and meaning to those of the helpee; below level 3 regard is negative while above level 3 it is increasingly positive and differentiating; below level 3 the helper allows all discussions to deal in vague and anonymous generalities while above level 3 he enables the helpee to develop in concrete and specific terms all instances of personal concern; below level 3 the helper is inauthentic and incongruent while above level 3 he is increasingly genuine and self-disclosing as appropriate; below level 3 the helper is closed to confrontations of helpee discrepancies while above level 3 he directly confronts the helpee with discrepancies in behavior; below level 3 the helper is closed to interpretations of immediacy while above level 3 he makes direct and explicit interpretations of immediacy.

We may say in general that *level 3 of all dimensions represents or establishes an openness or readiness to respond at the higher levels of the dimensions involved.* Only at the higher levels, however, is it possible ultimately to make a difference in the lives of the helpees. *"Minimally facilitative,"* then, *refers to the minimal level of conditions in which an effective and viable communication process of helping can take place.*

The introduction to the discrimination of the various dimensions may be accomplished in a more horizontally didactic fashion by treating every dimension individually before the trainee has had a prolonged experience in the rating of any one dimension. However, in our experience we have found it most effective to accomplish full discrimination training on each dimension before moving to the next dimension. Illustrations of the discrimination training procedures for the individual dimensions is warranted at this point.

The Discrimination of Empathy: Illustrations

We have found it most effective to begin with the dimension of empathy. Empathy is the key ingredient of helping. Its explicit communication, particularly during early phases of helping, is critical. Without an empathic understanding of the helpee's world and his difficulties as he sees them there is no basis for helping.

In focusing upon training in the discrimination of the level of communication of empathic understanding in interpersonal processes, then, we first emphasize the critical nature of this necessary ingredient. We study its functions and effects as well as its qualifications and modifications. Finally, we study those scales relevant to the assessment of the level of empathic understanding and apply them to taped material.

SCALE 1
EMPATHIC UNDERSTANDING IN INTERPERSONAL PROCESSES
A SCALE FOR MEASUREMENT[1]

Level 1

The verbal and behavioral expressions of the helper either *do not attend to* or *detract significantly from* the verbal and behavioral expressions of the helpee(s) in that they communicate significantly less of the helpee's feelings and experiences than the helpee has communicated himself.

EXAMPLE: The helper communicates no awareness of even the most obvious, expressed surface feelings of the helpee. The helper may be bored or disinterested or simply operating from a preconceived frame of reference which totally excludes that of the helpee(s).

In summary, the helper does everything but express that he is listening, understanding, or being sensitive to even the most obvious feelings of the helpee in such a way as to detract significantly from the communications of the helpee.

Level 2

While the helper responds to the expressed feelings of the helpee(s), he does so in such a way that he *subtracts noticeable affect* from the communications of the helpee.

EXAMPLE: The helper may communicate some awareness of obvious, surface feelings of the helpee, but his communications drain off a level of the affect and distort the level of meaning. The helper may communicate his own ideas of what may be going on, but these are not congruent with the expressions of the helpee.

In summary, the helper tends to respond to other than what the helpee is expressing or indicating.

Level 3

The expressions of the helper in response to the expressions of the helpee(s) are essentially *interchangeable* with those of the helpee in that they express essentially the same affect and meaning.

EXAMPLE: The helper responds with accurate understanding of the surface feelings of the helpee but may not respond to or may misinterpret the deeper feelings.

In summary, the helper is responding so as to neither subtract from nor add to the expressions of the helpee. He does not respond accurately to how that

---

[1] This scale is a revision of earlier versions of empathy scales (Carkhuff, 1968; Carkhuff & Berenson, 1967; Truax & Carkhuff, 1967).

person really feels beneath the surface feelings; but he indicates a willingness and openness to do so. Level 3 constitutes the minimal level of facilitative interpersonal functioning.

Level 4

The responses of the helper *add noticeably* to the expressions of the helpee(s) in such a way as to express feelings a level deeper than the helpee was able to express himself.

EXAMPLE: The helper communicates his understanding of the expressions of the helpee at a level deeper than they were expressed and thus enables the helpee to experience and/or express feelings he was unable to express previously.

In summary, the helper's responses add deeper feeling and meaning to the expressions of the helpee.

Level 5

The helper's responses *add significantly* to the feeling and meaning of the expressions of the helpee(s) in such a way as to accurately express feelings levels below what the helpee himself was able to express or, in the event of ongoing, deep self-exploration on the helpee's part, to be fully with him in his deepest moments.

EXAMPLE: The helper responds with accuracy to all of the helpee's deeper as well as surface feelings. He is "tuned in" on the helpee's wave length. The helper and the helpee might proceed together to explore previously unexplored areas of human existence.

In summary, the helper is responding with a full awareness of who the other person is and with a comprehensive and accurate empathic understanding of that individual's deepest feelings.

In the empathy discrimination training proper we concentrate initially upon the question of the interchangeability of the communications of helper and helpee: Is the helper expressing essentially the same affect and meaning, feeling and content that the helpee is communicating? On the five-point scale for the assessment of empathy level 3 is defined as follows: "The expressions of the helper in response to the expressions of the helpee(s) are essentially *interchangeable* with those of the helpee in that they express essentially the same affect and meaning." We have arbitrarily constituted level 3 as the minimal level of facilitative interpersonal functioning. At a minimum we are suggesting that the helper must communicate an understanding of at least as much material as the helpee has communicated in the first place. If the helper can add significant affect and meaning in that he extends the expressions of the helpee or enables the helpee to understand himself at even deeper levels, then he receives higher ratings.

The first determination, then, involves the question of interchangeability. This question can be answered by one helpee-helper exchange in that order. That is, one response by the helper to a helpee expression would conceivably be sufficient for rating purposes. Indeed, during the initial stages of communication training we employ only one exchange for rating. However, this is not to say that more exchange between helpee and helper is not helpful. Rather, one helpee-helper interaction is the minimum for making the determination of interchangeability.

If the helper's response is not interchangeable, it must be of an additive or subtractive nature. That is, it either adds noticeably or subtracts noticeably from the expressions of the helpee. Such helper expressions would seem to involve determinations more subjective than the operational interchangeability. This difficulty can best be handled by studying the effects upon the helpee. Does the helpee in fact tend to employ the helper's response effectively? Does the helpee in fact tend to explore himself meaningfully, searching out new meanings and new understanding, in response to the helper's response? If so, then we rate the helper above 3. If not, we rate him below 3. While the question of interchangeability may be answered by a helpee-helper interaction, then, the question of an additive or subtractive nature requires a minimum of a helpee-helper-helpee interaction.

If there is consensus that the helper's response adds noticeably, then, the trainee must assign the excerpt a rating above level 3. If there is consensus that the helper's response subtracts noticeably, then the trainee must assign the excerpt a rating below level 3. The questions of consensus are involved ones, however. Let us assume for the moment that our trainees are well-selected people relatively free from neurotic distortions. If, then, the helper in the excerpt continually does not communicate to the great majority of people that he understands the helpee, he will in all probability not communicate understanding to the helpee. The greater the number of excerpts sampled, the greater the probability that this will be so. In any event, over time and with continuous exposure to the helper's taped response and implied perception as well as to the perceptions of the trainer and the other trainees, each trainee will increasingly move toward some kind of group conformity in ratings. This conformity will be in large part a function of the skillful efforts of the trainer.

The key to empathy ratings is the relation of the helper's response to the helpee's expression, in terms of both the helpee's expressed affect and content. In particular, the relation of the tonal qualities as well as the verbal expressions of the helper to those of the helpee are critical. Although there has been some controversy concerning whether helper responses can be rated independently of helpee expressions, it is not a meaningful argument, with the level of warmth likely accounting for these independent empathy ratings. It is as meaningless to rate helper empathy in the absence of the helpee's expression as it is to rate helpee self-exploration in the absence of the helper's response. Neither may be related to its counterpart. Indeed, each, although apparently appropriate, when considered independently of the other may be a defensive maneuver calculated to avoid relating with the other.

Thus, if the helpee's initial expression relates to a deteriorating home situation and the attendant distressing affect, in order to achieve a level 3 rating the helper's communication must incorporate at least that much content and affect: "Right now things are just going so poorly at home that you just don't know if you can make any sense out of it any more." At higher levels the helper might not only reflect the helpee's expressions but also tap in on the feelings of depression and agitated hopelessness and extend the content of the helpee's expressions to all of his deteriorating relationships and the attendant area of self worth, enabling the helpee to explore himself at even deeper levels in the relevant areas: "It's really not just home but everything, everywhere, is falling apart and it's got you feeling pretty low, wondering about yourself." At lower levels the helper might not respond to the affect or the content, even in some cases redirecting the helpee's attention to those aspects of life, for example, his work situation, for which he should be happy and grateful ("You should be grateful for having such a fine job, though") or in more subtle ways simply subtracting affect and meaning from the helpee's expressions ("Although things aren't going well at home, there are other areas of your life that must be rewarding").

Some confounding in the rating process, then, is unavoidable. If available, the rater trainee may make his discrimination at least in part on the basis of the helpee's activities both prior to and following the helper's response. This is not to say that every empathic helper response is reflected immediately in helpee process involvement. However, on the average the utilitarian criterion of helpee response is supported by both experiential and research evidence. Indeed, if the helpee cannot understand the helper's responses, no matter how brilliant the helper's insights or "understanding," diagnostic or otherwise, we cannot say that the helper's understanding is immediately functional. If the helper does not understand the helpee well enough to communicate to the helpee in terms that the helpee can understand, then he does not understand the helpee, at least not well enough to help him.

The Discrimination of Respect: Illustrations

When the trainees have reached an adequate level of functioning in rating the empathy dimension the trainer will direct their attention to other dimensions. Criteria for satisfactory functioning on any one dimension might be set at no more than one half of a level of deviation from the standard ratings or those of the trainer-expert who has had rating experience and demonstrated the predictive validity of his assessments in treatment and training outcome studies. In addition, we would expect a very high level of rate-rerate reliability. That is, given the same excerpts one or two weeks later the trainees should emit very nearly the same levels of ratings. These criteria establish minimal group norms, and for the test trainees within the groups we might expect deviations of one third of a level or even less on the average. Even if there are time limitations on the training, if the trainees do not achieve the minimal criteria it is perhaps most meaningful to continue to concentrate upon the empathy dimension. This dimension is critical not only to the helping process but to the training process. If the trainees conquer the empathy-rating process, many of the remaining dimensions will come easily. Most of the other dimensions flow from this basic dimension. In addition, it is most important that the trainees learn this one dimension well rather than work poorly with all dimensions.

SCALE 2
THE COMMUNICATION OF RESPECT
IN INTERPERSONAL PROCESSES
A SCALE FOR MEASUREMENT[2]

Level 1

The verbal and behavioral expressions of the helper communicate a clear lack of respect (or negative regard) for the helpee(s).

EXAMPLE: The helper communicates to the helpee that the helpee's feelings and experiences are not worthy of consideration or that the helpee is not capable of acting constructively. The helper may become the sole focus of evaluation.

In summary, in many ways the helper communicates a total lack of respect for the feelings, experiences, and potentials of the helpee.

---

[2] This scale is a revision of earlier versions of respect or regard scales (Carkhuff, 1968; Carkhuff & Berenson, 1967; Truax & Carkhuff, 1967).

Level 2

The helper responds to the helpee in such a way as to communicate little respect for the feelings, experiences, and potentials of the helpee(s).

EXAMPLE: The helper may respond mechanically or passively or ignore many of the feelings of the helpee.

In summary, in many ways the helper displays a lack of respect or concern for the helpee's feelings, experiences, and potentials.

Level 3

The helper communicates the minimal acknowledgment of regard for the helpee's position and concern for the helpee's feelings, experiences, and potentials.

EXAMPLE: The helper communicates an openness to the prospect of the helpee's ability to express himself and to deal constructively with his life situation.

In summary, in many ways the helper communicates the possibility that who the helpee is and what he does may matter to the helper, at least minimally. Level 3 constitutes the minimal level of facilitative interpersonal functioning.

Level 4

The helper clearly communicates a very deep respect and concern for the helpee.

EXAMPLE: The helper's responses enable the helpee to feel free to be himself and to experience being valued as an individual.

In summary, the helper communicates a very deep caring for the feelings, experiences, and potentials of the helpee.

Level 5

The helper communicates the very deepest respect for the helpee's worth as a person and his potentials as a free individual.

EXAMPLE: The helper cares very deeply for the human potentials of the helpee and communicates a commitment to enabling the helpee to actualize this potential.

In summary, the helper does everything he can to enable the helpee to act most constructively and emerge most fully.

Following training in empathy, training in the discrimination of respect has both theoretical and experiential meaning. To be sure, the dimension of respect is often incorporated within a high-level empathy communication. However, that this is not always the case is particularly prominent in communications of the detached communications of a more diagnostic kind of empathy. Similarly, respect may be communicated to the helpee even in the absence of high levels of empathy. In this regard, although warmth often receives separate and distinct considerations, we view warmth as one of several possible vehicles for communicating respect; it is a critical vehicle that is essential under many and specifiable conditions but nevertheless only one vehicle for respect. In any event, without respect by the helper for some critical helpee characteristics helping is not possible.

With regard to discrimination it is also usually effective to begin with level 3, the minimal level of facilitative interpersonal functioning. The trainee must learn to make the discrimination whether the helper is open to the possibility that the helpee can act constructively in his own life. If this level of respect is communicated, however minimally, the rater trainee can assign a rating of 3. If the helper in a very clear and pronounced manner communicates a very deep respect for the value of the helpee and a commitment to the realization of his human potentials, then the rater trainee may assign ratings of 4 or 5, depending upon the intensity of the communication. In contrast, if there is no communication of respect but rather a lack of respect, or negative regard, for the feelings and experiences of the helpee by the helper, then the rater trainee assigns ratings of 1 or 2. The ratings depend upon whether the helper simply responds mechanically or passively (level 2) or communicates that the helpee's feelings and experiences are not worthy of consideration or that the helpee is not capable of constructive action (level 1).

Again the emphasis is upon the positive rather than the unconditional aspect of regard (which by this version of the respect scale would be best defined by level 3 in conjunction with level 3 empathy, a point to be discussed more fully in the section on treatment). Indeed, during later phases conditional regard involving differentially positive and negative reinforcements may be appropriate at the highest levels, particularly depending upon the mode of treatment employed.

The dimension of respect is not often directly communicated, in large part for lack of occasion. That is, the helper is not often heard to say, "I respect your ability to resolve your conflict." He says this implicitly by seeing the helpee in the first place. Indeed, the helper's continuous explicit expressions of respect, whether in warm tones or not, raise questions concerning his ability to communicate respect otherwise. Respect, then, is most often found in other communications, frequently those involving empathic understanding or genuineness. It deserves separate attention because sometimes even low-level empathy or genuineness in communications contain high levels of respect. For example, a genuine attempt by the helper to provide a depth of understanding to the helpee, while falling short, may nevertheless communicate high levels of respect.

When respect is communicated in relatively direct statements the expressions may be analyzed as follows: In response to the helpee's questions concerning his ability to deal with an increasingly debilitating work or school situation despite his diligent and obviously responsible work efforts, a helper functioning at low levels of respect may, for example, choose to encourage increased effort ("You'll just have to work harder"), as if he had never heard the helpee's expressions in the first place or has no confidence in the helpee's efforts, or to terminate the experience ("You'll just have to leave"), as if he had not heard both sides of the helpee's conflicts over leaving or as if he has no confidence in the helpee's ability to resolve his conflicts. At minimally facilitative levels, in turn, there is an explicit acknowledgment of the conflict and, while the helper expresses little direct positive regard, he does not communicate negative regard either ("You really don't know whether to leave or not"). Finally, at the highest levels the helper not only acknowledges the helpee's conflicts but, employing all of his resources, communicates a positive regard for the helpee's employment of all of his resources ("Although your efforts so far haven't worked, you're determined that this time, if you can get the right direction for you, you'll make it").

The Discrimination of Concreteness: Illustrations

Just as empathy at higher levels concentrates upon the helper's ability to communicate with accuracy the helper's fine discriminations of the helpee's experience, so does concreteness, during the initial phase of helping, serve a complementary role in its concentration upon the full development in specific terms of all instances of concern. Concreteness enables the helpee to discuss all personally relevant feelings and experiences in specific and concrete terms. Taking a range of forms from direct questions to reflections, concreteness is a catalyst that makes possible full exploration of relevant problem areas.

SCALE 3
PERSONALLY RELEVANT CONCRETENESS OR SPECIFICITY OF EXPRESSION IN INTERPERSONAL PROCESSES A SCALE FOR MEASUREMENT[3]

Level 1

The helper appears to lead or allow all discussions with the helpee(s) to deal only with vague and anonymous generalities.

EXAMPLE: The helper and the helpee discuss everything on strictly an abstract and highly intellectual level.

In summary, the helper makes no attempt to lead the discussion into the realm of personally relevant specific situations and feelings.

Level 2

The helper frequently appears to lead or allow even discussions of material personally relevant to the helpee(s) to be dealt with on a vague and abstract level.

EXAMPLE: The helper and the helpee may discuss "real" feelings but they do so at an abstract, intellectual level.

In summary, the helper does not elicit discussion of most personally relevant feelings and experiences in specific and concrete terms.

Level 3

The helper is open and at times facilitative of the helpee's discussion of personally relevant material in specific and concrete terminology.

EXAMPLE: The helper will help to make it possible for the discussion with the helpee(s) to center directly around most things that are personally important to the helpee(s), although there will continue to be areas not dealt with concretely and areas that the helpee does not develop fully and specifically.

In summary, the helper is open to consideration of personally relevant specific and concrete instances, but these are not always fully developed. Level 3 constitutes the minimal level of facilitative functioning.

Level 4

The helper appears frequently helpful in enabling the helpee(s) to fully develop in concrete and specific terms almost all instances of concern.

[3] This scale is a revision of earlier versions of the concreteness or specificity of expression scale (Carkhuff, 1968; Carkhuff & Berenson, 1967; Truax & Carkhuff, 1967).

EXAMPLE: The helper is able on many occasions to guide the discussion to specific feelings and experiences of personally meaningful material.

In summary, the helper is very helpful in enabling the discussion to center around specific and concrete instances of most important and personally relevant feelings and experiences.

Level 5

The helper appears always helpful in guiding the discussion so that the helpee(s) may discuss fluently, directly, and completely specific feelings and experiences.

EXAMPLE: The helper involves the helpee in discussion of specific feelings, situations, and events regardless of their emotional content.

In summary, the helper facilitates a direct expression of all personally relevant feelings and experiences in concrete and specific terms.

At minimally facilitative levels the helper demonstrates an openness to and may periodically enable the helpee to become involved in discussion of personally relevant material in specific and concrete terminology. In accordance with the operation of many other dimensions, whether or not an area is discussed fully and specifically appears more a function of the helper's interests or disposition rather than of what is most urgent or necessary for the helpee. At lower levels the helper leads or allows almost all discussion to deal with vague and anonymous generalities. While this approach may be helpful at times, particularly as an entry into troublesome material, it does not enable the helpee to come to grips with the specifics of his experience or the realities of his situation. At higher levels, in turn, the helper facilitates full, fluent, direct, and complete discussion by the helpee of specific feelings and experiences.

Thus, at relatively low levels of concreteness the helper might discuss all parental concerns on strictly an abstract or highly intellectual level: "One can't help but surmise that your current difficulties with your parents are a function of the long development of complex and heterogeneous interactions with them." At relatively high levels, in turn, the helper attempts to involve the helpee in the discussion of specific feelings, situations, and events regardless of their emotional content: "Although it's not easy for you to talk about because of strong feelings of guilt, it does seem that every time you make a move to find your own direction, your own autonomy, your mother gets sick and you get pulled back from your goal." At more intermediate or minimally facilitative levels the helper responds in a manner that is at least in part concrete and helpful: "In some way maybe you have related your mother's recurrent illnesses to your own struggles."

The Discrimination of Genuineness and Self-Disclosure: Illustrations

Empathic understanding and its often attendant dimension, warmth, are, we have seen, not the sole vehicles for communicating respect. For example, depending upon the persons and other conditions involved, helper genuineness and self-disclosure may communicate the very deepest levels of respect. In addition to constituting a necessary dimension of the experiential base, and indeed the goal of helping, one of the potentially critical contributions of genuineness is the respect that it communicates—we are most genuine with those for whom we care most. Similarly, in regard to self-disclosure we tend to make the most meaningful disclosures to those with whom we are most involved. Helper self-disclosure also offers an index of progress in helping. That is, we tend to disclose the most with those who are improving most, or, in another sense, with those who are approaching our own level of functioning. Discrimination training in empathy and respect, then, leads quite readily to a consideration of these dimensions.

SCALE 4
FACILITATIVE GENUINENESS IN INTERPERSONAL PROCESSES
A SCALE FOR MEASUREMENT[4]

Level 1

The helper's verbalizations are clearly unrelated to what he appears otherwise to be feeling at the moment, or his only genuine responses are negative in regard to the helpee(s) and appear to have a totally destructive effect upon the helpee.

EXAMPLE: The helper may appear defensive in his interaction with the helpee(s), and this defensiveness may be demonstrated in the content of his words or his voice quality. When he is defensive he does not employ his reaction as a basis for potentially valuable inquiry into the relationship.

In summary, there is evidence of a considerable discrepancy between the helper's inner experiencing and his current verbalizations, or where there is no discrepancy the helper's reactions are employed solely in a destructive fashion.

---

[4] This scale is a revision of earlier versions of genuineness and congruence scales (Carkhuff, 1968; Carkhuff & Berenson, 1967; Truax & Carkhuff, 1967).

Level 2

The helper's verbalizations are slightly unrelated to what he appears otherwise to be feeling at the moment, or when his responses are genuine they are negative in regard to the helpee and he does not appear to know how to employ his negative reactions constructively as a basis for inquiry into the relationship.

EXAMPLE: The helper may respond to the helpee(s) in a "professional" manner that has a rehearsed quality or a quality concerning the way a helper should respond in that situation.

In summary, the helper is usually responding according to his prescribed role rather than expressing what he personally feels or means. When he is genuine his responses are negative and he is unable to employ them as a basis for further inquiry.

Level 3

The helper provides no "negative" cues of a discrepancy between what he says and what he appears otherwise to be experiencing, but he provides no positive cues to indicate a really genuine response to the helpee(s).

EXAMPLE: The helper may listen and follow the helpee(s), committing nothing more of himself, but communicating an openness to further commitment.

In summary, the helper appears to make appropriate responses that do not seem insincere but that do not reflect any real involvement either. Level 3 constitutes the minimal level of facilitative interpersonal functioning.

Level 4

The helper presents some positive cues indicating a genuine response (whether positive or negative) in a nondestructive manner to the helpee(s).

EXAMPLE: The helper's expressions are congruent with his feelings, although he may be somewhat hesitant about expressing them fully.

In summary, the helper responds with many of his own feelings and there is no doubt as to whether he really means what he says. He is able to employ his responses, whatever the emotional content, as a basis for further inquiry into the relationship.

Level 5

The helper appears freely and deeply himself in a nonexploitative relationship with the helpee(s).

EXAMPLE: The helper is completely spontaneous in his interaction and open to experiences of all types, both pleasant and hurtful; and in the event of hurtful responses the helper's comments are employed constructively to open a further area of inquiry for both the helper and the helpee.

In summary, the helper is clearly being himself and employing his own genuine responses constructively.

As with the other dimensions it is most helpful to begin with level 3 of the five-point genuineness scale. At level 3 the helper provides no negative cues of a discrepancy between what he is saying and other indications of what he appears to be experiencing. Although he also provides no positive cues to indicate a really genuine response to the helpee, he may make otherwise perfectly appropriate responses, communicating an openness to responding genuinely. At the higher levels, 4 and 5, there are varying degrees of positive cues indicating a genuine response that, however, is communicated in a nondestructive manner. At the highest level in the event of hurtful responses the helper's responses are employed constructively to open a further area of inquiry for both the helper and the helpee. Analogously, at lower levels, 1 and 2, the verbalizations of the helper are unrelated to what he otherwise appears to be experiencing at the moment.

The cues are both content and voice and, if available, more visual cues are critical. For example, the defensiveness of the helper may be evident in either the content of his words or in the tone of his voice or, usually, in both. At the lowest levels the helper may respond to the helpee's questions concerning the helper's "leveling" with the helpee in a manner something like the following: "In regard to the conduct of psychotherapeutic processes, it is imperative that one make every possible effort to communicate as much veracity as is possible." At level 3, in turn, the helper may simply reflect the helpee's concern with the helper's essential honesty, giving no positive cues to his own genuine feelings other than his own understanding of the helpee's feelings: "You really want to know whether I have been completely honest with you." Finally, at higher levels there may be both acknowledgment of the helpee's feelings as well as some commitment of the helper's: "I know I hear you saying you really have to know and *now!*—but—No! I haven't shared all. You'll have to convince me that I should"; or, in a different context, "I hear the urgency of your question and am hurt by it—wondering if there is any more I have to offer—wondering, on the other hand, if you're trying to put me in that kind of position."

Helper self-disclosure, in turn, is often, although not necessarily, related to genuineness. That is, although a helper may be genuine and not self-disclosing or self-disclosing and not genuine, frequently, and particularly at the extremes, the two are related. When the helper is functioning at high levels of genuineness it is frequently quite natural for him to also disclose himself to the helpee; when the helper is functioning at low levels of genuineness he tends to disclose as little of himself as he can, often attempting to remain as ambiguous a figure as possible. The key to the self-disclosure dimension is the word "appropriate." It is most appropriate for a helper functioning at a high level to be self-disclosing with a helpee functioning at a high level and least appropriate with a helpee functioning at a low level.

SCALE 5
FACILITATIVE SELF-DISCLOSURE IN INTERPERSONAL PROCESSES A SCALE FOR MEASUREMENT[5]

Level 1

The helper appears to attempt actively to remain detached from the helpee(s) and discloses nothing about his own feelings or personality to the helpee(s). If he does disclose himself he does so in a way that is not tuned to the helpee's interests and may even retard the helpee's general progress.

EXAMPLE: The helper may attempt, whether awkwardly or skillfully, to divert the helpee's attention away from focusing upon personal questions concerning the helper, or his self-disclosures may be ego shattering for the helpee and may ultimately cause him to lose faith in the helper.

In summary, the helper actively attempts to remain ambiguous and an unknown quantity to the helpee, or if he is self-disclosing, he does so solely out of his own needs and is oblivious to the needs of the helpee.

Level 2

The helper, while not always appearing actively to avoid self-disclosures, never volunteers personal information about himself.

EXAMPLE: The helper may respond briefly to direct questions from the helpee about himself; however, he does so hesitantly and never provides more information about himself than the helpee specifically requests.

In summary, the helpee either does not ask about the personality of the helper or, if he does, the barest minimum of brief, vague, and superficial responses are offered by the helper.

[5] This scale is a revision of earlier versions of the self-disclosure scale (Carkhuff, 1968; Dickenson, 1965; Martin & Carkhuff, 1965; Truax & Carkhuff, 1967).

Level 3

The helper communicates an openness to volunteering personal information about himself that may be in keeping with the helpee's interest, but this information is often vague and indicates little about the unique character of the helper.

EXAMPLE: While the helper communicates a readiness to disclose personal information and never gives the impression that he does not wish to disclose more about himself, nevertheless, the content of his verbalizations are generally centered upon his reactions to the helpee and his ideas concerning their interaction.

In summary, the helper may introduce more abstract, personal ideas in accord with the helpee's interests, but these ideas do not stamp him as a unique person. Level 3 constitutes the minimum level of facilitative interpersonal functioning.

Level 4

The helper freely volunteers information about his personal ideas, attitudes, and experiences in accord with the helpee's interests and concerns.

EXAMPLE: The helper may discuss personal ideas in both depth and detail, and his expressions reveal him to be a unique individual.

In summary, the helper is free and spontaneous in volunteering personal information about himself and in so doing may reveal in a constructive fashion quite intimate material about his own feelings, values, and beliefs.

Level 5

The helper volunteers very intimate and often detailed material about his own personality and in keeping with the helpee's needs may express information that might be extremely embarrassing under different circumstances or if revealed to an outsider.

EXAMPLE: The helper gives the impression of holding nothing back and of disclosing his feelings and ideas fully and completely to the helpee. If some of his feelings are negative concerning the helpee, the helper employs them constructively as a basis for an open-ended inquiry.

In summary, the helper is operating in a constructive fashion at the most intimate levels of self-disclosure.

Again it is most effective to begin at level 3 where the helper communicates an openness to volunteering a minimal degree of personal information about himself. Although the helper may introduce more personal ideas in accordance with the helpee's interests and needs, these ideas do not stamp the helper as a unique person. At higher levels, in turn, the helper volunteers very intimate and detailed information about his personal ideas, attitudes, and experience in keeping with the helpee's interests and needs. At lower levels the helper may actively avoid self-disclosure in attempts to remain detached from the helpee.

Thus, at level 3 in response to a helpee's exploration of interpersonal difficulties the helper may acknowledge similar experiences in vague formulations: "I, too, at one point in my life, experienced similar difficulties." At higher levels the helper may respond more personally, not only acknowledging the commonality of experience but also the differences that make each unique: "Hey, I think I know some of this from personal experience only I think that you're a lot more introverted than I was—it's a degree of turning inward that I really don't fully understand yet. Can you help me?" On the other hand, at lower levels the helper might actively avoid all self-disclosures with a continuous stream of innocuous "professional" responses such as, "Tell me more about this," or reflections and interpretations that increase distance when a personal sharing might diminish it.

The Discrimination of Confrontation: Illustrations

Confrontation emphasizes the helper's experience of discrepancies in the helpee's behavior, independent insofar as it can be of the relationship with the helper. Thus, following a helpee's verbal or behavioral expression or series of such expressions if the helper communicates verbally to the helpee his experience of a discrepancy in the helpee's communications and/or behavior that the helper has experienced, a helper-initiated confrontation is said to have occurred.

SCALE 6
CONFRONTATION IN INTERPERSONAL PROCESSES
A SCALE FOR MEASUREMENT[6]

Level 1

The verbal and behavioral expressions of the helper disregard the discrepancies in the helpee's behavior (ideal versus real self, insight versus action, helper versus helpee's experiences).

[6] This scale is a revision of earlier versions of the confrontation scales (Anderson, Douds, & Carkhuff, 1967; Berenson & Mitchell, 1969; Carkhuff & Berenson, 1967).

EXAMPLE: The helper may simply ignore all helpee discrepancies by passively accepting them.

In summary, the helper simply disregards all of those discrepancies in the helpee's behavior that might be fruitful areas for consideration.

Level 2

The verbal and behavioral expressions of the helper disregard the discrepancies in the helpee's behavior.

EXAMPLE: The helper, although not explicitly accepting these discrepancies, may simply remain silent concerning most of them.

In summary, the helper disregards the discrepancies in the helpee's behavior and, thus, potentially important areas of inquiry.

Level 3

The verbal and behavioral expressions of the helper, while open to discrepancies in the helpee's behavior, do not relate directly and specifically to these discrepancies.

EXAMPLE: The helper may simply raise questions without pointing up the diverging directions of the possible answers.

In summary, while the helper does not disregard discrepancies in the helpee's behavior, he does not point up the directions of the discrepancies. Level 3 constitutes the minimum level of facilitative interpersonal functioning.

Level 4

The verbal and behavioral expressions of the helper attend directly and specifically to the discrepancies in the helpee's behavior.

EXAMPLE: The helper confronts the helpee directly and explicitly with discrepancies in the helpee's behavior.

In summary, the helper specifically addresses himself to discrepancies in the helpee's behavior.

Level 5

The verbal and behavioral expressions of the helper are keenly and continually attuned to the discrepancies in the helpee's behavior.

EXAMPLE: The helper confronts the helpee with helpee discrepancies in a sensitive and perceptive manner whenever they appear.

In summary, the helper does not neglect any potentially fruitful inquiry into the discrepancies in the helpee's behavior.

Confrontations fall into three main, broad categories, all based in the helper's experience of the helpee: (1) confrontation of a discrepancy between the helpee's expression of what he wishes to be and how he actually experiences himself (his ideal versus his real self); (2) confrontation of a discrepancy between the helpee's verbal expression of his awareness of himself (insight) and his observable or reported behavior; (3) confrontation of a discrepancy between how the helper reportedly experiences the helpee and the helpee's expression of his own experience of himself. At level 3, then, while the helper's expressions are open to the discrepancy in the helpee's behavior they do not relate directly and specifically to such while at higher levels they do. At lower levels the helper disregards the discrepancies in the helpee's behavior.

Thus, at the lowest levels of confrontation the helper may miss or avoid acknowledging his recognition of obvious discrepancies in the helpee's behavior. For example, in response to a listless, underachieving student the helper may simply reflect the student's verbally expressed goals in a passively receptive manner: "You want only to strive for higher and higher goals." At more intermediate levels the helper may acknowledge the helpee's expression while opening up the possibility for viewing behavioral discrepancies without giving them direction: "You say you want to achieve higher goals yet you have questions." At still higher levels the helper confronts the helpee directly and explicitly: "You say you want to succeed at higher levels yet you've been unable to get up enough energy to succeed at your present level."

In addition to the scoring of levels of confrontation, other relevant determinations may be made. Decisions can be made concerning whether or not the helper's verbal expression was directed toward the helpee's resources or limitations. If during helping, the helpee is presenting himself to the helper primarily in terms of his resources (/limitations), ignoring, minimizing, or apparently unaware of his limitations (/resources), and if the helper at this time verbally points out to the helpee a discrepancy between (1) how the helper experiences the helpee's feelings about himself or how the helper himself experiences the helpee and (2) what the helper is verbally or behaviorally expressing about himself, then the confrontation is categorized as being directed toward the helpee's limitations (/resources). In addition, discriminations may be made concerning whether the confrontations are experiential or didactic, that is, whether they are oriented toward the helpee's experiential understanding or whether they are oriented more toward teaching.

The Discrimination of Immediacy of Relationship: Illustrations

In a very real sense immediacy bridges the gap between empathy, which is responsive to the helpee's experience, and confrontation, which is initiated out of the helper's experience of the helpee. Immediacy of relationship makes possible a translation in the immediate present of the helper's insights into the helpee's expressions. The helper in responding immediately to his experience of the relationship with the helpee not only allows the helpee to have the intense experience of two persons in interaction but also provides a model of a person who understands and acts upon his experience of both his own impact upon the other and the other's impact upon him. Immediacy is probably one of the most critical variables in terms of communicating a depth of understanding of the complex interaction between the parties to a relationship. Very often the expressions of the helpee, whether direct or indirect, reflect his feelings and attitudes toward the helper in the present moment. Depending upon how sensitive the helper is to these expressions, whether or not he chooses to respond to them is critical to the helpee's feeling of really having his experience translated to action or interaction in the immediate context of helping. That is, the helper acts upon what he sees going on between himself and the helpee.

SCALE 7
IMMEDIACY OF RELATIONSHIP IN INTERPERSONAL PROCESSES
A SCALE FOR MEASUREMENT[7]

Level 1

The verbal and behavioral expressions of the helper disregard the content and affect of the helpee's expressions that have the potential for relating to the helper.

EXAMPLE: The helper may simply ignore all helpee communications, whether direct or indirect, that deal with the helper-helpee relationship.

In summary, the helper simply disregards all helpee messages that are related to the helper.

Level 2

The verbal and behavioral expressions of the helper disregard most of the helpee expressions that have the potential for relating to the helper.

---

[7] This scale is a revision of earlier versions of immediate relationship scales (Berenson & Mitchell, 1969; Carkhuff & Berenson, 1967; Leitner & Berenson, 1967).

EXAMPLE: Even if the helpee is talking about helping personnel in general, the helper may remain silent or simply not relate the content to himself.

In summary, the helper appears to choose to disregard most helpee messages that are related to the helper.

Level 3

The verbal and behavioral expressions of the helper, while open to interpretations of immediacy, do not relate what the helpee is saying to what is going on between the helper and the helpee in the immediate moment.

EXAMPLE: The helper may make literal responses or reflections to the helpee's expressions or otherwise open-ended responses that refer to no one specifically but that might refer to the helper.

In summary, while the helper does not extend the helpee's expressions to immediacy, he is not closed to such interpretations. Level 3 constitutes the minimum level of facilitative interpersonal functioning.

Level 4

The verbal and behavioral expressions of the helper appear cautiously to relate the helpee's expressions directly to the helper-helpee relationship.

EXAMPLE: The helper attempts to relate the helpee's responses to himself but he does so in a tentative manner.

In summary, the helper relates the helpee's responses to himself in an open yet cautious manner.

Level 5

The verbal and behavioral expressions of the helper relate the helpee's expressions directly to the helper-helpee relationship.

EXAMPLE: The helper in a direct and explicit manner relates the helpee's expressions to himself.

In summary, the helper is not hesitant in making explicit interpretations of the helper-helpee relationship.

At level 3 the helper makes no attempt either to go beyond or to relate what the helpee is saying to what is going on between the helper and the helpee in the immediate moment. He may make literal responses to the helpee's expressions or otherwise open-ended responses that might refer to anyone, including the helper. At higher levels the helper refers, either directly or indirectly, to the immediate relationship between the helper and the helpee, and at lower levels the helper ignores the helpee's references to their relationship, however direct or indirect.

Thus, in response to a direct reference by the helpee to her difficulty in relating to her physician the helper at the lowest levels might completely ignore the potential reference to himself by either remaining silent or by responding as if he had not heard that part of the helpee's expressions ("Perhaps we can proceed to more important material"). The helper shy of level 3 might make an appropriate reflection that does not, however, refer directly to the helper unless the helpee wishes to do so ("There are lots of aspects of relating to your physician that are just not easy experiences for you"). At level 3 the helper, however tentatively and cautiously, may attempt to relate the helpee's response to himself ("Perhaps it is difficult for you to relate to a helper in lots of different situations"), and at still higher levels the helper is much more specific in relating the helpee's expressions to the immediate relationship between the helper and the helpee ("What you're trying to tell me is how difficult it is for you to relate to me—here—now").

Immediacy of relationship may be interpreted with emphasis upon the immediacy or the action. We have concentrated primarily upon the dimension of immediacy. However, in relation to action, aside from the implementation of complementary techniques or preferred modes of treatment, the immediacy interpretations by the helper are, along with confrontation, among the most action-oriented indexes presently available to assess the helper's translation of his experience to active, assertive responses in the moment.

In summary, the dimensions reviewed are by no means exhaustive or all inclusive. There are other dimensions such as the "significant other" scale which emphasizes the discussion of the significant figures in the helpee's life, including in particular the helper as well as parents, boss, and spouse (Berenson & Mitchell, 1969). However, the significant contributions of this scale appear at their highest levels to be related to the immediacy dimension, where both helper and helpee are talking about what is going on between them. In addition, there are other dimensions in various stages of being made operational: intensity (Truax & Carkhuff, 1967); openness and flexibility (Piaget, 1968); confidence, intensity, and spontaneity (Barnard, 1968); and commitment (Berenson & Carkhuff, 1969).

The dimensions reviewed here have been made operational to a degree. In this regard it is noteworthy that the dimensions may be employed, and indeed have been employed, in a different manner. For example, much of the research on confrontation has been accomplished by frequency tabulations (Berenson & Mitchell, 1969) and, to be sure, the criterion of rigor calls for movement in the direction of such finite and precise categories of measurement for all dimensions (many of the complex problems involved here will be examined in detail in Volume II). However, for our purposes it has been of heuristic value theoretically to maintain some commonality and cohesiveness in the present scaling method.

In summary, the dimensions involved are those for which we have the most empirical evidence concerning the outcomes of helping processes. In addition, and perhaps most important, they are dimensions that make the most intuitive sense to us as helpers. By no means do they account for the totality of the human experience. In some respects they may account for a very limited amount. They represent only what we in this science-art of helping are able to account for at the present time. They represent what is knowable as we prepare to enter that area in which so much is—and will in all probability remain—unknown, the area of human relations.

REFERENCES

For a more detailed discussion of the issues considered in this chapter see the asterisked readings and the references upon which the readings are based.

Anderson, S., Douds, J., & Carkhuff, R. R. The effects of confrontation by high and low functioning therapists. Unpublished research, University of Massachusetts, Amherst, Mass., 1967.

Anthony, W., & Carkhuff, R. R. The effects of rehabilitation counselor training upon discrimination, communication and helping attitudes. *Journal of Counseling Psychology*, in press, 1969.

Barnard, W. M. Counselor spontaneity, confidence and intensity. In R. R. Carkhuff (ed.), *The counselor's contribution to facilitative processes.* Mimeographed manuscript, State University of New York at Buffalo, 1968.

Berenson, B. G., & Carkhuff, R. R. The nature, structure and functional commitment. *Journal of Rehabilitation*, in press, 1969.

Berenson, B. G., Carkhuff, R. R., Friel, T., & Leitner, L. Systematic training in written communication and discrimination in large groups. Unpublished research, State University of New York at Buffalo, 1968.

Berenson, B. G., & Mitchell, K. *Confrontation in counseling and life.* Mimeographed manuscript, American International College, 1969.

Burstein, J., & Carkhuff, R. R. Objective, client and therapist ratings of therapist-offered facilitative conditions of moderate to low functioning therapists. *Journal of Clinical Psychology*, in press, 1969.

*Carkhuff, R. R. *The counselor's contribution to facilitative processes.* Mimeographed manuscript, State University of New York at Buffalo, 1968.

*Carkhuff, R. R., & Berenson, B. G. *Beyond counseling and therapy.* New York: Holt, Rinehart and Winston, Inc., 1967.

Carkhuff, R. R., & Bierman, R. The effects of human relations training upon child psychiatric patients in treatment. *Journal of Counseling Psychology,* in press, 1969.

Carkhuff, R. R., Collingwood, T., & Renz, L. The prediction of the effects of didactic training in discrimination. *Journal of Clinical Psychology,* in press, 1969.

Carkhuff, R. R., Friel, T., & Kratochvil, D. The differential effects of training in responsive and initiative dimensions. *Counselor Education and Supervision,* in press, 1969.

Carkhuff, R. R., Kratochvil, D., & Friel, T. The effects of professional training: The communication and discrimination of facilitative conditions. *Journal of Counseling Psychology,* 1968, **15,** 68–74.

Dickenson, W. Therapist-disclosure as a variable in psychotherapeutic process and outcome. Unpublished doctoral dissertation, University of Kentucky, 1965.

Leitner, L., & Berenson, B. G. Immediate relationship scale. Mimeographed scale, State University of New York at Buffalo, 1967.

Martin, J. C., & Carkhuff, R. R. Facilitative self-disclosure in interpersonal processes. Mimeographed scale, University of Massachusetts, Amherst, Mass., 1965.

Piaget, G. Openness and flexibility. In R. R. Carkhuff (ed.), *The counselor's contribution to facilitative processes.* Mimeographed manuscript, State University of New York at Buffalo, 1968.

*Truax, C. B., & Carkhuff, R. R. *Toward effective counseling and psychotherapy.* Chicago: Aldine Publishing Company, 1967.

12

COMMUNICATION TRAINING

While insufficient in and of itself to effect significant changes in communication with most populations, discrimination training, whether it precedes or follows communication training, may act to increase understanding and to stabilize changes in communication. Again high levels of discrimination are a necessary but not sufficient condition of high levels of communication. High levels of communication constitute the essential goals of training.

Just as gains in the trainee's level of discrimination are dependent upon both the trainer and the trainee, the trainee's gains in communication are a function of the interaction between the levels of functioning of both the trainer and the trainee. The level of trainee communication, then, is dependent upon both the trainer and the trainee's initial level of discrimination and communication. These statements may be summarized briefly in propositional form.

Proposition I. The gains or losses in the trainee's level of communication are dependent in part upon the trainer's initial level of communication.

The trainer who communicates at high levels also discriminates at high levels and thus exerts the greatest over-all effect upon the trainee's level of communication. All of the sources of learning are integrated in the trainer who is communicating at a high level. The evidence is consistent, indicating that trainees of high-level–communicating trainers improve while those of low-level communicators demonstrate negative change in communication (Berenson, Carkhuff, & Myrus, 1966; Burstein & Carkhuff, 1969; Carkhuff, 1969; Carkhuff & Banks, 1969; Carkhuff & Bierman,

1969; Carkhuff, Collingwood, & Renz, 1969; Carkhuff & Griffin, 1969a, 1969b; Carkhuff, Friel, & Kratochvil, 1969; Carkhuff, Kratochvil, & Friel, 1968; Carkhuff & Truax, 1965; Kratochvil, 1969; Martin & Carkhuff, 1968; Pierce, Carkhuff, & Berenson, 1967; Pierce & Drasgow, 1969; Vitalo, 1969). Although the trainees of at least one program in which trainers were functioning at low levels of communication demonstrated positive change (Anthony & Carkhuff, 1969), the trainers were initially functioning above the trainees' still lower levels and discriminating at relatively high levels.

Proposition II. The gains or losses in the trainee's level of communication are dependent in part upon the trainer's initial level of discrimination.

Insofar as the trainer's discrimination level may be high while his communication level is low, this factor may nevertheless not only reinforce improved trainee communication but also enable the trainee to go on to function at higher levels of communication than the trainers. Here one study (Anthony & Carkhuff, 1969) is particularly relevant. Trainees who were communicating at extremely low levels demonstrated significant improvement in their communicative skills over the course of training with trainers who were functioning at (1) high levels of discrimination and (2) levels of communication that, while low, were higher than the initial levels of the trainees.

Proposition III. The gains or losses in the trainee's level of communication are dependent in part upon the trainee's initial level of communication.

The trainer's level of functioning operates in interaction with the trainee's level of functioning, particularly the trainee's initial level of communication. In training programs in which time is limited those trainees functioning at relatively high levels of communication demonstrate the highest level of final functioning, and where the differential between the levels of the trainer and the trainee are greatest relatively high-level trainees gain the most from trainers functioning at high levels, while relatively low-level trainees gain the least. Those trainees functioning at the highest levels of communication stand to lose the most over time if they do not terminate (Carkhuff, Kratochvil, & Friel, 1968; Holder, 1968), while those trainees functioning at the lowest levels lose the least in interaction with trainers communicating at low levels. The evidence both within and between groups points in general toward these effects (Berenson, Carkhuff, & Myrus, 1966; Carkhuff, 1969; Carkhuff & Bierman, 1969; Carkhuff & Berenson, 1967; Carkhuff, Collingwood, & Renz, 1969; Carkhuff, Friel, & Kratochvil, 1969; Carkhuff, Kratochvil, & Friel, 1968; Kratochvil, 1969; Martin & Carkhuff, 1968; Pierce *et al.*, 1967; Pierce & Drasgow, 1969).

Proposition IV. The gains or losses in the trainee's level of communication are dependent in part upon the trainee's initial level of discrimination.

The evidence to support this proposition is sparse. Although some of the studies suggest that trainees improve in discrimination over the course of training (Anthony & Carkhuff, 1969; Carkhuff, Collingwood, & Renz, 1968; Carkhuff, Friel & Kratochvil, 1969; Carkhuff, Kratochvil, & Friel, 1968), there is little evidence to indicate a predictive relationship between pretraining discrimination indexes and posttraining communication indexes. For many trainees there appears to be some kind of block between discriminating and communicating, so that, although high-level communication is related to high-level discrimination, the latter is not sufficient for high levels of communication. Some form of therapeutically beneficial experience or behavioristic shaping process may be a necessary intervening experience. In this regard it is appropriate at this point to make explicit the context within which lasting communicative changes have the highest probability of occurring.

THE CONTEXT OF TRAINING

In general, traditional professional programs tend to focus exclusively upon one or another mode of treatment, usually to the exclusion of other modes. Too, they tend to focus upon one or another source of learning to the exclusion of all others. In contrast, training programs that integrate all sources of learning and that focus in a systematic way upon primary, core conditions around which secondary dimensions or potentially preferred modes of treatment might be built (Carkhuff & Berenson, 1967; Truax & Carkhuff, 1967) have been found to be most effective.

The Experiential Base

The experiential base within which the program takes place is a crucial dimension. With high-level–functioning trainers high levels of communication enable the trainee to experience warm and sensitive as well as directionful and forceful communications, that is, the facilitative and action-oriented dimensions. In this context the trainee has the experience of having his own communications understood in depth with a fineness of discrimination that extends his communications and allows him to understand himself at even deeper levels. A sound experiential base also enables the trainee to experiment with different modes of functioning in the hope of finding those that in interaction with particular situations are most appropriate and functional for him.

However, other than perhaps initially, we are not suggesting an unconditional experiential base for training any more than we are for treatment. Ultimately the trainee can trust only that he will receive sensitive perceptions of practitioners functioning at high levels. These perceptions may reinforce the trainee's activities in a positive way or they may be negatively reinforcing. They will be honest and full. Similarly, we are not suggesting that the trainer focus exclusively and systematically upon the communication process. There are times when this approach is appropriate and times when it is not. Indeed, it is our experience that the individuals who make the finest discriminations know the value of their sensitivities and see no need to emphasize them in their communications. The trainees also know. Those who have contributions to make, make them. Within the helping professions those who do not have contributions to make hide the fact in communications that are usually exclusively and often inappropriately warm or more often in communications that are intended to be warm or, less frequently, in overly-reactive and negatively confronting assertions. Because of the inability of some individuals to make the necessary fine discriminations, usually all of these kinds of communications are independent of the needs of the persons with whom they are trying to communicate.

The Didactic Experience

In addition to providing a real, sensitive, and appropriately lifelike experiential base, with its punishments as well as its rewards, the high-level trainer has the responsibility for teaching the trainee in a structured and didactic fashion the components of his fine discriminations and communications, both inter- and intrapersonal. To be sure, as a "more knowing" trainer he is obliged to share with his students in as forceful a manner as he experiences them all of the constructs that he has developed as a function of his experience in helping and life. The effective helper, like the effective parent, teaches the products of his own experience while providing the experiential base within which the trainee can come to appreciate his own experience and, indeed, respond or react to the teachings of the trainer in an interactional process in which both parties are involved in a mutual search for more effective learnings. The helping field has existed for too long with the artificial dichotomy of didactic *or* experiential learning.

The Effects of Modeling

Finally, *the trainer is the key ingredient insofar as he offers a model of a person who is living effectively.* Without such a person there is no program. The trainer must be a person who is not only congruent and genuine but also one who has worked out an effective yet open-ended, working cosmology. He must not only be sensitive but must also be able to act on his fine discriminations. He translates his deep respect for constructive forces in his nourishment of them and also in his commitment to the destruction of destructive forces, both within and without individuals. In summary, without a person who in his dedication to his own integration at the highest levels can provide an integrated learning experience that draws upon all significant sources of learning the following discussion of communication training is meaningless.

INDIVIDUAL COMMUNICATIONS: PHASE 1 OF COMMUNICATION TRAINING

Just as we have dissected the communication process in moving from gross to individual discriminations, we now move from individual to gross communications in an attempt to reintegrate the communication process. Initially in communication training, then, the focus is upon communicating one dimension or the other. This may be done in three stages, the first involving responding to taped material, the second involving role-playing, and the third involving a helpee contact. Successful completion of the first two stages makes possible a viable communication process with a person in need of help, a person who cannot under any circumstances be used for the experimental purposes of the earlier stages.

Taped illustrations of helpee explorations of meaningful experiences may be employed as stimulus material. The trainees listen to this material as a group, and following the excerpt one trainee may be called upon to make an empathic response. Following this response, and in a manner similar to that used with discrimination training, the other trainees, including the trainee himself, rate the response, thus providing a basis for a shaping process based upon the immediate feedback. Following successful training with tape recorded material the program moves to role-playing and ultimately to helping experiences with real helpees.

In the early stages of communication training the trainee focuses upon the dimension empathy, the most critical of all helping process variables, the one from which all other dimensions flow in the helping process.

The Communication of Empathy: Guidelines for Formulation

Several guidelines are helpful in the formulation of empathic responses, particularly during the early stages of training. Again, whether we speak of depth reflections or sensitive interpretations, *the ultimate purpose of the empathic response is to communicate to the helpee a depth of understanding of him and his predicament in such a manner that he can expand and clarify his own self-understanding as well as his understanding of others.* The guidelines are as follows.

1. *The helper will find that he is most effective in communicating an empathic understanding when he concentrates with intensity upon the helpee's expressions, both verbal and nonverbal.*

The helper's intense concentration upon the helpee's verbal, postural, facial, and gestural expressions enables the helper to employ all possible cues to understanding the helpee's frame of reference. The key requirement for the helper here is a high energy level, made possible only by healthy and honest living, for such an existence leaves the helper free enough to listen and to hear another person. The helper's intense concentration minimizes the possibility of premature judgments and their resulting errors.

2. *The helper will find that initially he is most effective in communicating empathic understanding when he concentrates upon responses that are interchangeable with those of the helpee.*

Particularly during the early stages of communication training, as well as during the early stages of helping, it is critical that the helper insure for himself that he is attuned to the affect and meaning of the helpee's expressed experiences. The trainee does so by concentrating on formulating interchangeable, level 3 responses in an extension of the manner in which he learned to rate these responses. The ability to achieve interchangeable communication provides an accurate base from which to formulate higher-level empathic responses at a later point.

3. *The helper will find that he is most effective in communicating empathic understanding when he formulates his responses in language that is most attuned to the helpee.*

Since the purpose of empathic responses is, after all, to communicate to the helpee in a manner that the helpee is best able to employ for his own purposes, then the helper's language must reflect his ability to assume the helpee's frame of reference. This is not to say that the helpee's frame of reference is a healthy one. Rather, during the initial phases particularly, it is critical that a basis of communication be established in which the helpee has the experience of being understood.

4. *The helper will find that he is most effective in communicating empathic understanding when he responds in a feeling tone similar to that communicated by the helpee.*

Communication in a feeling tone analogous to that of the helpee provides the helpee with the experiential base of empathic understanding. The helpee becomes aware that the helper is tuning in on his wave length not only with an intellectual comprehension but also with an experiential understanding. At points the helper may even express more depression or anger or elation than the helpee in his restricted presentation has been able to express. In this manner the helper enables the helpee to experience and express feelings he was not before able to experience and express.

5. *The helper will find that he is most effective in communicating empathic understanding when he is most responsive.*

Particularly at the beginning of training as well as helping the helper will find that an increase in his verbal responsiveness will not only provide a model for an increasingly active helpee but will also serve to increase the probability of accuracy in communicated formulations. This does not mean, of course, that there is no place for relative inactivity or extended periods of silence when they are appropriate. However, the more frequently the helper responds to the helpee, the less likely he is to deviate from the way the helpee experiences the world or the more likely he is to be aware that he is deviating significantly from the helpee's phenomenology. In addition, the more frequent the responses on the part of the helper, the more likely the helpee is to take an active part in his own helping process.

6. *The helper will find that he is most effective in communicating empathic understanding when, having established an interchangeable base of communication, he moves tentatively toward expanding and clarifying the helpee's experiences at higher levels.*

The very limitations that lead the helpee to seek help necessitate that the helper ultimately go beyond the helpee in extending the intensity of the helpee's affect and the meaning of the helpee's content. The helper will find that tentative formulations are initially most effective in this regard, although this by no means negates the possibility of confrontations and immediacy interpretations of helpee resistance to such movement.

7. *The helper will find that he is most effective in communicating empathic understanding when he concentrates upon what is not being expressed by the helpee.*

The effective helper, both behaviorally and in his construct development, frequently finds himself concentrating upon what is not being said rather than upon what is being said. The helper may do this, for example, with a helpee who presents an issue from an exclusively feminine or exclusively masculine frame of reference. In each instance the other side of the experience must be developed in order to piece together a complete picture of the helpee. *The deepest level of empathy, then, involves filling in what is missing rather than simply dealing with what is present.*

8. *The helper will find that he is most effective in communicating empathic understanding when he employs the helpee's behavior as the best guideline to assesss the effectiveness of his responses.*

Ultimately the helper functions to benefit the helpee. If the helpee is unable to make constructive use of the helper's formulations, no matter how brilliant the formulations might otherwise appear, then the helping process has not been effective. However, if the helper initially lays a good communication base and then moves to higher-level empathic responses, he will find that the helpee also shifts to deeper levels within areas and to other significant areas of concern. Finally, he may find the helpee intensely and accurately attuned to the helper's own verbal and nonverbal expressions.

The Communication of Respect: Guidelines for Formulation

The communication of respect by a variety of means may accomplish its essential purposes: (1) to establish a relationship based upon trust and confidence in which the helpee can explore relevant concerns; (2) to establish a basis on which the helpee can come to respect himself in areas relevant to his effective functioning; (3) to establish a modality through which the helpee can with appropriate discriminations come to respect others in areas relevant to his own functioning. The guidelines for the communication of respect are as follows.

1. *The helper will find that initially he is most effective in communicating respect when he suspends all critical judgments concerning the helpee.*

In the absence of any other basis for respect it is initially most effective to be open to the helpee and his experiences. Thus, an initial kind of unconditionality, defined by an active encouragement of expression and an absence of negative regard, is perhaps the most effective vehicle for the communication of respect. The helpee knows at least that the helper will hear him out before he makes critical judgments.

2. *The helper will find that initially he is most effective in communicating respect when he communicates to the helpee in at least minimally warm and modulated tones.*

In the absence of any basis for warm feelings it is initially most effective for the helper to communicate in modulated tones at least the potential for warmth. However, just as warmth is only one of many vehicles for the communication of respect, depending upon the background and the circumstances of the helpee it may become readily apparent early in helping that the communication of warmth is inappropriate for the particular helpee involved.

3. *The helper will find that he is most effective in communicating respect when he concentrates upon understanding the helpee.*

There is no more direct communication of respect than that communicated in the intense attention and the commitment to understand the helpee, whether or not such understanding is accomplished. However, the ability to understand the helpee accurately is the richest source of understanding the variety of means for communicating respect to a particular helpee.

4. *The helper will find that he is most effective in communicating respect when he concentrates upon providing the helpee with an opportunity to make himself known in ways that might elicit positive regard from the helper.*

There is initially no basis for the helper's communication of positive regard to the helpee other than a disposition toward encouraging the helpee's self-expression specifically or possibly some general disposition toward humanity in general, which is questionable at best. However, with exposure to the helpee the possibility of the experience and, thus, the communication of a positive caring for the helpee emerges.

5. *The helper will find that he is most effective in communicating respect when he communicates in a genuine and spontaneous manner.*

The highest level of respect is communicated in a genuine and spontaneous sharing with another human being. There is initially no basis for such a relationship, and thus an unconditional stance is most effective. Upon the development of the intimate experience of helping, the helper may come to share his full range of feelings concerning the helpee, the positive as well as, ultimately, the very conditional regard that makes the helpee's emergence and actualization possible.

The Communication of Concreteness: Guidelines for Formulation

Initially at least concreteness or specificity of expression serves a function that is often complementary to empathy, enabling the helpee both within helping and ultimately outside of helping to deal specifically with all areas of personally relevant concern, a necessary precondition for effective problem resolution. During later phases of helping the focus is upon the specificity of problem resolution. The guidelines for the communication of concreteness are as follows.

1. *The helper will find that he is most effective in developing concrete and specific communications when he makes concrete his own reflections and interpretations.*

Thus, even in response to vague and abstract helpee communications the helper may attempt to formulate his reflections and interpretations with more specificity. In this manner not only does he sharpen the helpee's experiences but he also reduces the possibility of any kind of emotional remoteness from the helpee's current feelings and experiences. In addition, in this manner he encourages the helpee to formulate his own expressions with more concreteness and specificity.

2. *The helper will find that he is most effective in developing concrete and specific communications when he emphasizes the personal relevance of the helpee's communications.*

The helper must exercise enough control over the helping process to limit the helpee's discussion to personally relevant concerns. In this regard the frequent "storytelling" role that the helpee assumes and in which he gives the specifics of many irrelevancies must be regarded not only as an abuse of the necessary concreteness of helping but also as an abuse of the helper's valuable time.

3. *The helper will find that he is most effective in developing concrete and specific communications when he asks for specific details and specific instances.*

There is a very real place for the basic interrogatives of who, what, why, when, where, and how in regard to specific feelings, experiences, and events in helping. However, such questions should serve the function of entry and follow-through in an area only when the helpee cannot himself implement entry and follow-through in that area. In no way should questions and probing dominate helping because of the stimulus-response contingencies that it develops: one effective question should pave the way for the follow-up by numerous reflections and interpretations.

4. *The helper will find that he is most effective in developing concrete and specific communications when he relies upon his own experience as a guideline for determining whether concreteness is appropriate or not.*

Concreteness is particularly critical during the early stages of problem exploration in order to ascertain specifically and accurately the problems involved. Concreteness is again critical during the later stages of problem resolution and implementation when the helpee must once again return to the realities of his everyday environment. Between these stages abstract discussions of material not readily available to the helpee's conscious processes may be not only appropriate but most effective. The helper must rely upon the fine discriminations of his own experience in determining the applicability of such material.

The Communication of Genuineness and Self-Disclosure: Guidelines for Formulation

Genuineness provides both the goal of helping and the necessary contextual base within which helping takes place. Man's search in helping and in life is a search for authenticity, both intrapersonal and interpersonal. The dimension of self-disclosure is one facet of genuineness and serves a more complementary role in this regard, with its impact under some conditions more significant than under others. The guidelines for the communication of this dimension, while difficult to summarize, are as follows.

1. *The helper will find that he is most effective in communicating genuineness when he attempts to minimize the effects of his role, professional or otherwise.*

With full recognition that assumption of the helping role is guided by helpee benefits, when the helper minimizes the role façade and the concomitant role expectations he maximizes the possibility of involvement on the part of both the helper and the helpee. A real and integrated helper, courageous in the face of the unknown, offers the greatest hope for the development of a real and integrated helpee.

2. *The helper will find that he is most effective initially when he communicates no inauthentic responses while he demonstrates an openness to authentic ones.*

While there may be no basis initially for truly genuine responsiveness, at the same time the helper avoids inauthenticity and communicates an openness for the possibility of a rich and genuine sharing.

3. *The helper will find that he is most effective in communicating genuineness when he increasingly attempts to be as open and free within the helping relationship as is possible.*

While helping is not dedicated to the benefit of the helper and, thus, helper openness and freedom are not always possible or appropriate, the communication of the potential for these dimensions is critical. Indeed, over the course of successful helping the movement will be from technique to person, from the delimited freedom and rigid boundaries that bring the helpee to seek help to a growing and spontaneous openness and increasing degrees of freedom.

4. *The helper will find that he is most effective in communicating genuineness when he can share experiences with the helpee as fully as possible.*

Spontaneous sharing on the part of both parties is the essence of a genuine relationship. Here helper self-disclosure of personally relevant material may be important when appropriate; however, the moment-to-moment sharing of ongoing experiences is even more critical to the communication of genuineness.

5. *The helper will find that he is most effective in communicating genuineness when he can learn to make open-ended inquiries into the most difficult areas of his experience.*

The helper must learn to make open-ended inquiries into his experiences with the helpee that give him the most difficulty. Whether he experiences feelings of hostility or feelings of heightened conditionality, the helper must be able to inquire concerning the sources of these experiences, whether they are himself, the helpee, or both persons in interaction with each other.

6. *The helper will find that he is most effective in communicating genuineness when he relies upon his experience in the relationship as the best guideline.*

Whereas in empathy formulations the helper relies primarily upon his experience of the helpee, in the communication of genuineness he relies and acts primarily upon his experience of himself. Just as the helper's feelings for another person are based in his own experience, so also may his feelings for himself be in part a function of his experience of the other person in the relationship. Nevertheless, despite the apparent elusiveness of this entity, the focus is upon the helper's experiencing of himself in the moment.

The Communication of Confrontation: Guidelines for Formulation

The helpee plays a lot of tricks on himself as well as on others. He has smokescreens for everything that really matters to him. In order to enable him to confront himself and others effectively when appropriate, the helper must confront the helpee for the following discrepancies in the helpee's behavior: discrepancies between the helpee's expression of who or what he wishes to be and how he actually experiences himself; discrepancies between the helpee's verbal expression of his awareness of himself and his observable or reported behavior; discrepancies between how the helper experiences the helpee and the helpee's expression of his own experience. The following guidelines may be employed in formulating confrontation responses.

1. *The helper will find that he is most effective in confronting the helpee when he concentrates upon the helpee's expressions, both verbal and nonverbal.*

As in communicating empathy the helper must concentrate upon the helpee's verbal, postural, facial, and gestural expressions. Confrontation, however, serves not so much to communicate an understanding of the helpee's frame of reference as to provide the helpee with the experience of an external and, hopefully, a sensitive and accurate party. In this context the deepest level of empathy will tell the helper that the helpee wants not so much to be reinforced by a communicated understanding of his expressed phenomenological existence as he wants to be enabled to break free of its confusing and suffocating processes.

2. *The helper will find that he is most effective in confronting the helpee when he concentrates initially upon raising questions concerning discrepant communications from the helpee.*

During the initial stages of both training and helping it is most effective to concentrate upon raising questions rather than pointing up discrepancies in the helpee's behavior. For example, without any further comprehension of the dynamics involved the helper may phrase his experiences in a manner that says, "On the one hand you say this, while on the other hand you say that."

3. *The helper will find that he is most effective in confronting the helpee when he focuses with increasing specificity upon discrepancies in the helpee's behavior.*

Having raised questions concerning discrepancies in the helpee's behavior, the helper will find it most effective to focus with increasing specificity upon the implications of these discrepancies. The increasing specificity will lead to the development of an understanding of the distortions in the helpee's assumptive world and, hopefully, to a reconstruction of that world.

4. *The helper will find that he is most effective in confronting the helpee when he relies upon his experience of the helpee in the relationship as the best guideline.*

The helper must ultimately rely most heavily upon his experience of the helpee, particularly in contrast to the helpee's own view of his experience. This approach becomes most critical following confrontation, when the helpee will often engage in defensive maneuvers, including at times helpee-initiated confrontations in which the helpee pits his pathology against the helper's health. *Helping can be accomplished only on the terms of the healthier person in the relationship.*

The Interpretation of Immediacy: Guidelines for Formulation

With regard to interpretations of the immediacy of the relationship, the key question is, "What is the helpee really trying to tell me that he cannot tell me directly?" Obviously, the interpretations of such communications are critical to a helping process unconfounded by double messages, as well as to the helpee's ultimate ability to understand what is going on in his immediate relationships. The guidelines for communication of immediacy are as follows.

1. *The helper will find that he is most effective in interpreting immediacy when he concentrates upon his own personal experience in the immediate moment.*

The helper must employ his own immediate experiences, both positive as well as negative, as a basis for understanding attitudes that the helpee is directing toward him in the moment. For example, when the helpee says angrily, "So I have the insight; I still don't change," the helper must be able periodically to employ his own experience to understand the helpee's subverbal messages, emanating from the helpee's pathology and frustration, which are saying, "Even you aren't good enough to help me." Until the helper can do so the helpee cannot free himself of his sense of distortion, dependency, and alienation and achieve mature responsibility, freedom, and direction.

2. *The helper will find that he is most effective in interpreting immediacy if he disregards for the moment the content of the helpee's expressions.*

There are many moments in helping when the content of the helpee's expressions are misleading. The helper must learn to ignore the verbal content of the helpee's expressions and search for the subverbal messages. Usually when the helpee cannot express himself directly it is not so much a function of his inability to express himself as it is of the attitudes he holds about the helper in relation to himself.

3. *The helper will find that he is most effective in interpreting immediacy if he employs the frustrating, directionless moments of helping to search the question of immediacy.*

The meandering moments of helping are potentially rich sources for the understanding of immediacy if the helper can rise momentarily above his frustration to become an observer of the proceedings. If the helper has been concentrating intensely throughout helping, he may find, for example, that the directionless moments are just that—moments in which the helpee is trying to throw the helper off the track, or perhaps moments in which the helpee is simply seeking a rest period but does not know if it is appropriate from the helper's frame of reference or how to ask for it if it is appropriate.

4. *The helper will find that he is most effective in interpreting immediacy if he periodically sits back and searches the questions of immediacy.*

Since almost all helpee messages to the helper can be interpreted with immediacy, it is helpful periodically, whether helping is progressing positively or not, to sit back and ask questions concerning what is really going on. To be sure, there are other critical concerns, however, and therefore it is not always most appropriate and effective to make these interpretations. Again, the fineness of the helper's experience will dictate whether such interpretations would derail a meaningful experience or put it back on the track.

Thus, the helping process moves over time and with crises from an initial focus upon the helpee's experience to an increasing emphasis upon the helper's experience. The helper provides a model for a person who is living effectively, demonstrating first his ability to respond to another person and second his ability to respond to himself and to initiate actions accordingly. He knows full well that if the helpee is not equipped to both respond and initiate at least minimally facilitative levels he will encounter further difficulties in his life. *He knows that if there is any hope helping, as life, must ultimately be on the terms of the healthier party in the relationship.*

REFERENCES

For a more detailed discussion of the issues considered in this chapter see the asterisked readings and the references upon which the readings are based.

Anthony, W., & Carkhuff, R. R. The effects of rehabilitation counselor training upon discrimination, communication and helping attitudes. *Journal of Counseling Psychology*, in press, 1969.

Berenson, B. G., Carkhuff, R. R., & Myrus, P. The interpersonal functioning and training of college students. *Journal of Counseling Psychology*, 1966, 13, 441–446.

Burstein, J., & Carkhuff, R. R. Objective, client and therapist ratings of therapist-offered facilitative conditions of moderate to low functioning therapists. *Journal of Clinical Psychology*, in press, 1969.

Carkhuff, R. R. The prediction of the effects of teacher-counselor training: The development of communication and discrimination indexes. *Counselor Education and Supervision*, in press, 1969.

Carkhuff, R. R., & Banks, G. The effects of a human relations workshop for Negro parents and white teachers. Unpublished research, American International College, Springfield, Mass., 1969.

*Carkhuff, R. R., & Berenson, B. G. *Beyond counseling and therapy.* New York: Holt, Rinehart and Winston, Inc., 1967.

*Carkhuff, R. R., & Bierman, R. The effects of human relations training upon child psychiatric patients in treatment. *Journal of Counseling Psychology*, in press, 1969.

Carkhuff, R. R., Collingwood, T., & Renz, L. The prediction of the effects of didactic training in discrimination. *Journal of Clinical Psychology*, in press, 1969.

Carkhuff, R. R., Friel, T., & Kratochvil, D. The differential effects of training in responsive and initiative dimensions. *Counselor Education and Supervision*, in press, 1969.

Carkhuff, R. R., & Griffin, A. The effects of training in interpersonal skills in project "Head Start." Unpublished research, American International College, Springfield, Mass., 1969. (a)

Carkhuff, R. R., & Griffin, A. The effects of training in interpersonal skills in a Concentrated Employment Program. Unpublished research, American International College, Springfield, Mass., 1969. (b)

Carkhuff, R. R., Kratochvil, D., & Friel, T. The effects of professional training:

The communication and discrimination of facilitative conditions. *Journal of Counseling Psychology*, 1968, **15**, 68–74.

Carkhuff, R. R., & Truax, C. B. Training in counseling and psychotherapy: An evaluation of an integrated didactic and experiential approach. *Journal of Consulting Psychology*, 1965, **29**, 333–336.

Holder, B. T. A follow-up study of the activity-passivity and facilitative–non-facilitative dimensions of continuing and terminated graduate students. Unpublished research, State University of New York at Buffalo, 1968.

Kratochvil, D. Changes in values and interpersonal functioning of nurses in training. *Counselor Education and Supervision*, in press, 1969.

Martin, J., & Carkhuff, R. R. The effects of training upon changes in trainee personality and behavior. *Journal of Clinical Psychology*, 1968, **24**, 109–110.

Pierce, R., Carkhuff, R. R., & Berenson, B. G. The differential effects of high and low functioning counselors upon counselors-in-training. *Journal of Clinical Psychology*, 1967, **23**, 212–215.

Pierce, R., & Drasgow, J. The effects of human relations training upon V.A. neuropsychiatric patients. *Journal of Counseling Psychology*, in press, 1969.

*Truax, C. B., & Carkhuff, R. R. *Toward effective counseling and psychotherapy*. Chicago: Aldine Publishing Company, 1967.

Vitalo, R. The effects of training in interpersonal skills upon psychiatric inpatients. Unpublished research, V.A. Hospital, Buffalo, New York, and Buffalo State Hospital, 1969.

13
INITIAL HELPING INTERACTIONS

Perhaps the key means for developing effective communication in helping is role-playing. If there is one central ingredient to the training experience it is that the trainee will be involved over and over again in these training experiences. The implementation of the helping role provides the working and work-oriented structure within which the training process takes place. Both during the initial stages of communication training in attempting to make operational the individual dimensions and during the latter stages in attempting to put the process back together in more natural and global communications, we turn to role-playing. Role-playing enables us to involve the trainee in lifelike experiences (Carkhuff & Berenson, 1967; Truax & Carkhuff, 1967; Truax, Carkhuff, & Douds, 1964). In role-playing the trainee has an opportunity to interact with another person in an effective manner, perhaps for the first time. *The role-playing experience is as effective as the helper is.*

Role-playing enables the trainee to experience being the person in need of help as well as the helper. Of necessity the material of an ongoing, interactional communication process cannot focus exclusively upon one dimension or the other. Thus, the trainee must put the communication process back together again if he is to be an effective helper. In addition to offering continuing rating feedback, the role-playing experience has the benefit of making available the helpee's assessment of his experience of the helper-offered dimensions, although the degree of distortion in these assessments is in large part a function of how effectively the assessor is himself functioning. The same holds true for working with a person in need of help as that opportunity arises upon satisfactory completion of the role-playing experience.

Some simple guidelines may serve the helper trainee in his role-playing and finally in his helping experiences. We have seen that the helping process involves two principal phases: (1) the downward or inward phase in which a relationship is established and the helpee explores his areas of concern and (2) the phase of emergent directionality in which an attempt is made to search out and implement courses of action. We also noted earlier that the facilitative dimensions are most critical during the first phase and the action-oriented dimensions during the second, although each group of dimensions complements the other throughout both phases of helping. In general, however, there is movement from facilitative to action-oriented dimensions as well as movement within each of these categories. This subject will be explored further in the treatment section of Volume II. For now, the guidelines may be summarized as follows.

1. *In general, the helper will find that he is most effective during the initial stage of the first phase of helping if he focuses upon level 3 of the facilitative dimensions.*

The helper will usually find that initially he will be most effective if he communicates the following levels of facilitative dimensions: (1) empathic responses that are interchangeable in affect and meaning with those of the helpee; (2) a kind of open unconditionality and warmth that is appropriate during early phases; (3) a concreteness that is at least minimally facilitative of problem exploration; (4) a level of genuineness that connotes no incongruence or inauthenticity, although perhaps no spontaneous genuineness either. Concerning the duration of offering these conditions, the helper may be guided by the helpee's experience of having fully described the problems that brought him to seek help: the initial stage of phase 1 lasts as long as the helpee requires to present fully his problem area.

2. *In general, the helper will find that he is most effective in an intermediate stage of the first phase of helping when he attempts to move to higher levels of the facilitative conditions and to introduce the action-oriented dimensions at level 3.*

Following the helpee's presentation of his problem the helping process begins to shift to the helper's terms as he extends the helpee's presentation in determining further areas of exploration. Thus, the helper attempts to emphasize higher-level empathic responses that extend and clarify the helpee's expressions as well as a positive regard that relates appropriately to the helpee's characteristics. Except for the probings to gain entry into higher levels of exploration, however, concreteness may be less critical as the helping process comes to focus on material that is less readily available to the helpee's conscious processes. At the same time, the movement of genuineness to slightly higher levels (perhaps somewhere between levels 3 and 4) provides a bridge for introducing some of the more assertively action-oriented dimensions of self-disclosure, immediacy, and confrontation at level 3.

3. *In general, the helper will find that he is most effective during the initial stages of the second phase of helping when he is focusing upon the highest levels of action-oriented dimensions.*

Authentic and spontaneously shared interactions are the critical ingredients in preparing the helpee to act upon his difficulties. Thus, the helper focuses upon (1) a free, deep, and full expression of feelings and disclosures in a nonexploitative relationship; (2) direct and explicit confrontation of the discrepancies in the helpee's behavior; and (3) direct and explicit immediacy interpretations of the behavior of the helpee directed toward the helpee. Of course, dimensions such as empathy continue to be operative. Entry into a problem area often necessitates a follow-through at high levels of empathy. In addition, while positive regard for healthy helpee characteristics is very much in evidence, a more conditional type of helper attitude may be introduced at this point—that is, behavior that is conditional upon the helpee's improved functioning in areas where it is critical to his existence.

4. *In general, the helper will find that he is most effective during final stages of the second phase of helping when he focuses upon more cognitive kinds of problem-solving activities and considerations of concrete directionality.*

Finally, following all else we must return to the reasons the helpee entered helping or, more broadly, the reasons for which helping takes place. In an attempt to find solutions to the helpee's difficulties we must ultimately return the helpee to an environment, either the one he began with or another. Thus, we must consider alternative courses of action and the advantages and disadvantages of each. Although all conditions have their place at this final stage, the dimension of concreteness in the consideration and finally the implementation of the courses of action is perhaps most critical here. In this context a variety of potential preferred modes of treatment may be considered and implemented at this point.

Of course, the helping process may not flow directly as described here. It must be modified by the experience of both the helper and the helpee, and the helper must, accordingly, be sensitively attuned to each. However, the stages and phases do provide rough outlines for the highly complex processes of helping and human relations, outlines that many effective practitioners have found to be experientially validated.

It must be emphasized that different dimensions are of different significance at different stages of helping. Empathy, hopefully beginning at level 3, moves toward higher and higher levels throughout the helping process until during the final phases it may become implicit. Respect proceeds from an initial kind of unconditionality through to both positive and finally perhaps even conditional regard. Concreteness is most critical during the initial and the final stages of helping, first acting to complement the helpee's expressions and later to develop directionality. Genuineness and self-disclosure move toward higher levels throughout the helping process, with the important qualification that while authenticity is a desirable goal for the helpee, the helping process is not simply a forum for the spontaneous emissions of the helper. In turn, having established a facilitative relationship, the dimensions of immediacy and confrontation provide a direct translation of the helper's experience of the helpee into action-oriented considerations within the helping relationship. Finally comes the introduction of the more cognitive, problem-solving activities, including, in particular, the consideration and implementation of a variety of potential preferred modes of treatment. Let us consider for a moment in brief illustrative form the effects of the effective or ineffective implementation of such helping programs.

THE EFFECTS OF HELPING: ILLUSTRATIONS

The following examples are extensions of the material upon which the helpee stimulus expressions were based. These excerpts are role-played. The helper offers differential levels of conditions unknown to the helpee. The first involves a relatively distressed and depressed helpee exploring problems in social-interpersonal functioning. The helper, in turn, attempts to offer fairly high levels of both facilitative and action-oriented dimensions.

HIGH FACILITATIVE AND HIGH ACTION-ORIENTED CONDITIONS IN HELPING: AN ILLUSTRATION

HELPEE: Um, I don't know whether, whether I'm right or wrong in feeling the way I do, but, uh, I find myself withdrawing from people. I don't care to go out and socialize and play their stupid little games any more. Um, I get very anxious and come home depressed and have headaches—it seems all so superficial. There was a time when I used to get along with everybody; everybody said, "Oh, isn't she wonderful! She gets along with everybody; she's so nice and everybody likes her," and I used to think that was . . . that was something to be really proud of, but, uh, but, I think that only told how I, or who I was at that time, that I had no depth. I was sort of whatever the crowd wanted me to be, or the particular group I was with at the time. Um, I know it's important for my husband's business that we go out and socialize and meet people and make a good impression and join clubs and play all those stupid little games— Elks, and, you know, bowling banquets, and, uh, fishing trips and fraternity-type gatherings. Um, I . . . I just don't . . . I just don't care to do it any more, and, um, I don't know if that means that I'm a . . . that there's something wrong with me psychologically, or, uh, or is this normal. I mean . . . uh . . . people don't really know who I am and they really don't care who one another, who the other person is. They . . . it's all at such a superficial level.

HELPER: You're darn sure of how you feel, but you really don't know what it all adds up to. Is it you? Is it the other people? What are the implications of your husband's business? You? Where is it all going?

HELPEE: Uh, huh. It's an empty life. It's, um, there's, uh, no depth to it at all. I mean, you just talk about very, very superficial things, and the first few times, it's O.K. But then after that, there's nothing to talk about. So you drink and you pretend to be happy over silly jokes and silly things that people do when they all, uh, are trying to impress one another, and they're very materialistic, and, uh, it's just not the route I want to go.

HELPER: So your feelings are so strong now that you just can't fake it any more.

HELPEE: That's right, so what do you do? People say, "Oh, there's something wrong with you," then, "You need to see a psychiatrist or something," because you . . . you know the thing in society is that the normal person gets along with people, and, uh, can adjust to any situation. And when you . . . when you're a little discriminating, maybe very discriminating or critical, then that means there's something wrong with you.

HELPER: While you know how strongly you feel about all these things, you're not sure you can really act in terms of them and be free.

HELPEE: I don't know if I'm strong enough. The implications are great. It may mean, uh, a break up of the marriage, uh, and it means going it alone, and that's too frightening. I don't think I have the courage. But I do feel like I'm in sort of a trap.

HELPER: You know you can't pretend, yet you're really fearful of going it alone.

HELPEE: Yes, there's nobody I can really talk to, I mean, you know, it's one thing if you have a . . . like your husband . . . if you can share these things, if he can understand it at some level, but . . . um . . . he can't.

HELPER: It's like, "If I act on how I really feel, though, it frightens the people who mean most to me. They won't understand it, and I sure can't share that with them."

HELPEE: (*Pause*) So what do you do. (*Pause*) I mean . . . I . . . you know, I find myself going out and telling the people who I really feel about, about different topics and getting into controversial issues, and, uh, and that's, that's too anxiety provoking for me. I can't, because then you get into arguments and I don't want to do that either, that leads nowhere. I just get frustrated and anxious and upset and angry with myself for getting myself into the situation.

HELPER: You know that doesn't set you free, you know. . . .

HELPEE: No, it bottles me up.

HELPER: That only causes you more problems, and what you're really asking about is, how you can move toward greater freedom and greater fulfillment in your own life.

HELPEE: I . . . I think I know who I am now, independent of other people, and, uh, which most people aren't and . . . um . . . there's no room for that kind of person in this society.

HELPER: There's no room for *me* out there!

HELPEE: (*Pause*) So what do I do?

HELPER: We run over and over the questions that . . . you end up with. "Where do I go from here? How do I act on this? I know how I feel, but I don't know what'll happen if I act on how I feel."

HELPEE: I . . . have an idea of what'll happen.

HELPER: And it's not good!

HELPEE: No! It means almost starting a whole new life.

HELPER: And you don't know if you can make it.

HELPEE: Right, I know what I've got here, and if I don't make it all the way with the other, then I'm in trouble.

HELPER: While you don't know what'll happen if you act on your feelings, you know what the alternatives are if you don't. And they're not good either. They're worse.

HELPEE: I . . . I don't have much choice.

The helper tunes in quickly on the helpee's wave length and employs his facilitative communications as a lever to make deeper inquiries.

Never losing communicative contact with the client, he begins to employ open-ended, moderately action-oriented conditions to begin to consider the implications of the various alternatives available to the helpee. The helpee, in turn, moves smoothly and quickly to deeper explorations and consideration of courses of action. Even in this brief example an effective helping process has taken place.

In the following example a fairly depressed helpee explores some educational and vocational considerations. The helper, while offering relatively high levels of empathy and warmth (approximately level 3), does not direct the helpee toward more action-oriented considerations.

MINIMALLY FACILITATIVE AND LOW ACTION-ORIENTED CONDITIONS IN HELPING: AN ILLUSTRATION

HELPEE: Uh . . . uh . . . I enjoy being a mother. I love the children and my husband and I like doing most household things . . . uh . . . they get boring at times, but . . . uh . . . over-all, I think it's a very rewarding thing, but I don't miss working, going to the office every day. Um . . . I know most women complain about being just a housewife and just a mother, but . . . um . . . then again, I wonder if there is more for me. Others say there has to be, and then I really don't know. If a . . . ah . . . if there is . . . um . . . what do you do when the children grow up? Do you start . . . then do you start a new life for yourself? You can't continue to live for children when they're grown—or do you have to start now? Everyone goes to school and takes courses now, and they go to college so when the kids grow up 20 years from now they'll have a profession. But I just don't have the ambition to do it right now . . . um . . . but I do wonder what will happen. I can't live through my husband . . . uh . . . I enjoy his work and I get some rewards from it, but uh, I can't live just through him. I have an identity of my own. Um, what will I be, who will I be when the children are grown and they're gone? I'll still be a young women . . . 40 isn't very old . . . 40 or 50 . . . 45 . . . uh, where do I go?

HELPER: So, while you find a lot of meaning in being a housewife, you have to raise a lot of questions for yourself about where you are going.

HELPEE: Uh . . . yeah . . . but I don't think of it that much. I truly enjoy the here and now and what I'm doing but . . . uh . . . almost everybody that I'm associated with or talk with . . . uh . . . always worries about this, and so there's a part of me that worries about it. Um, do you have to worry about it more? Is it something that . . . that you have to start worrying about the future 10 or 15 years before it happens? Is this normal?

HELPER: Part of a lot of the pressures that you feel do come from other people.

HELPEE: Right! I know what I'd like to do. I know the things I'm best at doing, but they're not the things that society looks upon as the most meaningful or the best in their hierarchy. It isn't the thing that is looked upon as being the best thing to do . . . um, more of a menial-type job. It isn't like teaching or going out and being a social worker, going on for a master's or a Ph.D. I don't have that ambition.

HELPER: So you know something about who you are, but you have a growing feeling about whether your feelings about who you are are complete.

HELPEE: All right . . . but I . . . I don't know. Are they ever complete? This is looking to the future, something that's going to happen in the future. I have some ideas of the direction I'd like to go but I don't think you can know now what you're going to be 10 years from now, or 15 years from now, but I know . . . but I do know that my life's not going to be empty. I mean, that's, that's not my concern.

HELPER: So, while you ask the question about what's going to happen in the future, you, even though you don't know the answer, you kind of feel sure that you'll be able to handle it as it comes.

HELPEE: Right, I'm confident of that. But . . . um . . . but I don't know . . . Is it something? . . . I quit college . . . I really don't, I don't feel like going back, yet there's a part of me that feels guilty for not finishing. Uh . . . uh . . . society sort of puts this pressure on you . . . uh . . . that . . . uh . . . the best things come through a degree, and . . . uh . . . doing a professional job, instead of a secretarial or, or maybe something working with your hands . . . things like this that I enjoy doing. Um . . . uh . . . I find these things rewarding as opposed to going and listening to a lot of lecturers talk on things that aren't important to me.

HELPER: You feel the pressures, but they don't really come from the inside of you, they come from outside.

HELPEE: Right, and why should I be worried about that? Uh, I think I've outgrown that to a great degree . . . uh . . . there was a time when I felt very inferior, that I had to have a degree. This is to compete with everybody else, because everybody I know had a degree, and they automatically ask you, "Where did you get your degree?" and I feel sort of like, you know, it's like saying I'm a high school drop-out to say that I didn't finish college, and I get annoyed feeling that way.

HELPER: The real pressures do come from other people.

HELPEE: But why should I be worried about what other people think?

The helper communicates at a minimally facilitative level, essentially a level that is minimally respectful and interchangeable in affect and meaning with that of the helpee, yet is perhaps not as specific in his reflections as might otherwise be desirable. In spite of the helper's lack of orientation toward some directionality (at least in this brief excerpt), nevertheless, the helpee is able to explore herself at meaningful levels. However, these explorations do not approach culmination in directionality as in the interaction with the highly facilitative, action-oriented helper.

In the next example a relatively distressed mother explores child-rearing problems. The helper, although offering low levels of facilitative dimensions, is directionful and very highly action-oriented.

LOW FACILITATIVE AND HIGH ACTION-ORIENTED CONDITIONS IN HELPING: AN ILLUSTRATION

HELPEE: (*Sigh*) Sometimes I . . . uh . . . I question my . . . uh . . . adequacy at raising three boys. Um . . . um . . . especially with the baby . . . well, I call him a baby. He'll be four . . . uh . . . he's the last, I can't have any more, so . . . uh . . . I know I've . . . uh . . . kept him a baby longer than the others, and . . . uh . . . he won't let anyone else do anything for him. If . . . if someone else opens the door, he says, "I want Mommy to do it," and you have to close the door and then I have to open it, and, and I encourage this . . . I do it . . . and . . . um . . . I don't know if this is right or wrong. Um . . . he insists on sleeping with, with me at night . . . um . . . and I allow it . . . um . . . he says when he grows up he won't do it any more, but . . . um . . . right now he's, he's still my baby and I don't discourage this much. I, I don't know if this comes out of my needs . . . uh . . . or if I'm making too much out of this situation. Is it going to handicap him going to school . . . uh . . . breaking away from Mamma? Uh, is it going to be a traumatic experience for him? I don't know. Is this something I'm creating? Uh, I do worry more about my children than do most mothers. I, uh, I'm a little more watchful and I worry about things that can happen to them. I don't just let them run like most mothers do, just turn their kids out and don't worry about them till it's dinnertime or time to come in. I just can't seem to do that. I don't know if this is healthy on my part, or is it unhealthy . . . uh . . . uh . . . I really don't know. But . . . um . . . I don't have much to go on. I didn't have any brothers or sisters, or . . . uh . . . really parents that I can copy for models, and I don't know what is right or wrong. I know how I feel and how upset I get if . . . uh . . . if they go off . . . um . . . hither and yon, or so, where I can't see them or can't find them. I worry about them going to the creek and drowning or kids putting ropes around each other's necks in the woods and things like this. I don't know. Do I concentrate on that too much or . . . uh . . . is this normal?

HELPER: So, while baby certainly needs mother, there is some real question about whether mother needs baby in some, perhaps not so healthy, ways.

HELPEE: Well, I . . . uh . . . I have to admit I enjoy his being my baby. He's very affectionate . . . the other children are, too, but I find myself giving more to him and giving in to him, making the other children give in to him . . . um . . . he's much more demonstrative . . . uh . . . over a longer period of . . . well, he'll be four. Well, the others got a lot of love, but not for as long a period because there was always another child behind them . . . and, um, he's just a lingering, lingering baby.

HELPER: One thing you do know is that if you continue to rear this child as you have thus far, that, uh, that certainly is going to have deleterious effects on his behavior as an adult, but this is not the appropriate . . . this is not the healthy way to rear children.

HELPEE: Well, I don't know that . . . that's my question. Uh, I don't really feel that . . . that it's to the point where it's . . . I don't feel I'm neurotic or overprotective to that point where it's an unhealthy situation, but I'm sort of wondering, you know, like he'll be going to nursery school next year for 2 days a week. I think this is good for him, and . . . uh . . . to get away and see how he will react, but . . . uh . . . I really don't know if this, if it's unhealthy or not.

HELPER: But you do know that if you continue to defer to all his wishes . . . uh . . . you do know that if you continue to reinforce him for the requests he's making . . . opening the door, climbing in bed, all of these, these requests, you do know if you continue to do these things that, uh, the child will not be an independent, autonomous-functioning individual in society.

HELPEE: Uh, I don't, I don't, I don't really . . . Is this true? Is this what happens?

HELPER: Well, isn't this what you're concerned about?

HELPEE: Um, this is what I'm concerned about, but I'm not really sure that this is what happens. Uh, yeah, maybe I'm raving, maybe he is a little spoiled brat, but, uh . . .

HELPER: Doesn't one follow from the other?

HELPEE: Uh, not necessarily.

HELPER: I'm not sure what you mean, "not necessarily."

HELPEE: You're telling me this is what happens. Uh, I've read a lot of books, they tell you, "Do this. . . ."

HELPER: I don't think I'm telling you, I think I'm reflecting your doubts and concerns and extending them to what will, in fact, happen to your child.

HELPEE: But I don't feel as if I know how to end this, or how to . . . how to stop it . . . I mean . . . um . . . then I'd have to do a complete about face and . . . uh . . .

HELPER: O.K. Maybe the beginning point is with you, then, maybe what we're talking about here is the necessity for some form of longer-term psychotherapeutic treatment for you, and . . . uh . . . to prepare you for negatively reinforcing these kinds of behaviors on your child's part. Prepare you for not being so needy with your child, not needing to have your child around in a dependent way. These are . . . uh . . . your constructs . . . are based on a base with many, many flaws.

HELPEE: But isn't all child-rearing . . . I don't know if there's no . . . there's no . . . no perfect way of raising children. Uh, there's no set rules, and . . . uh . . . they're all individuals and unique and you sort of have to do what you feel.

HELPER: Perhaps not, but I think there are some universal errors in the assumptive world of the parent that we can be helpful with, and we can facilitate the parent's development so he can, in turn, facilitate the child's development.

HELPEE: Uh, but I don't think . . . I don't think he's that dependent upon me, where, where . . . um . . . you know, he doesn't hang on me every minute. It's when he's in the house, and we give in to him because he's the youngest.

HELPER: You don't think it or you don't want to think it. I think this is the question.

It becomes clear very early in helping that the helper has some very definite directionality, perhaps a directionality that is independent of the helpee, that is, an action direction that he had before entering helping, one that has been influenced very little by the expressions of the helpee. The helper, then, neither perceives nor communicates high levels of understanding of the helpee. The helpee, in turn, is derailed from her meaningful explorations and becomes, appropriately so, resistant to some of the helper's direction and argumentative with his rigidity in pursuing the direction.

In the final example a helpee depressed about prolonged sexual-marital problems discusses this problem with a helper who offers neither facilitative nor action-oriented dimensions at high levels.

LOW FACILITATIVE AND LOW ACTION-ORIENTED CONDITIONS IN HELPING: AN ILLUSTRATION

HELPER: Perhaps you can tell me a little bit about what brought you here today.

HELPEE: Well . . . um . . . it's not an easy thing to talk about. I guess the heart of the problem . . . I guess you'd call it a sexual problem. Um . . . I never thought I'd, I'd have this sort of a problem, but . . . uh . . . I find myself . . . um . . . not getting the fulfillment out of it that . . . uh . . . that I used to, and it's not as enjoyable. Uh, I don't think it is for my husband, either . . . uh . . . although we don't discuss it, but . . . um . . . uh . . . I . . . uh . . . used to enjoy and look forward to . . . uh . . . making love . . . uh . . . and I always got fulfillment and . . . uh . . . always had, had an orgasm, but I don't any more. I can't remember the last time that I've been satisfied, and . . . uh . . . I find myself being attracted to other men and wondering what it would be like to go to bed with them, and . . . um . . . uh . . . uh . . . I don't know, I don't know what this means, if this means, if this is symptomatic of something wrong with our whole relationship, our whole marriage, or . . . um . . . is this something wrong with me, or us, or what . . . um . . . uh . . . uh . . . I . . . um . . . uh . . . I don't like going to bed any more . . . um . . . it used to be . . . um . . . uh . . . it used to be the core of our marriage, but we keep finding excuses now for not making love . . . um . . . and we can't seem to talk about it . . . uh. . . . Is it, is this something that happens to most marriages? . . . or, uh, I always thought you'd look forward to better sexual relations as you got . . . were married longer and got older, but, uh, they've deteriorated.

HELPER: I see, you do have a sex problem.

HELPEE: Well, uh, that's the symptom, but is that symptomatic of something more? Um, it isn't something we always had. It's one thing if you get married and start off with a sexual problem . . . you never get in tune with it, but, uh, but this, this isn't so, uh, I think we always had a healthy attitude toward sex, and . . . um . . . making love, and . . . um . . . but it, and it was always, it was always very enjoyable and a very important part of our lives, but . . . um . . . but it doesn't seem to have the meaning to it that it had, and we don't get the fulfillment out of it that we used to get, but . . . um . . . isn't that symptomatic of something, uh, of something wrong with the whole marriage? Oh, how can you explain it?

HELPER: Perhaps you can figure that out.

HELPEE: Uh, but I can't, uh, um, I can't and I, uh, can't talk about it with my husband, and this is why I thought maybe you could help me figure out, uh, what could be wrong, or could it be me? Is there something, something wrong with me, that, uh, uh, that's causing this?

HELPER: Let me say that my role here will be to help you figure this out, but it will be your role to figure how to work on this.

HELPEE: But that, but that leaves me back where I started, um, I find that

I just can't explain it. I need somebody to, to help me explore this, to try to figure out why. I, I think I'm, I mean, I think I love my husband, and it isn't that I don't love him, um, I think he's a wonderful man but . . . uh . . . I do find myself more and more attracted to other men and . . . uh . . . uh . . . and daydreaming what it would be like to have an affair, and, uh, with many of those men, and, uh. . . . What could cause that, I mean, why?

HELPER: Well, maybe you could tell me a little bit more about that.

HELPEE: But . . . but I can't, and I don't know, and it's very upsetting because, because I feel very strongly that, uh, a satisfactory sexual life is very important to a marriage. I don't believe in platonic relationships and all this companionship thing without sex. Uh, it's very important to me, and, um, uh, uh. . . .

HELPER: What makes you feel that a marriage without sex is bad?

HELPEE: Well, because that's a basic, a basic . . . uh . . . thing in life and in human beings, and . . . uh . . . I found it a very, a wonderful feeling to have an orgasm. Maybe if I never had one, maybe if I had never felt fulfilled in a sexual relationship I wouldn't know what I was missing, but I had it and now it's missing, and uh, my life doesn't seem as complete, and, I want to find it again.

HELPER: Sort of a long search for recapturing the orgastic experience.

HELPEE: Oh, but I think it's more than that, uh, it, it's not just that . . . I mean, to have the relationship that I had with my husband . . . it has changed; we were much closer and, uh, and it was a wonderful experience all the way around. Um, uh, and it's sort of dividing us.

Perhaps most destructive of all is the passive-rejecting "helper" who in his very passivity communicates high levels of hostility. Offering neither understanding nor direction, he has absolutely nothing to give the helpee in an area where the helpee, no doubt with all her difficulties, is functioning at a higher level than the helper.

Perhaps the most significant learnings from these excerpts involves the potentially extreme effects of human relations. On the one hand, even the briefest interaction can make significant differences in the life of the helpee. On the other hand, some helping processes could continue in perpetuity and offer nothing but deterioration. The key again is putting the facilitative and action-oriented conditions together. The helper must have the potential for each group of dimensions as it becomes appropriate; the absence of either is handicapping. Although the offering of minimal facilitative conditions may, depending upon the level of helpee functioning, be relatively effective in providing the context within which fairly integrated persons can grow to function at even higher levels, it nevertheless is not maximally efficient and may place serious limitations upon the helpee's development. If the direction of the highly action-oriented but low facilitative helper does not happen to match up directly with the helpee's needs (and the chances of this are close to random), then about the only potential contribution the helper has to offer involves the possibility of the helpee's reacting to his direction. The low facilitative and low action-oriented helper is most destructive. Even in his more subtle forms it is as if he takes a grain of food away each day until the person living with him ultimately dies of starvation.

In this connection the same relatively high-level–functioning person (not a student or professor), without knowing the intentions of the same role-playing helper, was a standard client in each instance. Her response following the first interview (high facilitative-high active) was as follows: "What's so special about that? That's the way people should be able to relate in life." In response to the high facilitative-low active helper she said simply, "I didn't feel the therapist was any different this time but, without putting my finger on it, he didn't make me work as hard and I'm not sure I really got any place." To the interaction with the low facilitative-high active helper she responded, "He really didn't understand me and seemed only concerned with himself." Finally, in response to the low facilitative-low active helper she asked simply, "Are there really therapists like that?"

THE CONSTRUCTIVE CHANGE OF THE TRAINEE

All of this learning is valueless if it is not incorporated and integrated in the helper as a way of life. This is not to say that a person must go around offering high levels of conditions to everyone or, worse yet, involving them in long-term treatment programs. Quite the contrary, *it is an abuse of the helper's resources to offer high conditions to persons who cannot employ the experience constructively, whatever their motives.* Indeed, in many instances it might be most effective to avoid these interactions, or, if necessary, for the helper to direct toward the others the attitudes they direct toward him, whether consciously or not.

The effective helper, then, while he may suspend some attitudes temporarily in particular relationships for the good of the other person, in general lives at the highest level of authenticity. In addition, if he initially establishes a relationship with the implicit contractual agreement involving acceptance of the prospective helpee at less than he can be, then the helping process will encounter many future difficulties. The effective helper must have a full repertoire of responses to employ at any moment in time.

In order for the helper to have a large repertoire of potential responses as well as the trust in his experience that is necessary to employ these responses appropriately the helper trainee usually must become involved in constructive therapeutic change himself. Thus, the possibility for this change should be incorporated in the training program. Indeed, *the core of training involves the constructive change of the trainee.* With this change many of the core conditions and their implications for employment will become readily apparent and the necessity for learning a technique will diminish. However, involving the trainee in a lifelong learning process implies more than offering him the opportunity to change in training. It also requires to some degree, depending upon the inner-directedness of the individual trainee, the support and reinforcement of an environment that is favorably disposed toward such growth processes.

It is becoming increasingly obvious that the effective implementation of a training experience is contingent upon the skillful direction of a sensitive and directionful helper trainer. *The trainer must be expert yet open. He must be an expert in the whole area of training, treatment, and research, and he must be open to the potential contributions of the trainees, from whom he can learn so much if he makes them reach high enough.* Not only does the trainee raise critical questions that necessitate knowledgeable and communicative responses but he may also have psychological problems that demand an effective therapeutic agent. Finally, along with select other members of the group the trainer constitutes the greatest potential influencer or reinforcer of effective trainee discriminations and communications.

REFERENCES

For a more detailed discussion of the issues considered in this chapter see the references upon which the following readings are based.

Carkhuff, R. R., & Berenson, B. G. *Beyond counseling and therapy.* New York: Holt, Rinehart and Winston, Inc., 1967.

Truax, C. B., & Carkhuff, R. R. *Toward effective counseling and psychotherapy.* Chicago: Aldine Publishing Company, 1967.

Truax, C. B., Carkhuff, R. R., & Douds, J. Toward an integration of the didactic and experiential approaches to training in counseling and psychotherapy. *Journal of Counseling Psychology,* 1964, **11,** 140–147.

14

TRAINING IN CORE CONDITIONS

The jump from theory to practice is a large one, from the niceties of intellectual constructs to the complexities of real problems, from the clarity of hypotheses to the contingencies of life, from the systems of papers to the vagaries of people. Whether we begin theoretically with constructs gleaned from the evidence of previous efforts or atheoretically with generalizations from our immediate experiences, the learning process involves interaction between the raw material of human experience and the meanings we attach to this experience. We learn from one experience, whether experiential or experimental, and we generalize to other experiences that have common ingredients. We seek a system that orders these generalizations conceptually. In turn, we test hypotheses derived from these systems in further experiences in different areas and, according to what we find, we modify or qualify the systems with which we began. In this sense we and our systems are continually evolving and changing. *Our systems are only as useful as they are functional, and they are functional only insofar as they are attuned to the subtle nuances of changing times and people.*

A further ingredient in the study of human relations is the belief that wherever we begin our study, if we are open to and shaped by the results of our efforts we will be moving closer and closer to agreement with persons who may have begun from seemingly different positions but who have shared similar commitments to understand. The present chapter, then, describes some of our creative applications in training. We will consider here only a few of the most recent efforts in training in the core conditions.

Whereas the early programs that integrated the didactic and experiential approaches to training demonstrated significant results, many problems in interpretation were associated with them. For example, while hospital attendants as well as professional trainees functioned at posttraining levels commensurate with experienced professionals (Carkhuff & Truax, 1965a) and, indeed, produced significant positive outcomes (Carkhuff & Truax, 1965b), the projects lacked many necessary methodological controls. Accordingly, in designs that incorporated (1) training control groups that met at the same time for related purposes, (2) pre-posttesting, and (3) a variety of outcome indexes (Berenson, Carkhuff, & Myrus, 1966; Martin & Carkhuff, 1968) the training groups of dormitory counselors and guidance counselors demonstrated significantly greater differences in interpersonal functioning and personality change than either training control or control groups. These findings were replicated with different groups of trainees, including teachers (Carkhuff, 1969) and nurses (Kratochvil, 1969). Finally, increasing attention was paid to the level of trainer functioning as the critical ingredient in effective training of community volunteers as well as professionals (Pierce, Carkhuff, & Berenson, 1967). However, throughout these programs one critical condition was present: trainees were taught to discriminate in one operation, following which they were taught to communicate. The question of whether discrimination was a necessary condition for communication became explicit with the results from studies of the effects of professional clinical and counseling programs (Anthony & Carkhuff, 1969; Carkhuff, Kratochvil, & Friel, 1968) where discrimination and communication were found to be unrelated among persons who functioned at low levels in the helping role. Following this study a program that focused exclusively on discrimination, allowing no communication practice, was conducted with a group of undergraduate students (Carkhuff, Collingwood, & Renz, 1969). The results indicated that didactic training in discrimination led to positive changes in trainee discrimination but not in communication. There was little or no generalization from discrimination to communication among trainees functioning initially at low levels of both discrimination and communication. Accordingly, several experimental programs stressing practice in communication were conducted.

TRAINING PATIENTS IN INTERPERSONAL FUNCTIONING

Two recent and exciting projects involved groups of patients who were trained in more behavioristic ways to communicate effectively. With a group of Veterans Administration neuropsychiatric patients who were rejected from traditional groups Pierce and Drasgow (1969) essentially reconstructed the communication process. The group consisted of 7 male psychiatric inpatients selected at random from a group of patients who had not been assigned to individual or group therapy because it was believed that they could not meaningfully participate in or benefit from such programs. The patients ranged in age from 21 to 55 years and had been hospitalized from one to four times. Five of the patients were diagnosed schizophrenic and two as having psychiatric difficulties associated with chronic brain syndrome. The group met for an hour and a half to two hours a day for three weeks.

The purposes of the program were several. First, it was hoped that an improvement in interpersonal functioning would lead to improvement in other areas of functioning, in particular with significant others both within and outside the hospital. Accordingly, the patient's chances for discharge, staying out of the hospital, and retaining his job would be increased. Second, according to the helper therapy principle, the patient might be of benefit to other patients. Equipped with high-level interpersonal skills he might become a patient-helper to other persons in need of help.

With patients who were so severely disabled as to be unable to conduct a pretraining interview an index of functioning was obtained from responses to standard helpee stimulus expressions designed expressly for these individuals. The patients were functioning at such a low level that the trainers began with some very fundamental steps. In response to spontaneous helpee expressions the patients cast in the helping role were simply asked whether the helpee felt happy, sad, angry, and so on. If the patient accurately perceived sadness, for example, he was directed to construct a response beginning, "You feel . . ."; thus the response, "You feel sad." The trainees were reinforced for such accurate single-statement responses. Gradually trainee responses were built into two-statement interactions, then three, and so on, until they were able to sustain 15- to 20-minute interactions as "talkers" and "listeners." The groups clearly demonstrated an ability to function at more than a level higher than initially after little more than 20 hours over a three-week period of intensified training, with two of the patients finally functioning above level 3. In addition, the training group demonstrated significantly higher levels of interpersonal functioning than a pre-posttested time control group as well as a control group under drug treatment, a control group under individual psychotherapeutic treatment, and a control group under group psychotherapeutic treatment. Finally, all but the brain-damaged patients were discharged independently of the program, and, we might add, remained so. The brain-damaged patients were given weekend privileges as a result of their improved levels of functioning.

Of course, the focus of the groups was not exclusively training and shaping behavior. Many of the same phenomena that occur in traditional group therapeutic processes conducted by high-level–functioning therapists also occur in the training sessions conducted by high-level–functioning trainers, only they occur within the training structure. Thus, in addition to the original questions of some of the patients about whether they were going to live or die, they asked questions concerning the relevance of the program for them: "What good's this gonna do for me?" "What's in it for me?" The whole process of focusing upon someone else and actually trying to "hear" another person was alien to them. With these burning questions in mind, the program could not have been implemented successfully without the most effective leadership, and the patients could not have gone on to demonstrate for themselves the answers to their own questions.

TRAINING PARENTS TO WORK WITH
THEIR DISTURBED CHILDREN

In another study a group of parents on the waiting list of a child psychiatric clinic were directed toward a training group that met two nights a week for three weeks, one night a week for three additional weeks, and one night two weeks later, a very workable schedule for most clinic staffs (Carkhuff & Bierman, 1969). The group was comprised of five couples ranging in age from their 30's to their 50's. They were from many walks of life and included a truck driver, a sanitation worker, a small businessman, a production manager, and a professional counselor. The common bond among them was that their children had been diagnosed as emotionally disturbed.

A set of step-by-step training procedures was developed to meet the particular needs of this group. The method involved several early instructions concerning formulating responses to helpees: (1) listen for at least one minute (something that most people cannot do); (2) formulate your initial responses in terms of, "You feel that . . ."; (3) make no more than a single statement initially. Modifications in the formulation and the number of the responses were incorporated as the trainees moved toward higher levels of functioning. Assuming that the child's difficulties were a function at least in part of the interpersonal process (1) between parents and (2) between parents and children, the following stages were implemented: (a) a parent of one sex in one family unit and a parent of the other sex from another family unit were alternately helper and helpee with the focus upon problems in general; (b) in a similar manner a parent of one sex in one family unit and a parent of the other sex from another family unit were alternately helper and helpee with the focus on problems dealing with the child specifically; (3) parents from the same family unit served alternately as helper and helpee with the focus upon their own interpersonal problems; (4) parents from the same family unit served alternately as parent and child with the focus upon the difficulties between parent and child; (5) the children were brought in and parents and child interacted in play therapy situations and/or on common problems. Between sessions homework involving the child and the parent and leading up to the next stage of training was assigned, with the thought in mind that whatever really significant happens will happen between and after the termination of the training sessions. While the emphasis throughout training was upon communication practice, the trainer and the other trainees not only provided feedback on ratings of level of functioning but also attempted to enable the trainee involved to achieve new levels of understanding the problem area involved. The groups were extremely successful, achieving an improvement in functioning with each other of nearly a level and a half. However, the changes in functioning were not nearly as great for the parents in relation to their children, thus underscoring the need to incorporate more practice sessions directly involving the children as, for example, the promising training specific to the child's play (Santilli, 1969) which grew out of this project.

Again, there were problems to be worked through other than those involved directly with the training structure. On the one hand, there was active resistance on the part of the parents to the notion that their children's problems were in large part due to their problems. The burning question for them was whether they could surrender the defensive maneuvers they had incorporated as a way of life and replace them with more constructive behavior. On the other hand, the trainer had a hold on them—their children. To the reluctant the question could be put— as it was—of whether they would maintain their neurotic modes of behavior at the sacrifice of their children's welfare. *The group members found that just as the trainer must do in relation to them, they must go all the way in relation to their children.*

One of the experiences that was most clear in the fifth stage of training when the children were brought in and the interaction between parents and children was observed through a two-way observation room by the remaining parents was the absence of pathology. *There were no emotionally disturbed children!* Indeed, the parents with other children felt that these children now presented more problems than the child with the original problem. In order to change their behavior patterns, along with communication training the parents had to recognize themselves as a major source of their child's problems. They had to face themselves and work out their own conflicts, conscious or unconscious, or observe their children do so, so to speak, for them.

It is to be emphasized that of all the training programs for which extensive data are available, these groups, trained with a behavioral emphasis upon practice, demonstrated the most constructive change in interpersonal functioning. Indeed, they tended to demonstrate the greatest change in that which they had practiced most, communication between spouses. It is to be further emphasized that these groups were considered "patients" rather than professional or even subprofessional trainees. Contrary to our earlier expectations and orientations, then, we found that what was most critical was practice leading up to that which we wished to achieve. Rather than discrimination leading to communication, we assumed and found that with these groups of people discrimination followed communication, that is, insight followed action. Of course, the training sessions were conducted in a highly therapeutic atmosphere, and many of the conditions of group therapy as well as psychodrama were present. However, the discrete, step-by-step procedures involving practice at every stage appeared to be significantly more effective than the earlier training orientation of stressing discrimination in order to lead to communication.

TRAINING IN COMMUNICATION BETWEEN RACES

Obviously, the potential for the employment of the kinds of programs just described is great. Thus far we have emphasized personalized attention to personal problems. This is appropriate. However, there are many areas of social problems we did not consider. One such area is that of racial relations, and one of the major sources of difficulty in this area involves the communication gap between (1) white teachers and Negro students; (2) Negro parents and their children; and (3) Negro parents and white teachers. Accordingly, a human relations workshop was set up with the goal of bridging the communication gap experienced by these groups (Carkhuff & Banks, 1969).

In addition, other influences were studied. For one thing, the 25 trainees (15 white and 10 Negro) were divided into two groups, with half of the white teachers and half of the Negro parents in each group trained respectively by a white and Negro trainer in a counterbalanced fashion. Thus, for the first 12 hours one group of seven whites and five Negroes met with a white trainer while a second group similarly comprised met with a Negro trainer of a similar level of functioning and training orientation. For the second 12-hour period the groups and trainers were reversed so that the differential effects of white and Negro trainers could be studied.

Again step-by-step behavioristic procedures were developed for attaining each of these goals. The following stages were implemented in training, with each person alternately taking a turn as helper and helpee: (1) *communication between adults within racial groups:* white teachers practiced communication with other white teachers and Negro parents with other Negro parents; (2) *communication between adults of different races:* white teachers and Negro parents practiced communication with each other; (3) *communication between generations—role-playing:* white teachers alternately assumed the role of teacher and child while Negro parents alternately assumed the role of parent and child; (4) *communication between generations between races—role-playing:* white teachers and Negro parents alternately assumed the role of (a) teacher and child and (b) parent and child with each other; (5) *communication between generations between races:* white teachers and Negro parents counseled both white and Negro children. Thus, each group worked through phases 1 and 2 with one trainer and 3 and 4 with the other and were tested together at stage 5.

According to expectations gleaned from previous research and experience (Banks, 1969; Banks, Berenson, & Carkhuff, 1967; Carkhuff & Pierce, 1967), the trainees, both white and Negro, demonstrated uniformly positive change with each counselor and change significantly greater than that of previously assessed treatment control and control groups. Again the trainees demonstrated the greatest change in that which they practiced most, communication between adults, and the least change in that which they practiced least, communication between adults and children. The clear implication is that trainees learn the most in that in which they have had the most training.

While there was active resistance and defensiveness both within and between trainees, the problems were not insurmountable and were indeed overcome. The key to the results is the competence of the trainers. *Persons functioning at high levels can effect changes that neutralize the potential obstacles to communication between races.*

Other programs have demonstrated similar results. Thus, programs emphasizing practice in communication have demonstrated significant improvement in the interpersonal skills of teachers and teachers' aides (Bierman, Carkhuff, & Santilli, 1969; Carkhuff & Griffin, 1969a), counselors and counselors' aides (Carkhuff & Griffin, 1969b), and neuropsychiatric patients in both state and Veterans Administration hospitals (Vitalo, 1969). Again the key to increased interpersonal skills is practice in interpersonal roles.

Obviously, the question of retention always arises. There will be contingencies if we cannot influence or control critical aspects of the environment. However, the projects are persuasive in leading us to believe that the effects of practice will better enable the trainee to sustain his level of functioning upon returning to his environment than the more traditional approaches. Further preparation for his return to real life may be accomplished by practice in role-playing some of the difficulties that the individual may expect to encounter upon returning to his environment.

It should be underscored that the trainees did not gain as passive recipients of passively responsive trainers. They gained because they were active participants in programs directed by highly facilitative, action-oriented, and directionful trainers. The format for training bridged the gap between the experiential and the behavioristic. The trainees were trained behavioristically to communicate high levels of both facilitative and action-oriented dimensions. Had we been bound by the original experiential formulations we might never have achieved such pronounced results. On the other hand, had we and others not conceived of the original experiential formulations, there would have been no need for systematic, step-by-step procedures leading to desirable goals.

Further attempts have been made to shed light on the effective training process. One project concerned with training beginning graduate trainees not only stressed practice in communication but also counterbalanced the order for training in facilitative dimensions such as empathy and respect and action-oriented dimensions such as confrontation and immediacy in two training groups (Carkhuff, Friel, & Kratochvil, 1969). With trainers functioning at commensurate and minimally facilitative levels, one group concentrated initially upon the facilitative dimensions and subsequently upon the action-oriented dimensions while the other group reversed the sequence of training. The midtraining results indicated some generalization effect from the training on each to the other. Posttraining results indicated changes analagous with the patterns of change on each of the dimensions involved conforming to the trainer's style. The direct implication is that it may not matter if the trainee is trained first in responsive or initiative dimensions so long as the dimensions are put together through the efforts of an effective, or high-level, trainer.

In summary, we found a behavioristically oriented training program directed toward experiential conditions to be most effective for patient-helpers as well as for professional helpers and that such a program probably constitutes the preferred mode of treatment for many patient populations. In addition, these training programs under the guidance of trainers functioning at high levels may deal effectively with the major social problems of our times. Gains in levels of interpersonal functioning are one of the critical aspects of all effective interpersonal processes (Carkhuff & Berenson, 1967; Pagell, Carkhuff, & Berenson, 1967). A structured approach geared to the goals of the specific problems involved appears to provide the most economical and effective means of attaining the desired changes. For one thing, an open-ended structure appears to offer the trainee more rather than less freedom to experience and experiment with himself. For another, he knows that whatever the tasks he encounter he will have to put in a great deal of work if he hopes to surmount the obstacles to a full and effective life.

REFERENCES

For a more detailed discussion of the issues considered in this chapter see the asterisked readings and the references upon which the readings are based.

Anthony, W., & Carkhuff, R. R. The effects of rehabilitation counselor training upon discrimination, communication and helping attitudes. *Journal of Counseling Psychology*, in press, 1969.

Banks, G. The effects of race in the interview situation: A review. Mimeographed manuscript. State University of New York at Buffalo, 1969.

Banks, G., Berenson, B. G., & Carkhuff, R. R. The effects of counselor race and training upon Negro clients in initial interviews. *Journal of Clinical Psychology*, 1967, **23**, 70–72.

Bierman, R., Carkhuff, R. R., & Santilli, Muriel. The effects of a training workshop on project "Head Start." Unpublished research, University of Waterloo, Waterloo, Canada, 1969.

Berenson, B. G., Carkhuff, R. R., & Myrus, P. The interpersonal functioning and training of college students. *Journal of Counseling Psychology*, 1966, **13**, 441–446.

Carkhuff R. R. The prediction of the effects of teacher-counselor training: The development of communication and discrimination selection indexes. *Counselor Education and Supervision*, in press, 1969.

*Carkhuff, R. R., & Banks, G. The effects of human relations training upon communication between races and generations. Unpublished research, American International College, Springfield, Mass., 1969.

Carkhuff, R. R., & Berenson, B. G. *Beyond counseling and therapy*. New York: Holt, Rinehart and Winston, Inc., 1967.

*Carkhuff, R. R., & Bierman, R. The effects of human relations training upon child psychiatric patients in treatment. *Journal of Counseling Psychology*, in press, 1969.

Carkhuff, R. R., Collingwood, T., & Renz, L. The prediction of the effects of didactic training in discrimination. *Journal of Clinical Psychology*, in press, 1969.

Carkhuff, R. R., & Griffin, A. The effects of training in interpersonal skills in project "Head Start." Unpublished research, American International College, Springfield, Mass., 1969. (a)

Carkhuff, R. R., & Griffin, A. The effects of training in interpersonal skills in a Concentrated Employment Program. Unpublished research, American International College, Springfield, Mass., 1969. (b)

Carkhuff, R. R., Friel, T., & Kratochvil, D. The differential effects of training in responsive and initiative dimensions. *Counselor Education and Supervision*, in press, 1969.

Carkhuff, R. R., Kratochvil, D., & Friel, T. The effects of professional training: The communication and discrimination of facilitative conditions. *Journal of Counseling Psychology*, 1968, **15**, 68–74.

Carkhuff, R. R., & Pierce, R. The differential effects of counselor race and social class upon patient depth of self-exploration in an initial clinical interview. *Journal of Consulting Psychology*, 1967, **31**, 632–634.

Carkhuff, R. R., & Truax, C. B. Training in counseling and psychotherapy: An evaluation of an integrated didactic and experiential approach. *Journal of Consulting Psychology*, 1965, **29**, 333–336. (a)

Carkhuff, R. R., & Truax, C. B. Lay mental health counseling: The effects of lay group counseling. *Journal of Consulting Psychology*, 1965, **29**, 426–431. (b)

Kratochvil, D. Changes in values and interpersonal functioning of nurses in training. *Counselor Education and Supervision*, 1969, **8**, 104 107.

Martin, J., & Carkhuff, R. R. The effects of training upon changes in trainee personality and behavior. *Journal of Clinical Psychology*, 1968, **24**, 109–110.

Pagell, W., Carkhuff, R. R., & Berenson, B. G. The predicted differential effects of the level of counselor functioning upon the level of functioning of outpatients. *Journal of Clinical Psychology*, 1967, **23**, 510–512.

Pierce, R., Carkhuff, R. R., & Berenson, B. G. The differential effects of high and low functioning counselors upon counselors in training. *Journal of Clinical Phycology*, 1967, **23**, 212–215.

*Pierce, R., & Drasgow, J. The effects of human relations training upon VA neuropsychiatric patients. *Journal of Counseling Psychology*, in press, 1969.

Santilli, Muriel. Training parents in play-specific interpersonal skills. Unpublished research, Buffalo, N.Y.

Vitalo, R. The effects of training in interpersonal skills upon psychiatric inpatients. Unpublished research, University of Massachusetts, Amherst, Mass., 1969.

15

TRAINING IN THE DEVELOPMENT OF
EFFECTIVE COURSES OF ACTION

Effective discrimination and communication of the core, facilitative, and action-oriented dimensions enable the helpee to function effectively in response to many different kinds of stimuli in a variety of problem areas. Improved intrapersonal and interpersonal functioning will enable the helpee increasingly to resolve crises and make changes in his daily living. Often, however, the helpee needs additional help in handling the difficulties that brought him to seek help in the first place or to deal with new difficulties that have developed over the course of helping. Together the helpee and the helper will seek to develop and implement courses of action leading to the constructive resolution of the helpee's difficulties (Carkhuff, 1966a; Carkhuff & Berenson, 1967; Truax & Carkhuff, 1967). Briefly, the helping process may be described as follows: the more helpee self-exploration, the more helpee self-understanding; the more helpee self-understanding, the more clear the directionality; the more clear the directionality, the more focused the goals; the more focused the goals, the more clear the steps leading to the attainment of these goals. *Courses of action, then, are simply the means employed for attaining the goals focused upon in the helping process.*

In order to prepare trainees for implementing these courses of action with their future helpees their training must incorporate the following: (1) an introduction to the development of effective courses of action; (2) an introduction to and practice in a variety of potential preferred modes of treatment; (3) the development and implementation of courses of action and preferred modes of treatment with individuals and groups of trainees. Thus, consistent with all other aspects of an integrated program, the didactic and experiential approaches to training once again converge with the additional benefit of having the trainers as models for implementing these action modalities.

COURSES IN ACTION

Almost anything having to do with the procedures leading to physical, emotional, and intellectual goals, alone or as they relate to each other, may constitute a course of action. Accordingly, programs of rest, diet, and exercise constitute modalities geared toward healthy physical functioning. Similarly, programs of instruction, training, reading, and homework are only a few possible ways of meeting specifiable intellectual goals. The emotional and interpersonal areas are not always so clear. However, emotional changes and gains in the helpee's experience of himself accompany physical and intellectual gains and changes. In addition, training in responsiveness and assertiveness are examples of programs in the emotional-interpersonal area.

Again, however comprehensively the goals are described, they are only as meaningful and appropriate *for the helpee* as the helping processes that led to their delineation have been effective. *Only directionality firmly rooted in high levels of helpee self-understanding will lead to functional goals, the attainment of which will make a difference in the helper's life.* Similarly, however detailed the means of attaining these goals, the procedures are only as effective as they have meaning to the helpee's total experience of the helping process.

While we have treated the physical, emotional, and intellectual goals distinctively, the helping process has not been effective until the helpee is reintegrated as a whole person. Thus, the trainee must be taught to employ all available resources to enable the helpee to attain his goals. In this context those potential preferred modes of treatment that are essential to the helping programs for trainees should be made operational and implemented in training. The remaining approaches and the modalities for their acquisition should be introduced so that upon completion of training the trainee is at least equipped to make the appropriate referral or to call upon the appropriate consultant.

The development of directionality and the institution of a preferred mode of treatment may be made operational in training. Accordingly, as in Table 15-1, the earlier phases of helping serve to develop the relevant problem area *as experienced by the helpee*. That is, a depth of self-exploration and, with the helper's guidance, self-understanding on the part of the helpee leads readily to the definition and description of the helpee's problem area (I). A problem area, in turn, dictates

Table 15-1.   The Stages of Implementing a Course of Action in Helping

I.   The definition and description of problem area(s)
II. The definition and description of direction(s) and/or goal(s) dictated by the problem area(s)
III. An analysis of the critical dimensions of these direction(s) and/or goal(s)
IV. A consideration of the alternative courses of action available for attaining the dimensions of the direction(s) and/or goal(s)
V.   A consideration of the advantages and disadvantages of the alternative courses of action
VI. The development of physical, emotional-interpersonal, and intellectual programs for achieving that course with the most advantageous and fewest disadvantages in terms of ultimate success in goal achievement
VII. The development of progressive gradations of the programs involved

certain definable directions and goals (II), the critical dimensions of which can be analyzed in attainable terms (III). We mention directions as well as goals, since often there are no precise goals but only emerging and constantly modifiable directions. Several courses of action may be available for the attainment of these critical dimensions (IV). A consideration of the advantages and disadvantages of each alternative course of action will lead to the one that offers the highest probability of success (V). The programs that are initiated will be dictated by the course of action which is chosen. Thus, those physical, emotional-interpersonal, and intellectual means will be employed that offer the greatest prospect of implementing the course of action chosen to attain the directions or goals (VI). Similarly, gradations of these programs will be employed in order to insure the success of the different programs. The programs will be broken down into step-by-step progressions, and that behavioristic sequence that most effectively leads to the success of the program will be employed (VII).

A global description of a case will illustrate the implementation of a course of action in the helper-helpee training interaction. Thus, the helpee presented his concern over a deteriorating relationship with his deteriorating son. The process of self-exploration and self-understanding led to both helper and helpee confronting the helpee with his own deterioration or, in his terms, his inability to experience himself as a man. The helpee, so to speak, was not "on top" of himself and he was not "on top" of his family situation. The directional goal then became one not only of helping his son and other members of the family and of enabling his son to help himself but also one of enabling the helpee to help himself. Indeed, an analysis of the courses of action available indicated that only a changed father could make a difference in the other situations. A physical program involving rest, diet, exercise, and recreation was implemented in small stages. An emotional-interpersonal program involving training in responsiveness and assertiveness was implemented in gradations. An intellectual program was enacted involving the progressive development of the helpee's own ideas and his acting upon these ideas in such a manner as to develop his own effective working cosmology.

Gradually with successive success experiences the helpee came to achieve his physical, emotional, and intellectual programs, which, in turn, enabled him to take the course of action leading to the directions and/or goals involved in ameliorating the problem area. Thus, in what is apparently a very abstract experiential area, the experience of one's manhood, the helpee came increasingly to experience himself as a man. As he became comfortable with this new experience he was ready to deal with his relationship with his son and others and, finally, in the manner in which he had been helped, enable his son to help himself and others. To be sure, each individual case involves a myriad of complexities and a multitude of dimensions not illustrated here. However, a consideration of the step-by-step procedure in developing and implementing a course of action should lead to a greater perspective of preferred modes of treatment.

However grossly portrayed in this brief example, the principles involved are clear: (1) at all stages of development and implementation of a course of action we must check back with the helpee's experience with the question, "Is what we're doing relevant to the helpee's functioning?" (2) the individual helpee is usually presenting a problem that involves himself first and others only secondarily, and we must seek changes in the individual before we seek changes in his relationships with others; (3) we employ those means that insure the highest probability of constructive change or gain; (4) we remain outcome oriented, or geared to the achievement of attainable goals and shaped by the feedback we receive in terms of the achievement of these goals.

In this regard the helper must often employ his expertise and experience as the basis for developing courses of action that the helpee cannot himself develop. That is, based upon the helper's experience of the helpee, the helper may structure assignments and programs for the helpee when the helpee cannot do it alone or in conjunction with the helper. The helping process is always guided by the course of action that offers the best prospect for the helpee's success. If the helpee cannot share as fully in a conjunctive process, then it is the helper's responsibility to develop programs that enable the helpee to carry some of the burden of responsibility for his own life. For an example in the extreme, if an institutionalized patient does not demonstrate adequate levels of either intrapersonal or interpersonal functioning, then the helper may make value judgments in the interest of the helpee and independent of the helpee's expressed or unexpressed interests. Having made such a judgment, the helper may proceed to employ all of the means available to enable the helpee once again to function effectively. The helper may direct the courses of action and, indeed, the lives of those who cannot direct them for themselves.

TRAINING IN PREFERRED MODES OF TREATMENT: AN ILLUSTRATION

There are a variety of traditional or classical approaches that may constitute effective courses of action given a particular interaction of relevant variables. The real question concerning any of these approaches is what are their unique contributions, over and above those accounted for by the core, facilitative, and action-oriented dimensions (Berenson & Carkhuff, 1967; Carkhuff, 1966b). That is, do these approaches make a significant, additional contribution to the constructive change or gain of the helpee? Thus, in a given instance the client-centered, existential, or psychoanalytic approach may constitute a preferred mode of treatment. More frequently in the context of an adequate experiential base a combination of the trait-and-factor and behavioristic approaches will yield the most promising programs. One program does not operate to the exclusion of the other, and frequently the more experientially oriented positions may be integrated with the behavioristic in building the most successful approach to treatment.

Again the emphasis is upon the translation of the treatment programs to tangible human benefits. While the ends of helping may be loosely described by the more traditional therapeutic orientations, neither the description of the goals nor the means developed to attain them is sufficient to warrant the term "preferred modes of treatment." Only those means that enable us to achieve constructive change or gain may be so designated.

The two treatment modalities that appear to offer the most promise in this regard, then, are the trait-and-factor and the behavioristic (Carkhuff & Berenson, 1967). The trait-and-factor approach, with its emphasis upon assessing both man and his environment along relatively stable and measurable dimensions, provides us with the most comprehensive means for describing the critical dimensions of the directions or the goals involved. With a comprehensive description of the critical aspects of the goals, the behavioristic approaches provide us with the most effective procedures for attaining these goals.

In addition to exposure to making full and detailed descriptions of the critical dimensions of treatment goals and delineating step-by-step procedures for attaining these goals, then, the trainee should be given sufficient experience with all of the available treatment modalities. He should be fully aware of the advantages and disadvantages and the contributions and limitations of each treatment modality. The more treatment modalities he understands, the greater the probability of his matching up the treatment modality with the helpee's directionality. Accordingly, different treatment modalities may be integrated in total treatment programs. The following description of counterconditioning, or systematic desensitization, illustrates how a treatment modality that richly deserves the designation "preferred mode of treatment" may be made operational in training.

COUNTERCONDITIONING IN TRAINING: AN ILLUSTRATION[1]

A given helpee may be disabled in his functioning in one or another area of his life as reflected in phobic reactions or ideas, bodily sensations, or some external situations. Systematic counterconditioning or desensitization has as its objective the minimization of the disrupting effects of anxiety that prevent the helpee from dealing with his problems effectively. In this procedure objects, persons, or events that are upsetting or distressing to the helpee are gradually placed before him, either ideationally or physically or both, while he is in a state of deep relaxation. In order to utilize the desensitization technique the helper must develop skill in three critical aspects of the procedure: (1) deep muscle relaxation; (2) the construction of anxiety hierarchies; and (3) the counterposing of relaxation and anxiety-provoking stimuli from the hierarchy constructed. The purpose of deep muscle relaxation is to induce a highly relaxed state in the helpee, so that when he is confronted with anxiety-provoking stimuli the helpee will remain at ease and gradually "unlearn" his formerly distressing response. The anxiety hierarchy, in turn, is simply a list of stimuli (objects, persons, events) to which a helpee reacts with different degrees of anxiety. The most disturbing

[1] These training experiences lead readily to a consideration of the need for more detailed methodology in this treatment procedure. The example of systematic desensitization given in Appendix B illustrates just such a program developed for instructional purposes.

item is placed at the top of the list, the least disturbing at the bottom. Hierarchy construction may begin at the same time as relaxation training, with modifications or additions being made in the hierarchy at any point during treatment. After the relaxation training has been completed and initial hierarchies have been constructed the next phase in treatment involves the systematic presentation of items in the helpee's anxiety hierarchy while he is in a state of deep relaxation. Again the helper introduces the helpee to what will take place and what is hoped for—the elimination of disabling symptomatology preventing more effective action on his part by replacing these obstacles (anxiety responses) with feelings of relaxation. The helpee is told that he will enter a deeply relaxed state and that while relaxed he will be asked to imagine clearly and vividly scenes from his hierarchy. He is instructed to indicate by raising his finger if a particular scene is upsetting to him.

Training in desensitization may be structured in a simplified fashion. The trainer or an outside expert in behavior therapy may serve first as a model for the implementation of this approach. The trainees can incorporate the initial experiences firsthand as helpees in the desensitization, moving to interchangeable helper and helpee roles with each other under direct supervision and trainee observation, and finally to individual treatment with regular supervision. The time allotted may be structured or open-ended, with the former practice insuring some control over the training experience and the latter serving the individual needs of the helpee trainees involved.

Initially, then, sessions for muscle relaxation training and practice and exploration of the reaction and construction of the hierarchy must be allotted. Based upon a depth of helpee self-exploration and self-understanding, a full exploration of the reaction must be conducted and the construction of the hierarchy detailed. Some relatively isolated phobic reaction, such as a fear of spiders or snakes, may be employed as the most direct and simple entry into this treatment area. Indeed, a research project involving systematic pre- and postassessments of approach-avoidance gradients in relation to the distressing object may be implemented. Another possibility that will structure the experience even further might involve a number of predetermined experiences (designed to cover the given reaction as comprehensively as possible) which would be presented to the helpee-trainee in card form. Those items most relevant to the helpee-trainee's concerns would be indicated and ordered in a step-by-step progression from the least to the most difficult experiences. Thus, the items may range from helpee experiences of seeing a word for an object in a book to waking up in the middle of the night and finding the object in bed with him. This phase may be followed by a series of desensitization sessions. These sessions might run from a half hour to an hour each depending on the purposes of the program.

With this structure *one possible training-treatment schedule* may be outlined as follows.

A TRAINING EXPERIENCE IN COUNTERCONDITIONING

I. *Training sessions*
   A. Time allotted for full exploration of reaction and comprehensive construction of hierarchy
      1. Based upon helpee self-exploration, present the helpee with alternate cards with the following instructions
         a. Choose the least bothersome and the most bothersome
         b. Choose the remaining relevant cards in a step-by-step progression of equal increments from the easiest to the most difficult scene
   B. Time allotted for relaxation training and practice
      1. Explain relaxation of specific muscle groups
      2. Demonstrate how to flex and relax muscles of arms and legs and point out relaxation experienced after flexion
      3. Have the helpee close his eyes and begin general relaxation
      4. Have the helpee flex each limb, following each flexion with relaxation
      5. In later training sessions have the helpee learn to flex and relax the muscles in his stomach, shoulders, neck, and face
      6. Follow with general relaxation
   C. Time allotted for visualization practice
      1. While the helpee is relaxed have him visualize any object that stands out clearly to him
         a. Have the helpee signal with his index finger when visualization is clear
         b. Have the helpee hold visualization for a period of seconds, stop the scene, and return the helpee to relaxing muscles
         c. Repeat this procedure several times
      2. Have the helpee visualize the scene that he is in
         a. Have the helpee signal with his index finger when visualization is clear
         b. Have the helpee hold visualization for a period of seconds, stop the scene, and return the helpee to relaxing muscles
         c. Reactivate the helpee slowly
         d. Quiz the helpee on the details of visualization, making sure that the helpee was looking out at the world from within himself

3.   Give the helpee a homework assignment
    a.   Relaxation practice
    b.   Visualization practice
II.   *Treatment sessions*
   A.   Time allotted for relaxation
      1.   Run through specific muscle groupings
         a.   *Note*: Muscles are focused upon and relaxed, not flexed
         b.   Count and complete general relaxation
   B.   Presentation of the scene
      1.   Initially deal with only one scene in each session
      2.   Indicate to the helpee before the start of the first treatment session what you are going to do and tell him if any scene causes overwhelming discomfort while he is visualizing it to raise his finger and the scene will be terminated immediately
      3.   The scene may be presented for two seconds in the following way
         a.   "While you are relaxed I want you to visualize that you . . ."
         b.   After two seconds say, "Stop the scene, turn it off, and return your attention to relaxation"
         c.   Return to general relaxation
      4.   Ask two questions of the helpee
         a.   Whether the scene was clear or not
            1)   If the scene was unclear, present it again
         b.   Whether the scene was bothersome or not
            1)   If the scene was bothersome, present it again for two seconds
            2)   If the scene was clear and not bothersome, increase the duration of the scene from 2 to 3 to 5 to 10 to 15 seconds
   C.   Repeat the procedure with the next scene
   D.   Repeat the procedure until the most difficult scene in the hierarchy is effectively handled

The outline describes only one of many possible programs in desensitization training and only one of many possible preferred modes of treatment. These programs may serve as training models for the operationalization in training of those treatment modalities essential to a given setting. Perhaps the major contribution of training in these different modalities is to equip the helper with the necessary openness and flexibility to discern the potential applications of the various treatment modes and the necessary knowledgeability and competence to make creative applications to meet the helpee's goals. It is to be underscored that subprofessionals as well as professionals can be trained in many of these procedures. Indeed, in regard to the subprofessionals programs have been conducted employing them as treatment agents. Again the train-

ing programs employed should be tailored to meet the needs of the treatment setting for which the trainees are being prepared. It remains for trainers and trainees to put into operation all existing treatment modalities.

PERSONALIZED DIRECTIONALITY: AN ILLUSTRATION

Courses of action, then, constitute the means by which the directional goals of treatment are achieved. By definition they represent an action orientation toward life. However, these modes of functioning may also represent a directionality with less specifically defined goals, or perhaps goals that may become more clear as a particular direction is followed. The preferred approach could even involve an "actionless" approach. For example, an individual who has set and acted upon many goals may also have to experience fully the consequences of his efforts. This characteristic may indicate a more passive kind of inward growth in which the individual "lets things happen" in exploring the nooks and corners of his experience. *Life is a process of "being" as well as "becoming" and each phase in its turn has a function. There are moments when an individual is simply not entitled to " 'more' than 'less' " and moments when he cannot have " 'less' than 'more.' " Each must find out what is his.*

Courses of action, then, are not always most effectively represented by the more classical treatment approaches, although, to be sure, there are aspects of the more traditional approaches that might be integrated in any given treatment program. Courses of action may instead be conceived of as very simple, common sense procedures for attaining goals that are relevant to the helpee's functioning. In order to introduce trainees to the basics of the development of courses of action and in order to insure that the trainees do not lose contact with the very individualistic and simplistic nature of meaningful and effective approaches, they may be asked to develop courses of action for themselves. That is, having attained some depth of self-understanding, whatever their developmental level they are asked to treat themselves as helpees and to develop effective modes of treatment for themselves. This training approach serves several purposes, not the least of which is the trainee's increased appreciation for the helpee's experience of the imposition and implementation of a treatment program. In this regard perhaps the most important learning gleaned from these practices is that the reinforcements, both positive and negative, must come out of the helpee's own phenomenology. In this context the following brief analysis was worked out by one of the trainees for himself. He developed the courses of action as if he were doing so for one of his helpees.

FOR JOHN, FROM JOHN

I. *Diagnosis and description*
    A. Severe work problem—not able to direct energies in a continuous, intrinsically meaningful way
        1. Successful and fortunate by society's standards—college graduate; university teacher; good athlete; good looking; healthy; soon to be married
        2. Little self-respect for those accomplishments; feels he has certain natural endowments that enable him to "cheat" past society's goals but has never worked to utilize them fully for himself
        3. Childlike and adolescent; won't assume full responsibility for self—not willing to put self on the line. Doesn't like to lose yet sometimes won't risk winning. Unconscious and almost conscious masochism. Believes a lot of past and present life is smokescreen
        4. Certain recurring patterns
            a. Won't work until last moment, then will work like a maniac, never really feeling good about it
            b. Trying to "save" others—using them as a substitute for himself and trying to justify self by his attitude toward them. Always trying to tell his parents in some way they are not failures in life and with him. He is filled with guilt and shame about this. Sometimes he even blames them for what he is, although he knows he is most to blame
            c. Forgetting too often about day-to-day life until he goes too far, then reacts like lion in a cage when he realizes where he is. Fights his way out of the cage only to find later that he never bothered to break chains that allowed the cage to form
            d. History—ashamed of family—fear of being like father (a trapped, fearful man)—fear of marrying a woman like his mother who gives him all the external things just like his father—this is their love. Hates his mother at times and even blames his father's "failure" (business-financial) on her. Father is a strong man (physically) who is afraid to show his emotions (stoic attitude)—a man doesn't do this he thinks—never asserts himself with John. Mainly very afraid of being hurt and who lives his life through and for the children, in particular John. His father is a hard worker and a proud man who never lives for himself. John loves

him but hates him and his life. Some things good he has gotten from his father and can learn some things from him. His mother is an unconditional over-hugging woman who is a slave to her children and wants her children that way. Not sure what she has to offer him. Both his mother and father were mothers. His mother is very jealous, an unsatisfied woman. John is strong (physically) like his father—even stronger. He is much brighter than either one and more emotionally alive but has a great fear—substantiated in life at times—that he will be like his father. Great guilt about being everybody's favorite, getting everything and not feeling he deserves it. Psychoanalytic interpretation of stealing mother from father may be appropriate here in John's mind, although his mother never belonged to his father. He is afraid the world will do the same to him as it did to his father and he may even want this at some level. But he is not his father

B. Conclusion—Part I: Too much John has to hide at this point—has to act for himself honestly—must fill himself and work toward self-respect and actualization first and now

II. *Strong natural abilities and strong desire to change*
A. Physically strong and aggressive (especially on field)
B. Bright
C. Tremendous amount of energy
D. Overwhelming nausea—desire to be honest with self and life
E. Realizes too much life has been spent with intellectual insights and now wants to act, has to act
F. Has a vague sense of manliness and desires to actualize
G. Has broken with certain people where much neurotic energy has been spent
H. Has been relating better to his parents—more understanding and less resentment; has even talked with and felt his father for the first time in his life. His father never talks; feels good about this
I. Seeking his own internal standard of worth and judgment on which to act
J. Has come to realize that he is strong; has overcome early image that was quite different. Learned to see himself better from the field where he gives it his all. He has accepted that part of him with pride. This is where the preferred mode of treatment must begin. He realizes that words are worth shit without action. Doesn't talk as much garbage anymore. Part of program must give him weapons—a good brain without knowledge—strong arms without knowing how to use them—strong feelings which he has been afraid to show, even to himself. Fill these gaps so there are no excuses (built-in beforehand) for not facing the moment

    K. Living for self; the rest must come second for now

III. *Program and goals*

    A. Goals

        1. Long range

            a. To become the best man John can be in terms of himself, nobody else

            b. To do all that has to be done to experience and express feelings

            c. To be doing those things that are meaningful to *him*, so *he* can hold his head up high and feel good about the time being spent, like when he rebounds in basketball

            d. To be able to express himself fully to himself in each moment

        2. Short range

            a. To study and pass in a major area

            b. To be in top physical shape

            c. To give the above two things 100 percent

            d. To assert and express feelings about the future and to act on them from day to day this summer

    B. Program—WORK!!!!!

        1. Physical

            a. Proper and regular rest

            b. Proper diet

            c. Build by stages to point where can run a mile regularly

                (1) First, alternately walking and running as able

                (2) Finally, running every day

            d. Build body by exercise

                (1) First, doing as many sit-ups and push-ups, and so on, as possible

                (2) Gradually and systematically adding tasks

            e. Engaging in basketball and recreational activities

            f. Guided by anything that makes John feel stronger

                (1) Work harder when strong in order to increase sharpness of edge

                (2) Abandon work when weak in order to recuperate strength

        2. Intellectual

            a. Building gradually, an hour at a time, develop to a point where can study several hours a day as appropriate

            b. Find one book I desire to read and read it through

            c. Think all my ideas through

            d. Record ideas in journal

            e. Develop own working cosmology in systematic form

        3. Emotional

            a. To act on those things described above—work each day and every day

b. Increasingly to seek out those relationships that are honest and leave him stronger and breaking those that are dishonest and leave him weaker

c. Not to do anything consciously believed to be wrong

d. To keep an emotional journal recording feelings

e. Not to talk just to talk

f. To go with feelings all the way

g. To keep in a corner of his mind the disgust toward what he may become if he doesn't change. When self-respect grows and a constructive meaningful life becomes more a part of self this self-conscious aspect will not be needed; hopefully, he will be moving toward a positive goal then and not just away from an extremely negative one

While this approach does not so much delineate step-by-step procedures, perhaps the most critical aspect of a preferred treatment program is that, growing out of the directionality borne of the helpee's experiences, it mobilizes the helpee to act. In this regard the training experience of designating treatment programs by the trainees for themselves is not a mere exercise in creativity. Just as with helpees, *the trainees are expected to follow through on the treatment programs they have designated for themselves*. To be sure, just as in the case of helpees to whom they might assign such a program, *they will modify the programs as they are shaped by what is effective*.

Following the development and the continuing modification and re-development by the trainee of his own individual course of action, it is beneficial for him to get additional practice. This practice is again available in the role-playing experiences of training. As a helper he may obtain the necessary experience in describing meaningful dimensions of meaningful goals and in taking the steps necessary to attain these goals. As a helpee he will have the experience of the "fit" of the program developed or the congruence of his needs and the means developed to meet these needs. Accordingly, the trainee can learn to develop courses of action in the most effective manner in preparation for the helpees he will encounter in his posttraining experiences.

In summary, the development of courses of action constitutes the answer to the question, "Now that we understand, what are we going to do about it?" Courses of action are effective because they encourage the helpee to mobilize all of his resources to act upon his world in some significant way. In acting the helpee learns about himself and his world. In learning he modifies his stance in such a manner as to achieve the fullest possible emergence at a given moment in time. In so doing the trainee is no different from the helpee in his concerns for "putting himself on the line" and "meeting his moments" in the step-by-step criteria for functioning which he has developed. John has the full experience of the helpee when he has dialogue with himself as helper about the risks of acting to find out what he can do about "it."

WILL I CHANGE?

HELPEE: Why will this time be different?
HELPER: You're really wondering if you can do it.
HELPEE: I feel so bad, I have to.
HELPER: You don't know if you can but you know you must.
HELPEE: I'm so afraid.
HELPER: It's not just what you're going to that you're afraid of but also what you're leaving—what you have to give up if you go.
HELPEE: I've got to grow up and leave the security of—of no real responsibilities—of irresponsibility—the security of childhood—the security of, of. . . .
HELPER: Of a patient?
HELPEE: Much as I don't like what I know, I feel more secure with it.
HELPER: And afraid of what I don't know.
HELPEE: I'm afraid I might not make it.
HELPER: You're hung up on the wrong alternative.
HELPEE: What do you mean?
HELPER: You should be hung up with what you know and where that's leading.
HELPEE: But if I don't make it, I'll be nothing.
HELPER: You are nothing.
HELPEE: I can't stand myself this way. Either I do it or I kill myself.
HELPER: If you don't have the guts to live, you don't have the guts to die.
HELPEE: I guess if I had the guts to kill myself I'd have the guts to live. I've got to go all the way this time. I've got to go all the way once.

REFERENCES

For a more detailed discussion of the issues considered in this chapter see the asterisked readings and the references upon which the readings are based.

*Berenson, B. G., & Carkhuff, R. R. *The sources of gain in counseling and psychotherapy.* New York: Holt, Rinehart and Winston, Inc., 1967.
Carkhuff, R. R. Counseling research theory and practice—1965. *Journal of Counseling Psychology,* 1966, **13,** 467–480. (a)
*Carkhuff, R. R. Training in counseling and psychotherapy: Requiem or reveille? *Journal of Counseling Psychology,* 1966, **13,** 260–267. (b)

*Carkhuff, R. R., & Berenson, B. G. *Beyond counseling and therapy.* New York: Holt, Rinehart and Winston, Inc., 1967.

Truax, C. B., & Carkhuff, R. R. *Toward effective counseling and psychotherapy: Training and practice.* Chicago: Aldine Publishing Company, 1967.

Overview and Transition

PART FIVE SERVES to summarize briefly and to put into perspective the preceding chapters of this volume. In addition, with its focus upon trainer and trainee level of functioning, Chapter 16 develops a model for a formula for effective selection and training. Finally, the three R's of helping—right, responsibility, and role—that have been interwoven through this text culminate in a consideration of the fourth R of helping, the realization of individual resources.

16
SELECTION AND TRAINING
IN HELPING AND LIFE

We have found that the conditions of human nourishment are not exclusively the province of the professional helper (Chapter 1) and that these conditions are simply the very human dimensions that one person can offer another. We have found that right is not given by role and that intervention by one person into the life of another can have profoundly constructive or destructive consequences, physically, emotionally, and intellectually, and that the effects over time may be cumulative (Chapter 2). We studied the sources of these effects and found that one of the greatest contributors to change in an individual is the level of facilitative and action-oriented dimensions offered by other individuals, often persons who have assumed a helping role (Chapter 3). In turn, these dimensions interact with dimensions of the person being helped, in particular in terms of the level at which the helpee is functioning in relevant problem areas as well as in terms of the process movement of self-exploration and self-experiencing which the facilitative and action-oriented dimensions elicit in the relevant problem areas (Chapter 4). We have searched the environment from which the helpee comes and to which he returns and found that for most considerations related to the helpee's growth the environment consists of people who can influence him to grow or deteriorate (Chapter 5). Thus, we developed and presented the evidence for a model for growth that is very humanistic and personalistic in orientation, although not, to be sure, to the exclusion of physical and socioeconomic bases of survival. In the face of ever-increasing numbers of disabled persons, the problem is how to populate the world with individuals who can most effectively assume the *responsibility* for the welfare of others.

We developed selection procedures that for the first time are based upon meaningful indexes of functioning in the helping role (Chapter 6). In particular, crossing differing affects with differing problem areas, we developed representative helpee stimulus expressions and presented the validating data for the responses to these expressions by prospective helpers (Chapter 7). In addition, crossing level of facilitation with level of action-orientation, we developed representative helper responses to the helpee expressions and presented the data on the accuracy of the ratings of the prospective helpers (Chapter 8). Thus, we developed functional indexes of both communication and discrimination of facilitative and action-oriented dimensions, and we employed these indexes in making applications in selection (Chapter 9). Under ordinary circumstances, of course, selection procedures apply to training programs, and, accordingly, we attempted to make effective training procedures operational.

We found that the critical ingredients of effective training processes are the level of functioning of the trainer and trainee and the type of program implemented, with the level of trainer functioning being the most significant source of training effectiveness (Chapter 10). We developed effective procedures for training in discrimination, and we gave special attention to cues for rating the trainee (Chapter 11). Similarly, we developed effective procedures for training in communication, and we focused on cues for formulating effective responses (Chapter 12). An effective transition into helping interactions was provided by our consideration of role-playing, which affords the trainee an apportunity to put all of his learnings into operation (Chapter 13). An overview of applications in training in the core, facilitative, and action-oriented conditions was provided, with special emphasis upon the training of patients and the development of innovating approaches to problems in human relations (Chapter 14). Finally, since the core conditions must often be complemented by other activities, applications in training in the development of courses of action were introduced, with special emphasis in training upon the trainee's development of individualized preferred modes of treatment (Chapter 15). Again, training is preparatory for helping, or *treatment programs and helping programs are, hopefully, preparatory for life.*

SELECTION AND TRAINING: A FORMULA

Selection and training share the same goal—the development of the effective helper. This goal may be described most fully by the level of functioning of the trainee when he is finally cast in the helping role.

The direct implication for selection, of course, is that those prospective helpers should be selected who are functioning at the highest levels prior to training. However, leaving aside for a moment the ultimate criterion of helping effectiveness—absolute level of functioning in the helping role —the effectiveness of the training program can best be assessed by the degree of change elicited in the trainee over the course of training. Thus, two potential criteria emerge, one focusing upon the absolute level of effectiveness in the helping role and the other on the relative effectiveness of the training program. *The selection procedure can make the greatest contribution to the trainee's absolute functioning at the highest level. The training program can make the greatest contribution to the relative changes in the level of functioning of the trainee over training by employing those training personnel and those programs that elicit the most constructive change.* In effective programs the orientations merge.

The most critical index in selection effectiveness is obviously the level of functioning of the trainee. The most critical index of training effectiveness is the level of functioning of the trainer. In regard to the latter, regression formulas have been worked out that measure the level of functioning of the trainee in the helping role. These prediction formulas are summarized in Figure 16-1. Roughly, on the average, *we may simply*

$$-\tfrac{1}{2} \text{ (initial level of trainee functioning)} \quad +\tfrac{1}{2} \text{ (initial level of trainer functioning)} \quad +\tfrac{1}{20} \text{ (discrepancy between initial levels)} \quad +0.2 \text{ (a constant)} \quad = \text{Total trainee change in level of functioning}$$

Figure 16-1. Formula for the effects of training upon level of trainee functioning.

halve the differential between the levels of functioning of the trainer and the trainee in order to estimate the potential change of the trainee in a given time period. Potential trainee change, then, is in large part a function of the differential between the levels of functioning of the trainer and the trainee. These findings must be qualified in programs that have limitations of time, where trainees functioning at the very lowest levels may gain very little even when the discrepancy with trainer's level of functioning may be great.

Since, as the base rate data indicate, the initial level of functioning of the prospective helper ranges somewhere between slightly above level 1 to slightly above level 2, *the key to the training formula is the trainer's level of functioning.* In order to effect maximal changes the trainer must be functioning at a high level. For example, in order to achieve a gain of a level or more in the trainee's level of functioning over the course of a reasonable, time-limited program with trainees entering at level 2 the trainer must himself be functioning at level 4. It is noteworthy that the trainees in such a program will conclude training functioning at minimally facilitative levels or above. On the other hand, in order to achieve a similar level of change with trainees entering at level 1.5 the trainer need only be functioning at level 3.5; however, such trainees will not, on the average, conclude training functioning above minimally facilitative levels. They could achieve minimal levels only if the trainers were functioning well above level 4. Conversely, if the trainers—as many are—are functioning only at level 2, then we would predict essentially no change for a group of trainees entering at level 2, slightly positive change for trainees entering at level 1.5, and slightly negative change for trainees entering at higher levels. As can be seen, the formula is reversible, with negative changes predicted where trainees enter at levels exceeding those of their trainers.

Thus, the key to trainee change is the trainer's level of functioning while the key to future functioning is the trainee's level of functioning. The two may converge in effective programs, where trainees entering at relatively high levels interact with trainers functioning at very high levels. Accordingly, trainees functioning between levels 2.0 and 2.5 initially may gain significantly over the course of training with trainers functioning between levels 4.0 and 4.5. *We can select the highest-level trainees if and only if we have the highest-level trainers.* Indeed, if we do not have the highest-level trainers we can anticipate difficulties in training. If we have low-level trainers, we can plan on trainee termination or deterioration.

SELECTION AND TRAINING: A PERSPECTIVE

Of course, training represents only a small segment of the trainer's life. Indeed, the formulas we have developed are predicated upon time-limited programs, whether they are 20 hours or four or more years. Nevertheless, as our data indicate, these programs have a very significant impact. Sometimes one very potent constructive agent can in only a few hours counterbalance forces that have been a lifetime in building. This situation would become even more apparent if we were to extend the time periods. However, this is neither economical nor efficient in terms of the trainer's investment. Long, extended, open-ended periods of training sound more like treatment and reflect upon the inadequacy of our selection procedures.

Just as with the helpee we must be attuned to the dominant influences of the environment from which the trainee comes. Unlike most helpees, however, following training the trainee will very likely be going to a new environment and we must similarly be attuned to that. In any event the level of support from a given environment will be most influential in determining the degree to which the trainee-product of a successful program maintains his gains. If the work or helping environment in which he functions, for example, offers low levels of conditions or if the people with whom he is associated do not recognize him as an agent of change, then the trainee-product must be prepared for long and arduous trials if he is to continue to grow or even to maintain his level of functioning. On the other hand, if the work setting offers high levels of conditions and support or if the people in it recognize the trainee-product as an agent of their change, then the trainee-product and the setting can be flourishing centers of health in a world that is often unhealthy. There are, of course, obligations on the part of the trainer, as well as upon his trainee-product, to nourish the development of healthy helping settings as well as actively to discourage the development of unhealthy settings, for we can do more about where our trainee-product is going than we can about where he came from.

We must, then, not only extend our models for selection and training to incorporate the other potentially influential persons or groups of persons in an individual's life, whether trainee or helpee, but we must also do what we can about these forces. We must seek to exercise control over the potentially destructive forces. We know a great deal about what forces make for good and what forces make for bad, and we can no longer afford the luxury of delay in acting upon our knowledge. In this regard we consider ourselves fortunate in our work in the area of training. It is one area in which the goals of functioning in the helping role are universally held if not attained. It is one area in which we can assess the trainers and the trainees and the effects of training by similar indexes of levels of functioning in the helping role. In a sense, then, training in human relations represents a contained process that allows us to understand aspects of real-life functioning which we might not otherwise discern so readily. For example, while we know experientially the critical nature of the teacher's contribution to student learning or the parent's contribution to child-rearing, we have not been able to apportion the sources of variance or effects as neatly as we have in the area of training simply because other significant dimensions are involved. Nevertheless, the working principles developed in our training paradigms hold—with modifications—for other areas of interpersonal functioning. In this regard we might briefly add that *the huge body of experimental work involving direct experimenter-subject contacts upon which the social and behavioral sciences are based is subject to question on this basis. We know nothing about the levels of functioning of experimenter and subject and the lack of this knowledge, probably more than anything else, accounts for negative results in one series of studies and positive results in another on the same phenomenon. Of course, low-level–functioning persons cannot replicate the results of high-level–functioning persons, whatever apparent roles such individuals assume.*

CONCLUSIONS AND DIRECTIONS

The selection procedures that have dominated training programs in helping have not been related to functional criteria by which we can measure the effectiveness of training. Similarly, the training programs themselves have not demonstrated their ability to fulfill these functional criteria. Two simple remedies have been incorporated. Based upon extensive evidence relating helper-offered facilitative and action-oriented dimensions to helpee process movement and outcome, effective selection and training programs have been developed. Simply stated, indexes of present functioning in the helping role have been developed as the best index of future functioning in the helping role. Similarly, training programs emphasizing practice in functioning in the helping role have been developed as the best means of preparing individuals to function in the helping role.

In general, we have found that a functional approach to helping puts together things that were previously disparate. We select and train helpers to function effectively on dimensions that enable the helpee to function effectively on dimensions that make a constructive difference in his life. We assess his environment with regard to those dimensions that will make a difference in the helpee's life. We research the entire selection, training, and treatment process with regard to those dimensions that will make a difference.

In this context we have seen in the formula developed that implementation of the selection and training procedures does not come easily. We have seen that if the promulgators of training programs are to attempt to select the best trainees available, they must themselves be functioning at very high levels. We have spoken about minimally facilitative levels of conditions as being level 3. This level, then, represents the minimal levels of conditions at which we can consistently demonstrate constructive change in the persons with whom we are working. However, now we see that unless the trainers are functioning around level 4 they will not be able to effect significant change in the lives of others. And, even if such trainers do effect significant changes in the trainees, the trainee-products will not be functioning at minimally facilitative, self-sustaining absolute levels. When we combine this finding with what we know about most of the environments in which the trainee-products will be functioning, we can predict only deterioration for the trainee-product over time.

What can the promulgators of these training programs, both lay and professional, do in order to implement programs that maximize the possibility of trainee change over the course of training as well as absolute level of trainee functioning? First, those who have the responsibility of training others can begin with themselves. If they are not themselves functioning at the highest possible levels, they must become involved in processes that lead to higher levels of functioning. At a minimum systematic training programs conducted by trainers who are functioning at the highest levels are necessary. Second, those in charge of training programs can select trainees who are functioning at the highest levels. Depending upon the circumstances and the means available, they can obtain that index of functioning that most closely approximates real-life functioning in the helping role. Third, they can institute procedures and practices that most effectively achieve the goals of their programs. In this connection the programs may be predicated upon the unique interaction of variables in a given setting. Thus, for example, with a population of trainees or trainers functioning at a high level (level 3 or above) discrimination training may more effectively precede communication training, while with a population functioning at a low level communication training may more effectively precede discrimination. In addition, the program must equip the trainee with all of the tools and ancillary modes of treatment that he will need to employ in his helping relationships. Obviously, the trainer must be similarly equipped in order to transmit these tools.

Briefly, then, the formula for selection and training simply gives us a rough approximation of what effects to anticipate according to the conditions that dominate a particular program. The approximation will change as the conditions change, and the conditions will change as the trainers change. *The trainers will change as they themselves enter and live their own lives most fully, for only then can they help another person who in turn can help still another person.*

In summary, the three R's of helping with which we began this volume—the *right* of intervention, the *responsibility* for intervention, and the *role* in intervention—lead quite readily into the fourth R of helping—the full *realization* of the helper's resources, the subject with which we begin the second volume.

Appendix A
RELEVANT PUBLICATIONS
OF THE AUTHOR

1963

Role conflicts of beginning therapists. Buffalo, N.Y.: Psychology and Education Tapes, 1963 (with M. J. Feldman).

The ambiguity dimension in psychotherapy. *Discussion papers, Wisconsin Psychiatric Institute*, 1963, No. 46, pp. 1–7.

On the necessary conditions of therapeutic personality change. *Discussion papers, Wisconsin Psychiatric Institute*, 1963, No. 47. pp. 1–7.

1964

For better or for worse: The process of psychotherapeutic personality change. Chapter 8, *Recent advances in the study of behavior change.* Montreal, Canada: McGill University Press, 1964, pp. 118–163 (with C. B. Truax).

Significant developments in psychotherapy research. Chapter 7, *Progress in clinical psychology* (L. E. Abt and B. F. Reiss, eds.). New York: Grune and Stratton, 1964, pp. 124–155 (with C. B. Truax).

Concreteness: A neglected variable in research in psychology. *Journal of Clinical Psychology*, 1964, **11**, 67–71 (with C. B. Truax).

Kuder neuropsychiatric keys before and after psychotherapy. *Journal of Counseling Psychology*, 1964, **11**, 67–71 (with J. Drasgow).

The old and the new: Theory and research in counseling and psychotherapy. *Personnel and Guidance Journal*, 1934, **42**, 860–866 (with C. B. Truax).

Age and role reversal in therapy. *Journal of Clinical Psychology*, 1964, **20**, 398–402 (with M. J. Feldman and C. B. Truax).

Toward an integration of didactic and experiential approaches to training in counseling and psychotherapy. *Journal of Counseling Psychology*, 1964, **11**, 140–147 (with J. Douds and C. B. Truax).

1965

The counselor's handbook: Vol. III, scale and profile interpretations of the MMPI. Urbana, Ill.: Parkinson (Follett), 1965.

Client and therapist transparency in the psychotherapeutic encounter. *Journal of Counseling Psychology*, 1965, **12**, 3–9 (with C. B. Truax).

The experimental manipulation of therapeutic conditions. *Journal of Consulting Psychology*, 1965, **29**, 119–124 (with C. B. Truax).

Personality change in hospitalized mental patients during group psychotherapy as a function of the use of alternate sessions and vicarious therapy pre-training. *Journal of Clinical Psychology*, 1965, **21**, 225–228 (with C. B. Truax).

Training in counseling and psychotherapy: An evaluation of an integrated didactic and experiential approach. *Journal of Consulting Psychology*, 1965, **29**, 333–336 (with C. B. Truax).

Lay mental health counseling: The effectiveness of lay group counseling. *Journal of Consulting Psychology*, 1965, **29**, 426–431 (with C. B. Truax).

1966

Toward effective counseling and psychotherapy: Training and practice. Chicago, Ill.: Aldine Publishing Company, 1966 (with C. B. Truax).

Toward explaining success or failure in interpersonal learning processes. *Personnel and Guidance Journal*, 1966, **44**, 723–728 (with C. B. Truax).

Changes in self-concepts during group psychotherapy as a function of alternate sessions and vicarious therapy pre-training in institutionalized mental patients and juvenile delinquents. *Journal of Counsulting Psychology*, 1966, **30**, 309–314 (with C. B. Truax).

Training in the counseling and therapeutic processes: Requiem or reveille? *Journal of Counseling Psychology*, 1966, **13**, 360–367.

Process variables in counseling and psychotherapy: A study of counseling and friendship. *Journal of Counseling Psychology*, 1966, **13**, 356–359. (with J. C. Martin and B. G. Berenson).

The interpersonal functioning and training of college students. *Journal of Counseling Psychology*, 1966, **13**, 441–446 (with B. G. Berenson and P. Myrus).

Counseling research, theory and practice—1965. *Journal of Counseling Psychology*, 1966, **13**, 467–480.

(Invited to do review of counseling literature for 1965 by Division 17, Committee on Scientific Affairs, A.P.A.).

1967

The sources of gain in counseling and psychotherapy. New York: Holt, Rinehart and Winston, Inc. (with B. G. Berenson).

Beyond counseling and therapy. New York: Holt, Rinehart and Winston, Inc., 1967 (with B. G. Berenson).

The client-centered process: As viewed by psychoanalytic, existential, eclectic and client-centered theorists. Chapter 19, *The therapeutic relationship and its impact: A study of psychotherapy with schizophrenics.* Madison, Wisc.: University of Wisconsin Press, 1967, pp. 419–505. C. R. Rogers, E. T. Gendlin, and C. B. Truax, eds. (with P. Bergman, C. S. English, W. C. Lewis, R. May, J. Seeman, C. B. Truax, and C. A. Whitaker).

Toward a comprehensive model of facilitative interpersonal processes. *Journal of Counseling Psychology*, 1967, 14, 67–72.

The differential effects of the manipulation of therapeutic conditions upon high and low functioning clients. *Journal of Counseling Psychology*, 1967, 14, 63–66 (with B. G. Berenson and T. Holder).

The effects of the manipulation of client depth of self-exploration upon high and low functioning counselors. *Journal of Clinical Psychology*, 1967, 23, 210–212, (with M. Alexik).

The differential effects of high and low functioning counselors upon counselors-upon counselors-in-training. *Journal of Clinical Psychology*, 1967, 23, 212–215 (with R. Pierce and B. G. Berenson).

The search for an identity. *Counselor Education and Supervision*, 1967, 6, 311–316.

The differential effects of counselor race and social class upon patient depth of self-exploration in an initial clinical interview. *Journal of Consulting Psychology*, 1967, 31, 632–634 (with R. Pierce).

The differential effects of the manipulation of client self-exploration upon high and low functioning counselors. *Journal of Counseling Psychology*, 1967, 14, 350–355 (with M. Alexik).

The differential effects of absolute level and direction of growth in counselor functioning upon client functioning. *Journal of Clinical Psychology*, 1967, 23, 216–218 (with D. Kratochvil and D. Aspy).

The predicted differential effects of the level of counselor functioning upon the level of functioning of outpatients. *Journal of Clinical Psychology*, 1967, 23, 510–512 (with W. Pagell and B. G. Berenson).

The differential effects of the manipulation of therapeutic conditions by high and low functioning counselors upon high and low functioning clients. *Journal of Consulting Psychology*, 1967, 31, 481–486 (with G. Piaget and B. G. Berenson).

The contributions of a phenomenological approach to determine approaches to counseling. *Journal of Counseling Psychology*, 1967, 14, 570–572.

1968

The counselor's contribution to facilitative processes. Buffalo, N. Y.: State University of New York at Buffalo, 1968.

The development of skills in interpersonal functioning. *Counselor Education and Supervision*, 1968, 7, 102–106 (with G. Piaget and R. Pierce).

The "non-traditional" assessment of graduate training in the helping professions. *Counselor Education and Supervision*, 1968, 7, 252–261.

The effects of professional training: The communication and discrimination of facilitative conditions. *Journal of Counseling Psychology*, 1968, **15**, 68–74 (with T. Friel and D. Kratochvil).

The effects of training upon changes in trainee personality and behavior. *Journal of Clinical Psychology*, 1968, **24**, 109–110 (with J. Martin).

The differential functioning of lay and professional helpers. *Journal of Counseling Psychology*, 1968, **15**, 417–426.

Plastic and reconstructive surgery as an instance of crisis therapy. *Journal of Rehabilitation*, 1968, **33**, 15–18 (with B. G. Berenson).

The effects of training and experience upon the manipulation of client conditions. *Journal of Clinical Psychology*, 1968, **24**, 247–249 (with T. Friel and D. Kratochvil).

Lay mental health counseling: Prospects and problems. *Journal of Individual Psychology*, 1968, **24**, 88–93.

Helper communication as a function of helpee affect and content. *Journal of Counseling Psychology*, 1969, **16**, 126–131.

Objective, client and therapist ratings of therapist-offered facilitative conditions of moderate and low functioning therapists. *Journal of Clinical Psychology*, in press, 1969 (with J. Burstein).

Critical variables in effective counselor training. *Journal of Counselor Psychology*, in press, 1969.

The prediction of the effects of didactic training in discrimination. *Journal of Clinical Psychology*, in press, 1969 (with T. Collingwood and L. Renz).

The prediction of the effects of teacher-counselor training: The development of communication and discrimination selection indexes. *Counselor Education and Supervision*, in press, 1969.

The effects of rehabilitation counselor training upon discrimination, communication and helping attitudes. *Journal of Counseling Psychology*, in press, 1969 (with W. Anthony).

The effects of experience and level of functioning on accuracy of discrimination. *Journal of Consulting Psychology*, in press, 1969 (with J. Cannon).

The effects of parent and teacher-offered levels of facilitative conditions upon indexes of student physical, emotional and intellectual functioning. *Journal of Educational Research*, in press, 1969 (with D. Kratochvil).

The effects of human relations training upon parents of emotionally disturbed children. *Journal of Counseling Psychology*, in press, 1969 (with R. Bierman).

The nature, structure and function of commitment. *Journal of Rehabilitation*, in press, 1969 (with B. G. Berenson).

The counselor is a man and a woman. *Personnel and Guidance Journal*, in press, 1969 (with B. G. Berenson).

The effects of human relations training upon relations between races and generations. *Journal of Counseling Psychology*, in press, 1969 (with G. Banks).

Developments in eclectism. *Journal of Individual Psychology*, in press, 1969.

Appendix B

SYSTEMATIC DESENSITIZATION MANUAL FOR HELPER INSTRUCTION AND TREATMENT PROCEDURE*

INTRODUCTION

The purpose of this manual is to serve as a guide in the performing of one type of behavior therapy, namely, systematic desensitizaton. In this procedure objects, persons, or events that are upsetting or distressing to the client are gradually put before him while he is in a state of deep relaxation. The aim of this approach is to minimize the disrupting effects of anxiety that inhibit his more effective and efficient coping with real-life problems. A knowledge of or belief in "learning theory" per se is not necessary for the adequate implementation of this therapeutic approach. In essence, one is confronted by a client having difficulties in some or many areas of his life. If it appears, after a careful assessment of these difficulties, that the client is hampered in action by his own feelings of anxiety, it behooves any good therapist to intervene in such a way as to reduce these obstacles. Systematic desensitization is one technique for effective intervention in such instances. Its range of applicability is not limited to the classical phobias. It may be used to deal with numerous less obvious and often complex sources of distress. These may involve ideas, bodily sensations, or external situations. The most common external source of anxiety occurs in the context of dealing with other people. For example, a client may react with anxiety to the mere presence of other persons, especially those in authority. As a consequence, he may begin to doubt his adequacy, gradually withdraw from contacts with others, and appear depressed. Another person experiencing the same anxiety in the presence of others may develop different reactive behaviors—although similarly self-defeating. He may become boisterous or overaggressive. In both instances anxiety is the root diffi-

---

* Prepared by Raphael Vitalo, University of Massachusetts, Amherst, Mass. An illustration of one set of elaborated procedures which have been developed for training, this manual draws upon the writings of Joseph Wolpe, Peter Lang, and David Lazovik for its informative and procedural guidelines.

271

culty that, at the same point in treatment, must be dealt with if the client is to institute more self-beneficial behaviors.

In order to utilize the desensitization technique, a therapist must have knowledge and develop skill in the three sets of operations involved: (1) training in deep muscle relaxation; (2) the construction of anxiety hierarchies; and (3) the counterposing of relaxation and anxiety-provoking stimuli from the client's hierarchy.

DEEP MUSCLE RELAXATION

The purpose of this training is to induce a highly relaxed state in your client, so that when he is confronted with the anxiety-provoking stimuli, either through his imagining or verbalizing them, he will remain at ease and gradually "unlearn" his former distressing response. The client should be informed of this purpose and of the beneficial emotional effects that relaxation holds.

The training begins with the therapist choosing a particular muscle group to demonstrate, with the client's aid, the contrast between tension and relaxation. The hand or forearm is usually chosen as a beginning point and the therapist instructs the client to make a tight fist (in the case of the hand) and maintain it for a period of 15 to 20 seconds. While the client is performing this action, the therapist calls to his attention the feelings of tension that he, the client, is experiencing. The therapist then instructs the client to allow his fist to open and rest while bringing to his notice the now different, pleasant sensations of relaxation.[1]

During the training period the following muscle groups are focused upon:

A. Extensor Muscles
   1. Right hand and forearm
   2. Entire right arm
   3. Left hand and forearm
   4. Entire left arm
   5. Right thigh and calf
   6. Entire right leg
   7. Left thigh and calf
   8. Entire left leg
B. Abdominal Muscles
   1. Stomach muscles
   2. Lower back muscles
C. Facial Muscles
   1. Forehead
   2. Eyes
   3. Nose

[1] Besides pointing out this contrast, the therapist will usually give the suggestion to his client to allow himself to feel this relaxation ever more and to allow this feeling to spread throughout his entire body.

D. Upper Trunk and Neck
   1. Neck
   2. Shoulders
   3. Chest

The training proceeds from one to another muscle group following the same format of first tension and then relaxation. Usually the therapist focuses on one muscle group per session. At the following session there is a brief review of each previous muscle group before the therapist and client move on to the next. Between sessions the client is instructed to practice at home what he has thus far learned for a period of 20 minutes a day. Commonly, five to seven sessions are sufficient for training a client. After this period, the therapist need only give general suggestions of relaxation to his patient. He may accompany these suggestions with a cursory review of the muscle groups. There is no longer any need to contrast tension with relaxation, so the exercises for inducing tension are omitted. Once the client has achieved a relaxed state, the therapist should use direct suggestion to further increase his relaxation. For example:

THERAPIST: You are now quite calm and your body is very much relaxed. However, you may still become even more deeply relaxed, and—as I count backwards from ten to one you will achieve even greater depths of relaxation. . . Ten, nine, . . ., and so on.

It should be stressed that for the training to be successful the full cooperation of the client is essential. In addition, the therapist will find it of some benefit in conducting the training of his client if he himself has experienced deep relaxation. His suggestive descriptions will come more easily and will tend to have greater effectiveness.

THE CONSTRUCTION OF ANXIETY HIERARCHIES

An anxiety hierarchy is a list of stimuli (objects, persons, events) to which a client reacts with graded amounts of anxiety. The most disturbing item is placed at the top of the list, the least disturbing at the bottom. Hierarchy construction usually begins at the same time as relaxation training. Modifications or additions may be made at any point during treatment.

The information needed for the construction of the hierarchies is obtained from: (a) conversations with the client about his past history, especially the history of his complaints; (b) client responses to a fear inventory or questionnaire such as the Willoughby Personality Schedule; and (c) a listing made by the client himself of situations he finds upsetting, embarrassing, or in any way distressing. In each instance the therapist looks for the specific circumstances that provoke the client's unnecessary and self-defeating reactions. Usually the stimuli fall into definable groups of themes. The themes may be obvious ones like fear of enclosed places or less obvious ones like fear of rejection. In most cases the themes and the subsumed anxiety-provoking stimuli are clearly related to the client's expressed complaints.[2] For example, a student comes to a university clinic with the complaint that he is too upset to study and that, although he is generally relaxed and easygoing, when he has to study he becomes tense and unable to concentrate. The most pertinent anxiety-eliciting stimulus in this case would be "sitting at a desk and doing an assignment." A hierarchy using this situation as its highest point might be constructed.

Once a major theme and its most powerful stimulus has been identified, it becomes the therapist's task to construct other related stimulus situations that in varying degrees elicit the same distressing response. In the case of the student, other levels in the studying hierarchy could be developed by using the dimension of distance (temporal or spatial) from the actual event (that is, studying) or by using the dimension of similarity. In the former instance, the therapist might propose as a lower level on the hierarchy "standing across the room facing your desk one hour before you must sit down and study." Using the similarity dimension, one might propose as a lower-level situation "reading a book unrelated to your course work." There are other possible dimensions that the therapist may use, for example, number and intensity. The student might imagine studying for several exams versus one exam or for a final exam versus a daily quiz. The dimension that the therapist uses to graduate to a particular hierarchy will depend upon what the client experiences as meaningful in terms of representing variations in his level of experienced distress.

In more than 50 percent of the cases seen by a therapist, more than one thematic grouping or stimulus hierarchy is involved in the client's presentation of his difficulties. To return to the example of the student, it might well turn out that a rather intense fear of failure may have tainted his reactions to studying A hierarchy dealing specifically with the theme of failure would also be constructed and worked with. As the treatment progressed a further refinement might occur. The student's undue and self-defeating fear of failure might partially have its roots in a more general fear of being rejected by others. Such a development would not be unexpected, and a hierarchy dealing with this problem would also be constructed.

In each instance of hierarchy building the same successive steps occur: (a) identification of a major theme; (b) identification of the most potent stimulus event; (c) development along some dimension (temporal or spatial distance, similarity, number, intensity) of related but less potent stimulus events; and (d) evaluation by the client of the proposed levels in the hierarchy. With reference to the last step (d), the therapist may supply the client with a list of proposed stimulus items and have him rank them according to how threateningly he experiences them. After the ranking is completed, it is advisable to review the listing with the client, instructing him to alert you to any sequence

---

[2] See case A (below) for an instance in which the anxiety-provoking stimuli are not self-evidently related to the client's expressed complaints.

that may seem too abrupt a transition in terms of the degrees of distress experienced. The beginning therapist should be especially cautious about the beginning items on the hierarchy. A common difficulty encountered by therapists inexperienced in the construction of anxiety hierarchies is to find that even the weakest item in a thematic group produces more anxiety than can be counteracted by the patient's relaxation. No harm is ever done by including and presenting a stimulus that is too weak.

As with the relaxation training, again it must be stressed that client cooperation is essential. There will be occasions when a client will be genuinely unable to render a clear description of his complaints or of the circumstances that instigate them. In these instances, the therapist must "tease out" the significant elements in the information he does receive from the client.

Sample Hierarchies

CASE A—A man of 22 who had suffered from impotence for three years before seeking help. This case is important because it underlines the need for the correct identification of the relevant sources of anxiety. Although his difficulty was in the sexual sphere, the crucial stimuli eliciting his anxiety and in turn hindering his potency were not specifically sexual. Rather, they centered around his sensitivity to pain and tissue damage in other people.

(Wolpe, 1958)

Hierarchies

A. Injury and Suffering
1. Idea of uterus being scraped.
2. An untreated fractured limb (what is most disturbing is the idea of the broken ends scraping together).
3. A raw wound bleeding (worse if large; worse on the face than on trunk and not so bad on a limb).
4. A person being injected (would be worse if Mr. L had to give the injection himself).
5. A very small facial wound with much bleeding.
6. Dissecting an animal.
7. Injecting a drug into an animal.
8. The sight of a dead human body.
9. Watching someone else dissect an animal.
10. Seeing a patient propped up in bed short of breath.
11. An old unhealed wound; the larger the worse.
12. Seeing an animal that has just been killed by a car.
13. Seeing an animal that has died evidently of disease.
14. A small facial wound with slight bleeding.
15. Traumatic epistaxis.
16. A schoolboy being caned.

B. Vocalizing of Suffering
   1. An unseen hospital patient groaning.
   2. His father groaning.
   3. A child groaning.
   4. A customer comes in groaning and says he has abdominal cramps.
   5. A kicked dog howling.
C. Vocal Violence
   1. A quarrel in his family.
   2. A quarrel anywhere else.
   3. A child being shouted at.

(Wolpe, 1958, pp. 155–156)

CASE B—An unmarried 46-year-old woman came to therapy with an extreme sensitivity to other people in many social contexts. Her proneness to anxiety further exacerbated her ulcer, which she had suffered with for one year.

The importance of this case is in demonstrating a hierarchy (A) that includes a broad range of social stimuli.

Hierarchies
A. Broad Range of Social Stimuli
   1. Having an interview with any doctor or lawyer (her own doctor was the stimulus figure used in the desensitization).
   2. Unexpectedly finding a strange man when visiting at her brother's house.
   3. Being phoned by a man to whom recently introduced.
   4. Speaking, in company, to a man to whom just introduced.
   5. Meeting her girl friend's boy friend.
   6. Making a speech to the employees of her firm at the end-of-the-year party.
   7. Going up to receive a prize at the end-of-the-year party.
   8. Having an interview with the representative of the Industrial Council because of sick pay not received from employer.
   9. Telling her employer that an error of which she has been accused is due to someone else's wrong instruction.
   10. Being told by her employer that a hem she has made is not straight.
   11. Criticisms from members of her family.
   12. Criticisms from fellow-workers.
   13. Being at a party with other girls who work with her.
B. Shouting and Arguments between Others
   1. Men across the road punching each other; with Miss T. the only witness.
   2. Men across the road punching each other in the presence of other people besides Miss T.

3. A man across the road punches another man with whom he is quarreling without being punched in return.
4. Men across the road engaged in argument.

(Wolpe, 1958, p. 148 ff)

CASE C—A 41-year-old medical resident who had felt anxious and insecure most of his life came to therapy with the sensitivities listed below.

The importance of this case is in the material and problems dealt with—namely, feelings of being "at fault" even when there was no justification. The hierarchies deal with insecurity, unjustified guilt, and self-devaluation, topics not usually associated with conditioning therapy.

Hierarchies

A. Unjustified Feelings of Being "At Fault" and Guilty
   1. "Jackson (the dean of the medical school) wants to see you."
   2. Thinks, "I did only 10 minutes' work today."
   3. Thinks, "I did only an hour's work today."
   4. Thinks, "I did only six hours' work today."
   5. Sitting at the movies.
   6. Reading an enjoyable novel.
   7. Going on a casual stroll.
   8. Staying in bed during the day (even though ill).

B. Insecurity and Devaluation Series
   1. A woman doesn't respond to his advances.
   2. An acquaintance says, "I saw you in Jefferson Street with a woman." (This kind of activity had locally acquired a disreputable flavor.)
   3. Having a piece of writing rejected.
   4. Awareness that his skill at a particular surgical operation left something to be desired. (Anxiety in terms of "Will I ever be able to do it?")
   5. Overhearing adverse remarks about a lecture he delivered that he knows was not good.
   6. Overhearing, "Dr. B. fancies himself as a surgeon."
   7. Hearing anyone praised, for example, "Dr. K. is a fine surgeon."
   8. Having submitted a piece of writing for publication.

(Wolpe, 1961)

CASE D—A 50-year-old housewife whose main complaints were phobic in nature and referred to enclosed places, death, and illness. This case is included to give the beginning therapist exposure to a large number of items, their phrasing, and the manner in which the difficulty of an item may be varied along the distance dimension.

Hierarchies

A. Claustrophobic Series
    1. Being stuck in an elevator. (The longer the time, the more disturbing.)
    2. Being locked in a room. (The smaller the room and the longer the time, the more disturbing.)
    3. Passing through a tunnel in a railway train. (The longer the tunnel, the more disturbing.)
    4. Traveling in an elevator alone. (The greater the distance, the more disturbing.)
    5. Traveling in an elevator with an operator. (The longer the distance, the more disturbing.)
    6. Stuck in a dress with a stuck zipper.
    7. Having a tight ring on her finger.
    8. Visiting and unable to leave at will (for example, if engaged in a card game).
    9. Being told of somebody in jail.
    10. Having polish on her fingernails and no access to remover.
    11. Reading of miners trapped underground.

B. Death Series
    1. Being at a burial.
    2. Being at a house of mourning.
    3. The word "death."
    4. Seeing a funeral procession. (The nearer, the more disturbing.)
    5. The sight of a dead animal, for example, a cat.
    6. Driving past a cemetery. (The nearer, the more disturbing.)

C. Illness Series
    1. Hearing that an acquaintance has cancer.
    2. The word "cancer."
    3. Witnessing a convulsive seizure.
    4. Discussions of operations. (The more prolonged the discussion, the more disturbing.)
    5. Seeing a person receive an injection.
    6. Seeing someone faint.
    7. The word "operation."
    8. Considerable bleeding from another person.
    9. A friend points to a stranger, saying, "This man has tuberculosis."
    10. The sight of a blood-stained bandage.
    11. The smell of ether.

12. The sight of a friend sick in bed. (The more sick looking, the more disturbing.)
13. The smell of methylated spirits.
14. Driving past a hospital.

(Wolpe, 1961, pp. 196–197)

THE COUNTERPOSING OF RELAXATION AND ANXIETY-PROVOKING STIMULI: SYSTEMATIC DESENSITIZATION

After the relaxation training has been completed and initial hierarchies have been constructed, the next phase in treatment is the systematic presentation of items in the client's anxiety hierarchy while he is in a state of deep relaxation. The therapist should introduce the client to what will take place and what is hoped will be achieved, namely, the elimination of obstacles preventing more effective action on his part by replacing these obstacles (anxiety responses) with feelings of relaxation. The client is told that he will enter a deeply relaxed state and that, while relaxed, he will be asked to imagine clearly and vividly scenes from his hierarchy. He is instructed to indicate (usually by raising a finger or a hand) if any of the scenes are upsetting to him.

The client is then placed in a deeply relaxed state and given a "neutral" scene to imagine—for example, standing before an open field under a bright blue sky with a pleasant warm breeze blowing or reclining in a hammock on a lazy Sunday afternoon. After a period of 10 seconds, the therapist instructs the client to stop imagining this scene and to turn his attention once more to relaxation. This may last for approximately 30 seconds. This is followed by a small number of presentations (3–4) of the mildest items from one or two of the client's hierarchies. Each presentation is alternated with an interval of relaxation. At the completion of the session, the therapist interviews the client to discover how well relaxed he felt, whether he was able to clearly visualize the scenes presented,[3] whether these scenes produced any discomfort and, if they did, how much.

At subsequent sessions, the same basic format (that is, imagined scene 10 seconds, relaxation 30 seconds, imagined scene 10 seconds) is followed. If, at the end of the previous session, the client reported slight *and* decreasing discomfort with the repeated presentation of a particular item, that item becomes the first one dealt with at the new session. If, at the close of the last meeting, the client reported an undiminishing reaction to a particular item, the therapist should construct a new item of less strength. This new item should be dealt with before the therapist returns to the original disturbing item. Finally, if the client reported no further reaction to an item presented at the previous

---

[3] Occasionally a client will not be able to visualize at all or his reactions to the imagined scenes will not reflect his reactions to the actual scenes. In such cases, verbalization of the scene by the client may be successfully substituted.

session, the therapist should move on to the next highest item on the client's hierarchy. In order to gauge progress during a session and to decide whether it is appropriate to move on to a new item, the therapist should ask the client to indicate, via the prearranged sign, if he experienced even the slightest discomfort to the last presentation of a particular item. If the signal is not given, the therapist moves on to the next item in the hierarchy.

The therapist must be prepared for several contingencies that may interfere with the normal course of the procedure. First, with the presentation of an item, the client may signal distress. In this event, the therapist immediately instructs the client to stop imagining the particular scene and to turn his attention to relaxation. Extra time should be spent in returning the client to his former relaxed state. If the client's distress is noticeable (that is, if he becomes uneasy in his seat, grimaces, and so on), it is wise to discontinue desensitization for the remainder of the session. Again, before the distressing item is reintroduced, one of slightly lesser strength should be constructed and dealt with. A second possible occurrence is that the client will not signal distress, yet he will evidence physical signs of discomfort. In this case the therapist should shorten the period of visualization, from 10 seconds to perhaps 5 seconds, and emphasize relaxation. An alternate scene of less strength may be substituted, or the therapist may elect to present the same scene for a shorter time (5 seconds). A third possibility is that the client will be unable to relax at the beginning of a session. The therapist may try to aid the client by reviewing sequentially the muscle groups. If this is not completely successful, desensitization should not be attempted. The session may be postponed or given over to discussing what may be interfering with the client's relaxation.

The number of hierarchies dealt with in a given session as well as the number of scenes from each hierarchy and the number of presentations of a particular scene vary greatly. It has been suggested that up to four hierarchies may be drawn from at a particular meeting (Wolpe, 1961). The number of new scenes presented will depend upon the client's reaction to past scenes and the amount of time available in a session. It is good procedure for a beginning therapist to limit his presentations to four new scenes per session. The number of repetitions of a scene is generally 3 to 4, however, as many as 15 to 20 may be needed before a client ceases to report discomfort. The continued repetition of an item may become tedious for a client. To offset this, it is wise for a therapist to mix his presentations. For example, client X has hierarchies A, B, and C; the sequence of presentations used could be as follows: item A_1, relaxation; item B_1, relaxation; item A_1, relaxation; item C_1, relaxation; item A_1, relaxation and inquiry concerning reaction to item A_1.

The interval of relaxation will generally remain at 30 seconds; however, if the need arises to emphasize relaxation, the period may be extended until the desired effect is achieved.

The length of a session varies from 30 minutes to an hour and is governed by the client's desire to continue the procedure and the amount of work that needs to be completed. The number of sessions per week is generally but not necessarily two. During the period of relaxation training, it is worthwhile to have at least two meetings per week to facilitate the client's learning how to relax.

In general, the therapist should be consistently aware of the client's state. He should stand ready to modify existing hierarchies, to alter the order of items, to add new items, and if the need arises, to construct entirely new hierarchies. While guidelines concerning the exposure time to an imagined scene, the length of an interval of relaxation, the number of items presented in a session, and so on, should be adhered to, the therapist must remain flexible and ready to alter any of these to meet the needs of the client.

REFERENCES AND SUGGESTED READINGS

Wolpe, J. *Psychotherapy by reciprocal inhibition.* Stanford, Calif.: Stanford University Press, 1958.

Wolpe, J. Systematic desensitization of neuroses. *Journal of Nervous and Mental Diseases,* 1961, **132,** 189–203.

Wolpe, J., Salter, A., & Regna, L. *The conditioning therapies.* New York: Holt, Rinehart and Winston, Inc., 1964.

THERAPY PROCEDURE°

Session I: Initial Interview with Client

The client is interviewed by the therapist, with the initial focus on his presenting difficulties and their history. An attempt is made to identify any precipitating events and any factors that noticeably aggravate or ameliorate the client's symptoms. The interview may gradually unfold to cover related areas in the client's life. The therapist seeks information in order to determine what stimuli (objects, persons, situations) provoke the client's neurotic reactions.

Session II: Introduction: Beginning of Muscle Training and Hierarchy Building

1. The patient is informed of the type of treatment he is to receive and is given a brief description of it.

> After going over your test results and after considering what we discussed at our last meeting, it appears that a special type of treatment may well be of benefit in your case. This type of treatment deals directly with one's anxieties, fears, and feelings of distress by first attempting to identify what circumstances, situations, persons, or

° This section is adapted in part from P. Lang and A. Lazovik, *Systematic desensitization: An experimental Analogue.* Mimeographed research manual, Sept., 1966.

objects presently give rise to these feelings in you, and second, by training you to no longer react to these situations, persons, and so on, that upset. As you can see, there is a twofold process involved. The first is to gather relevant information—our conversation last time was a step in this direction. The second is to put this information to use to your benefit. Before beginning this second phase we will devote some time to training you in relaxation.

I will have more to say about the treatment as we go along, but for now, how do you feel about it?

The patient is encouraged to verbalize any fear or apprehension that he or she may feel about the treatment. In each case an attempt at reassurance is made. However, it is stressed that the patient should not feel any concern about the therapist's feelings if at any point he decides not to continue treatment. It is also stressed that frankness with the therapist is important. It is explained that the treatment will have little if any benefit unless the patient is willing to cooperate to the best of his ability. If the patient indicates in some manner his willingness to continue, he is then given more information concerning the treatment. It is stressed that he will be fully informed as to what is going on and that questions are always appropriate:

As you have already been told, the treatment will last 20 sessions, and we will be meeting about twice a week. Our next five meetings— of about 45 minutes to one hour—will be devoted to gathering information and training you to relax your muscles. You perhaps think that you already know how to relax, but I think you will find that you can relax even more. During this time we will also be compiling a list of things and situations that are upsetting to you. You will be asked to order these items in terms of the degree to which they make you frightened, anxious, or uncomfortable. For example, _____. [Here, choose an example suitable to your patient's problems, for example, if his complaint is of a fear of heights, contrast his standing on a table with his standing on the roof of a building; if his complaint is shyness, contrast his conversing with a friend with his speaking to a total stranger.] After the training sessions we will see each other for 14 more meetings of about 45 minutes each. During these sessions we will be working with the list of situations you describe as upsetting. The relaxation will be important in desensitizing you to these things. I'll be able to tell you more about this as we go along. Any questions now?

2. At this point an interview is conducted, focusing on the feared objects. As an aid the therapist may refer to the client's response on the Willoughby Schedule and the FSS-III. The patient is encouraged to describe real or imagined experiences with the feared object and to attempt to rate these

incidents as more or less frightening. The therapist notes these and instructs the client to think further of experiences with the feared situations or objects and attempt to place them in order from least to most fearful. He is instructed to bring this list to the next session.

3. Progressive relaxation procedure—introduction

> Now I am going to start teaching you to relax your muscles. In essence, muscle relaxation consists of doing nothing with your muscles —making them completely free of tension. You know what muscle tension is; relaxation is the opposite—freedom from tension.
> You learn to relax your muscles through your own conscious effort. First you must learn where the muscles are that you wish to relax. You will learn to locate these muscles by tensing them or contracting them and then by concentrating on where the muscular tension is and what it feels like. Once you have learned to locate the muscle and to recognize the tension in it, I want you to concentrate on the feeling of relaxation you will produce by doing nothing with the given muscle—just letting it go completely limp. Most people don't realize that when they think they are relaxed they are capable of consciously producing an even greater degree of muscular relaxation by just letting their muscles go—letting them become limp, by doing nothing. We will be working with a number of different muscle groups, taking them one at a time. Our goal is a state of general bodily relaxation. I will want you to practice this relaxation at home for about 15 to 30 minutes a day. We shall go into the details of this later.

Muscle relaxation takes place while the patient sits upright in the chair, with his eyes closed. Two muscle groups are relaxed in Session II. The instructions and periods of relaxation are as follows.[4]

> Now that you are beginning your muscle relaxation training, I'd like to say a word about your role in this phase of our work. You have a very active role in this procedure, as you will have throughout the treatment. You will be the one that will be relaxing your muscles. You will be the one who determines how much relaxation you can experience. You will do this by learning to do nothing with your muscles except to relax them. I'm sure as we proceed with muscle relaxation training you will see just how important a role you play in being in charge of your relaxation.

> *Left Arm Extensor (remarks in brackets are for the therapist and are not to be spoken)*

[4] For a general discussion of the progressive relaxation procedure, see Jacobson, *Progressive Relaxation* (Chicago: University of Chicago Press, 1938).

1. Bend your hand back at the wrist, maintaining this for one minute. Notice the tension in your wrist, hand, and forearm.
2. Let your hand fall relaxed. Don't put it down. Pretend your hand is held up by a string. I cut the string and your hand falls limp.
3. [Relax!] Let your hand be limp. Notice the now different sensation of relaxation and enjoy this feeling.
4. [Repeat steps 1, 2, and 3, contracting the hand at the wrist *for only 10* seconds]
5. [Repeat steps 1 and 2 and then let your arm relax for 3 minutes. Give suggestions to client to allow the pleasant feeling of relaxation to fill his entire arm]

Left Arm Extensor
1. Bend your left arm at your elbow and tense your biceps—tense them harder—harder—hold it and study the tension. [Gradually build up the tension for about 30 seconds]
2. Relax the arm completely. [One minute]
3. Now relax the arm even more. [For another minute]
4. [Repeat step 1. Contract the arm for only 15 seconds]
5. Now relax the arm completely. [For about three minutes]

I'd like you to practice relaxing your muscles at home. Simply relax them. Don't contract the muscles when you practice at home. Find a comfortable chair, away from distractions, where you can be alone for 15 to 30 minutes. Practice relaxing your muscles in the same order you have learned to relax them here.

Session III: Hierarchy Building, Muscle Training Continued

The therapist should inquire about the amount of muscle relaxation practice in which the patient has engaged and encourage him to continue his practice. The therapist then examines with the patient the list of fear-provoking incidents the patient has prepared between meetings. Items are added if there are too few at a particular level of difficulty. Items are eliminated if they are inappropriate or unrealistic. An effort is made to select items suitable for an "anxiety hierarchy." The final ranking is not done until Session IV.

1. Muscle relaxation training
   A. Muscle review
      (1) Gradually close your eyes. [15 seconds]
      (2) Relax your left forearm. [30 seconds]
      (3) Relax your entire left arm. [30 seconds]
   B. Right arm extensor
      (1) Bend your right hand back at the wrist. Maintain this

for one minute and notice the tension in your wrist and right forearm.

(2) Let your hand fall relaxed. Don't put it down; just let it fall. Pretend your hand is held up by a string. I cut the string and your hand falls limp.

(3) Now relax . . . let your hand be limp and enjoy the pleasant feelings [one minute]

(4) [Repeat steps 1, 2, and 3, bending your wrist for only 10 seconds]

(5) [Repeat steps 1 and 2 and then let your arm relax for three minutes]

C. Entire right arm

(1) Bend your right arm back at the elbow and tense your bicep—harder, harder . . . hold it. [Gradually build up tension for 30 seconds]

(2) Relax the arm completely [one minute]

(3) Now relax it even more [one minute]

(4) [Repeat step 1. Contract for only 15 seconds]

(5) Now relax the arm completely [About five minutes]

D. Both arms

(1) Now raise both arms and stretch them out in front of you—stretch them further. Feel the tension build up in your arms and in your tricep muscles. [Gradually build up tension for 30 seconds]

(2) Now relax . . . let your arms fall gently by your side and enjoy the pleasant, relaxed feeling. [one minute]

(3) Now relax even more and allow the feelings of relaxation to travel throughout your body. [one minute]

(4) [Repeat step 1 for 15 seconds]

(5) Now let your arms completely relax. [two minutes]

The patient is reminded that home practice should be continued.

Session IV: Final Ranking of Anxiety Hierarchy and Muscle Training Continued

1. Muscle relaxation training.
   A. Muscle review
      (1) Gradually close eyes [15 seconds]
      (2) Relax left forearm [30 seconds]
      (3) Relax entire left arm [30 seconds]
      (4) Relax right forearm [30 seconds]
      (5) Relax entire right arm [30 seconds]
      (6) Relax both arms [one minute]
   B. Left leg
      (1) Create tension in the leg muscle [the muscle group at

the front of the leg below the knee] by bending the
left foot back toward the knee [30 seconds]

(2)   Let the foot relax. Just release the foot abruptly. Let
it go limp. Relax this muscle group for one minute.

(3)   [Repeat steps 1 and 2 twice. In these repetitions contract the foot for only five seconds]

(4)   Now relax your leg completely [four minutes]

C.   Right leg

(1)   Repeat the same procedure as for the left leg.

Remind the patient to add these new muscle groups to his home practice.

Prior to this session, the therapist types or prints the hierarchy items on
individual three by five cards. The cards are given to the patient, who is instructed to put them in order from least frightening to most frightening.
Initially the patient is given 15 cards, with an additional number of blank
cards. He is instructed to place one or more of these blank cards between
items that seem to represent relatively large jumps in experienced anxiety.

Here is a deck of cards. Each card has a statement on it which describes a situation involving your problem area. Some of these situations are ones you have described as part of your own real or imagined
experience. Some are situations I have added that you may not have
considered before. I would like you to put the cards in order, starting
with the situation that does not seem to be fear-provoking at all or
only mildly so. The next card should describe a situation slightly more
fearful, then a little more, until the last card should represent the
most frightening situation. In other words, the first situation might
make you feel just a tinge of squeamishness or perhaps not affect you
at all; the next would represent a slight increment in your feeling of
discomfort or apprehension, then a little more, and so on. If at some
point the next card seems to be a relatively big increase in fearfulness,
place one or more blank cards between it and the card that follows.

(3)   After the patient has completed this task attempt
jointly to add still more items. This may be done in one
of three ways: (1) an item that is spontaneously suggested by the client; (2) an item proposed by the
therapist which the patient holds to be appropriate;
and (3) an item selected by the patient from a stack
of reserve items which the therapist should prepare
before this session. These last items may be drawn
from the patient's test responses.

Session V: Muscle Training Continued

1.   Muscle relaxation training. [Inquire about home practice]

A.   Muscle review

(1)   Gradually close your eyes [15 seconds]
(2)   Relax your left forearm [15 seconds]
(3)   Relax your entire left arm [15 seconds]
(4)   Relax your right forearm [15 seconds]
(5)   Relax your entire right arm [15 seconds]
(6)   Relax your left leg [15 seconds]
(7)   Relax your right leg [15 seconds]

B.   Neck and shoulders
(1)   Tense up your neck and shoulders; hunch your shoulders up . . . try to touch your ears . . . hold it. [30 seconds]
(2)   Relax your neck and shoulders completely for one minute.
(3)   Relax even more. [one minute]
(4)   Tense your neck and shoulders again. [15 seconds]
(5)   Relax your neck and shoulders completely. [one minute]
(6)   Relax, just sit quietly, and relax even more. [three minutes]

C.   Forehead [keep eyes open during tension, but allow the eyes to close slowly while relaxing this muscle group]
(1)   Wrinkle forehead. [30 seconds]
(2)   Relax forehead completely. [one minute]
(3)   Wrinkle forehead again. [15 seconds]
(4)   Relax forehead completely. [one minute]
(5)   Relax forehead even more. [three minutes]

D.   Eyes
(1)   Close your eyes tightly. [30 seconds]
(2)   Relax your eyes completely. [one minute]
(3)   Relax your eyes even more. [one minute]
(4)   Shut them tightly again. [15 seconds]
(5)   Relax your eyes. [one minute]
(6)   Just sit quietly and relax even more. [three minutes]

E.   Nose and mouth
(1)   Wrinkle your nose, wrinkle it tighter, tighter. [Gradually for 15 seconds]
(2)   Relax your nose, smooth out its surface. [30 seconds]
(3)   Repeat steps 1 and 2.
(4)   Now press your lips together—harder, harder—hold it. [15 seconds]
(5)   Relax your lips. [30 seconds]
(6)   Repeat steps 4 and 5.

F.   Abdominal muscles
(1)   Draw in your abdominal muscle slowly as you would if you were told to hold your stomach in. [30 seconds]

(2)   Relax your stomach completely. [one minute]
(3)   Draw your abdominal muscles in again. [15 seconds]
(4)   Let go completely; relax your stomach. [one minute]
(5)   Let go even more; relax. [four minutes]

Session VI: Introduction to Desensitization Procedure

A.   Muscle review. (*Inquire about practice.*)
    1.   Gradually close your eyes. [10 seconds]
    2.   Left forearm. [10 seconds]
    3.   Entire left arm. [10 seconds]
    4.   Right forearm. [10 seconds]
    5.   Entire right arm. [10 seconds]
    6.   Left leg. [10 seconds]
    7.   Right leg. [10 seconds]
    8.   Neck and shoulders. [10 seconds]
    9.   Forehead. [10 seconds]
    10.   Eyes. [10 seconds]
    11.   Nose and mouth. [10 seconds]
    12.   Abdominal. [10 seconds]
B.   Theoretical introduction (*Note*: The following is to be modified for each case)

We have now finished the major part of the muscle training procedure (although I want you to continue to practice muscle training) and are ready to move on to the next stage of the traetment.

Perhaps if I impart a little bit of psychological theory to you it will help you to understand our next procedure. You have now learned what your muscles feel like when they are relaxed and when they are tense. If you think back you will recall that tension in a muscle is not only associated with work but also with fear, anxiety, and apprehension. In fact, we frequently refer to anxiety as tension—a tightness in the muscles of the body. This tension is a normal part of fear and anxiety. Some psychologists hold that it is also a necessary part of fear. That is, it is impossible to have a feeling of fear or anxiety if your muscles are relaxed. Stated another way, fear and anxiety are responses, things your body does. Relaxation is also a response, a different response, in fact, one that may be incompatible with fear. What I hope to do in the rest of our sessions together is to train you to make a relaxation response to certain situations that normally cause you to feel fearful or upset. We are going to work with the problem hierarchy that you have created. Specifically, I am going to ask you to visualize the scenes described by the different items of the hierarchy. At the same time, you will be asked to relax, as you have learned to do here. We will start at the bottom of the hierarchy and progressively, as you learn to make relaxation rather than fear responses to items, move on to items that you ranked higher. In this

way you will learn to overcome your difficulties. Any questions?
C. Instruction for desensitization
    1. Desensitization
    I want you now to sit in a comfortable chair and close your eyes. Concentrate on relaxation—that wonderful, pleasant feeling of relaxation. I want you to listen carefully to my voice and relax yourself as you have learned to do. [Pause] You are now deeply relaxed, you feel heavy . . . heavy . . . heavy and relaxed, but you are going to become even more relaxed . . . let relaxation grow deeper and deeper. We shall concentrate on the various zones of your body in turn, and you will relax these more and more deeply. Relax the muscles of your left forearm . . . the entire arm. [Pause] Relax the muscles of your right forearm. [Pause] Relax the muscles of the entire arm. [Pause] Relax the muscles of your left leg. [Pause] The right leg. [Pause] Relax the muscles of your abdomen. [Pause] Your forehead. [Pause] Relax the muscles of your neck and shoulders. [Pause] Relax the muscles around your eyes. [Pause] Relax all the muscles in your face, all the muscles in your body. Let go more and still more. You become so calm, you feel so comfortable, nothing matters except to enjoy this pleasant, calm, relaxed state. [Pause] Now I want you to achieve an even greater degree of relaxation than you have experienced before. And now as I count backwards from ten to one you will move ever more deeply into a state of complete relaxation . . . 10, 9, 8, 7, . . . you are now very much relaxed, . . . 6, 5, 4, 3, 2, 1. Now as you are sitting there, deeply relaxed, I am going to give you some scenes to imagine and you will imagine them very clearly and calmly. If, however, by any chance anything that you imagine disturbs you, you will at once indicate this to me by raising your left hand two or three inches.

    First, I am going to give you a very commonplace scene. Remember you will imagine this scene quite vividly. Imagine that you are sitting alone in an armchair in your home. It is a very pleasant, sunny day and you are sitting in this chair perfectly at ease. [Pause of about five seconds] Stop imagining that scene and relax.

    Next I want you to imagine [insert a scene from the bottom of the hierarchy]____[Pause of about 5 to 10 seconds]

    Stop imagining____and concentrate on relaxing your muscles. [10 seconds] If the last scene disturbed you in the slightest, please raise your left hand. [Pause] Now relax your muscles. Let them go completely. Enjoy this calm state. [Silence for 20 seconds]

    If the patient is undisturbed by the first scene from the hierarchy, up to three more scenes may be presented in this session; this will depend, of course, on the patient's subsequent reactions. Remember, do not move on to a higher scene in the hierarchy until the patient reports *absolutely no further reaction* to the lower scene. After repeating a scene two or three times, ask your client to indicate by raising his hand if he felt the slightest discomfort at the last presentation.

2. Inquiry

The patient is interviewed to determine: (1) the extent and quality of the anxiety associated with each scene; (2) the vividness of his visualization; and (3) any change in either of the above factors with repeated presentations. Inquire also about the degree of relaxation.

GENERAL RULES FOR THE CONDUCT OF DESENSITIZATION

Each session begins with the muscle review. The amount of practice is noted. The patient is then relaxed. Scenes are presented as described above.

1. No more than four new items a day.

2. Allow 10 seconds of visualization after a scene is presented unless indexes of anxiety appear.

3. Relaxation for a minimum of 30 seconds following each presentation—more if necessary.

4. Present each item no less than twice.

5. Do not move on to a higher item until you establish that the client has no longer any reaction to the lesser item.

6. Observe the facial expression, body tension, respiration, and so on, of your client. If disturbances occur, attempt to be aware of them before your client needs to signal. When they occur immediately withdraw the stimulus and give suggestions of relaxation.

7. Do not abruptly end a session when a disturbance occurs. Before rousing the client, the therapist should present an "easy" stimulus, one the client has already overcome. Do not present the easy stimulus, however, until you are sure the state of relaxation has fully returned.

AUTHOR INDEX

Alexik, M., 88, 90-91
Allen, T. W., 13, 80
American Personnel and Guidance Association, 13
Anderson, S., 189n., 195
Andronico, M. P., 6, 15
Anker, J. M., 6, 7, 11, 13
Ansbacher, H. L., 12, 15
Anthony, W., 5, 14, 82, 86, 87, 90, 105, 110, 128, 133, 150, 157, 161, 164, 168, 169, 195, 198, 199, 213, 231, 238
Antonuzzo, R., 82, 90, 108, 110, 131, 133
Appleby, L., 6, 14
Arnhoff, F. N., 5, 14
Aspy, D., 22, 32, 87, 91, 153, 166

Banks, G., 11, 14, 107, 111, 150, 151, 152, 159, 165, 197, 213, 236, 238
Barker, E. N., 4, 15
Barnard, W. M., 194, 195
Beck, J. C., 6, 14
Berenson, B. G., 4, 5, 7, 8, 9, 11, 14, 17, 21, 22, 23, 30, 31n., 32, 33, 36, 37, 38, 39, 41, 43, 44, 45, 49, 51, 53, 54, 60, 62, 63, 67, 74, 79, 82, 83, 87, 88, 90, 91, 92, 93, 104n., 105, 106, 107, 110, 111, 112, 130, 133, 150, 151, 152, 153, 157, 160, 161, 162, 163, 164-165, 166, 167, 168, 169, 174n., 178n., 182n., 184n., 189n., 194, 195, 196, 197, 198, 199, 213, 214, 215, 229, 231, 236, 238, 239, 240, 244, 254, 255
Bergin, A., 5, 8, 14, 80, 90, 150, 154n., 165
Bierman, R., 32, 38-39, 45, 87, 91, 107, 111, 150, 151, 152, 159, 165, 168, 197, 199, 213, 233, 236, 238-239
Brand, M. S., 12, 18
Brown, D. F., 6, 12, 17
Brown, W. F., 6, 14, 18
Burstein, J., 82, 90, 105, 110-111, 151, 165, 168, 195, 197, 213

Cannon, J., 38-39, 45, 83, 90, 163, 165
Caudill, W., 64, 74
Coggeshall, L. T., 12, 14
Colarelli, N. J., 6, 14, 17

291

SUBJECT INDEX